M000106635

3/93

The Feminism and Socialism of Lily Braun

Lily Braun in 1902 (Friedrich-Ebert-Stiftung, Bonn)

THE
FEMINISM AND
SOCIALISM
OF LILY BRAUN

ALFRED G. MEYER

INDIANA UNIVERSITY PRESS • BLOOMINGTON

Photo credits:
The photographs of Lily von Kretschman in 1876 and Lily Braun in 1916 were used
by permission of Ullstein Bilderdienst, Berlin. The photographs of Georg von
Giżycki in 1890 and Lily Braun in 1902 were used by permission of the
Friedrich-Ebert-Stiftung, Bonn. The photographs of Heinrich Braun ca. 1895 and
Lily Braun ca. 1905 are used by permission of the SPD Archive and the Karl
Kautsky Archive at the International Institute for Social History, Amsterdam.

Copyright © 1985 by Alfred G. Meyer

All rights reserved

No part of this book may be reproduced or utilized in any form
or by any means, electronic or mechanical, including photocopying
and recording, or by any information storage and retrieval system,
without permission in writing from the publisher. The Association
of American University Presses' Resolution on Permissions constitutes
the only exception to this prohibition.

Manufactured in the United States of America
Library of Congress Cataloging in Publication Data

Meyer, Alfred G.
The feminism and socialism of Lily Braun.

Bibliography: p.
Includes index.
1. Braun, Lily. 2. Feminists—Germany—Biography.
3. Women and socialism—Germany—History. I. Title.
HQ1625.B73M49   1985   305.4'2'0924   84-43077
ISBN 0-253-32169-7

1   2   3   4   5   89   88   87   86   85

To the memory of my parents
Gustav Meyer
   born 6 June 1884 in Herford
   left to die in Theresienstadt concentration camp, 1944
and
Therese Meyer-Melchior
   born 14 December 1890 in Dortmund
   exterminated 1944 in the gas chambers of Auschwitz
Had the likes of Lily Braun prevailed, they would have
been granted to die in dignity.

CONTENTS

PREFACE

Lily Braun (1865–1916) was one of those pioneers of feminism who because of the radical nature of her ideas was notorious in her lifetime, but, because no existing social movement cared to claim her as its own, was thereafter quickly forgotten. That is to be regretted, because she anticipated by several generations many of the ideas which constitute today's feminist ideology. At the same time, students of the contemporary American women's movement might also be interested to find out how the concerns and demands of a Marxist feminist in the Germany of William II differ from those raised by people who wage a similar struggle in America today.

I discovered Braun some years ago while doing research for an essay on the relationship between Marxism and feminism,[1] and I have been studying her life and contributions ever since.

Her life and her ideas can be treated separately only at the risk of tearing asunder an organic whole, or of dissecting in the way a cadaver is cut up in the laboratory. To separate life from ideology is an altogether artificial separation, particularly in the case of Lily Braun, who very self-consciously sought to live out her philosophic and political convictions, which, in turn, she very self-consciously derived from her own personal experiences. Feminist theory, after all, derives much of its force from the tension between women's private and public roles. All the more reason, then, to write about Braun in such a fashion as to treat her private and her public persons as a whole.

The groundwork for my research was laid in 1979/80 during a year's sabbatical leave granted me by the University of Michigan. I gratefully acknowledge not only this help, but also repeated small allocations for research and clerical assistance granted me by the Center for Russian and East European Studies of the University of Michigan. My special thanks go to the Director and the archival staff of the Leo Baeck Institute, New York, which allowed me to read the voluminous unpublished correspondence of Braun and her family even before these materials had been catalogued. I owe thanks to the following institutions for their helpfulness in making available to me materials and/or advice: the Bundesarchiv in Bonn; the Bundesmilitärarchiv in Koblenz; the Zentralarchiv der DDR, Berlin; the Institute for Social History, Amsterdam; the Kungl. Biblioteken, Stockholm; Honnold Library; Wiener Stadt- und Landesarchiv; Österreichische Nationalbibliothek, Wien; Verein für Geschichte der Arbeiterbewegung, Wien; and Staatsarchiv der DDR, Potsdam.

I am grateful to Patricia Willacker for her intelligent and sensitive editorial work; to Melody Fill for her hours of typing; to Shebar Windstone for locating some hard-to-get source material for me; and to the many colleagues, students, and friends in the field of women's studies who provided encouragement and criticism.

INTRODUCTION

Lily Braun was born and raised in a Prussian noble family and spent the first twenty-five years of her life preparing herself—reluctantly— for a conventional life as an aristocrat's wife. From early youth, however, she began to rebel against the restrictions that her status as a woman of the upper classes imposed on her. When circumstances forced her to fend for herself sometime in her mid-twenties, she rapidly sampled a variety of radical causes, became active in them, and soon found herself participating in movements on the far left of the political and cultural spectrum. During the last fifteen or twenty years of her relatively short life, she published a major scholarly work on the political economy of female labor, a number of lengthy monographs, 120 or so articles ranging from one to about eighty pages, a two-volume autobiography, and several large works of fiction—novels, a drama, and an opera libretto. She was active as a political organizer and lecturer, carried on an active correspondence with large numbers of people, and through all this bore a double burden as housewife and mother. She led a life of self-sacrifice that destroyed her health prematurely, and at the age of fifty-one she collapsed and died.

During her life, Braun earned fame and notoriety, but after her death she was quickly forgotten, presumably because most of her ideas were too advanced, and made people feel uncomfortable. Discovering her, I immediately felt the urge to share my sense of discovery with others. I recognized Lily Braun as a radical feminist whose ideas, developed between 1895 and 1915, anticipated many of the views discussed by American and European feminists during the last ten to twenty years, and who therefore has things of great interest to say to today's women's movement. I recognized her also as an unorthodox Marxist; and unorthodox Marxists are the only kind of Marxists that can be of interest to radical social theorists, since orthodoxies freeze the mind while rebellion against orthodoxy, however radical that orthodoxy may be, is essential to genuine radicalism as Marx defined it, i.e., as an attempt to go to the human roots of all problems.

Braun had come to Marxism from feminism. But the ultimate sources of her radicalism were even more unusual: they included the deep sense of social obligation that had been instilled in her during her conventional aristocratic and Christian upbringing, and her early acquaintance with controversial literary works, chiefly those of Goethe and Nietzsche. All these influences helped determine both the style and the substance of her radicalism. In her style, she self-consciously avoided the tone of invective in which the Marxist movement of her time carried on its discussions. Deeply committed to the idea of class warfare, she nonetheless insisted that even this struggle should be waged according to rules of decency, for a humane society without exploitation and domination could be created only by a proletariat that had learned to rise above its slum culture in language, manners, morals, and enlightenment. Throughout her life, Braun encountered brutality in many forms, and she devoted herself to the struggle against it; but she absolutely refused to allow herself to be brutalized in this endeavor. She firmly believed that noble ends could only be attained by resorting to noble means. It is precisely this highmindedness that originally attracted me to her.

For her first twenty-five years, this daughter of a Prussian general led a giddy debutante's life, preparing herself for, and displaying herself in, the aristocratic marriage market, a pursuit that she recognized as insane and demeaning, even though it did provide pleasures and excitements. But she did dream of a more useful life for herself that would not waste her many talents in the distasteful routines of housekeeping. She also fantasized about sexual pleasures in a way that came into sharp conflict with upper-class marital conventions. The resulting conflicts between secret ambitions and permissible prospects nearly drove her to suicide.

From early youth Braun had been a voracious reader, not only of children's books but also of serious literature, with a predilection for unconventional fiction, poetry, and drama. In this literature she found support for her democratic, pacifist, feminist, and socialist ideas long before her actual break with her class. But reading Wagner's essays or Ibsen's dramas did not by itself give her sufficient courage to make the break and to speak out publicly for radical causes. Also necessary were a few wrenching experiences that would shake her forcefully from her conventional life. Three such experiences hit her more or less at the same time: her father's unexpected dismissal from military service; a sudden opportunity to do some original research on Goethe and his circle in Weimar; and a passionate love for a man who turned her down.

Once forced out of her accustomed life, she then, in rapid succession, sampled a variety of radical activities. She published numerous essays in literary criticism, generally supporting the literary avant-garde who voiced social criticism in their works of fiction, but even more often criticizing them for not going far enough. She became a leader in the Ethical Culture movement, where unconventional ideas on religion, politics, social problems, and family morality were freely discussed, but soon left this movement as being too tepid. She became active as a feminist and quickly found herself one of the leaders of the most radical wing of the German women's movement. Finally, she joined the German Social Democratic Party (SPD) and thus became a member of the international Marxist movement. In the SPD she was welcomed as a spectacular "catch," but soon found herself shunted aside because her ideas and her entire bearing seem to have made the leadership of the movement uncomfortable. In the last ten years of her life, having alienated all her former associates in all these movements, she supported herself and her husband by her eminently successful books of fiction and a scandalously revealing autobiography. In all these writings her radical views on politics and society, on women's liberation, sexuality, children's upbringing, working-class culture, and related matters emerge clearly.

As a writer and an activist, Lily Braun fought against two principal enemies—patriarchy and capitalism. She sought to liberate workers from all forms of exploitation that condemned them to short, joyless lives of toil and made all attainable pleasures the exclusive possession of the rich, who, in their turn, were rendered incapable of enjoying them properly. Capitalism, she believed, was evil not only because it turned productive labor into mindless drudgery and made the wealth of the few dependent on the misery of the many, but also because it led to the commercialization of all values and ultimately to the destruction of culture, art, sexuality, the family, and the very existence of the human species.

Women, she believed, had been doubly exploited and degraded. They had always functioned as the reserve army of the work force and hence at the bottom of the economic order; but patriarchal culture had, in addition, alienated them from their sexuality and had thus systematically crippled their emotions. As a result, Braun argued, all innate creativity in women had been stifled; meaningful, creative activity had become a male privilege. Macho attitudes and macho principles were ruling the world. Moreover, a pernicious system of child rearing, fed by harmful and deceitful ideologies, was perpetuating all the evils of capitalism and patriarchy, of greed, lust for power, violence, barbarism, and hypocrisy. To make this a world fit for human beings, workers would have to free themselves from capitalism by a proletarian revolution, children would have to rebel against the miseducation they received from parents, pastors, and pedagogues, and women would not only have to emancipate themselves from oppression, but would have to assert their influence over society. Ultimately, what Lily Braun demanded was the feminization of a world sick with the masculine spirit.

Underlying all her ideological positions was her belief in the uniqueness of the feminine experience, especially the close bond between mother and child, which for her was the paradigmatic relationship for any society of the future, replacing the master-slave relations that had hitherto prevailed. This exaltation of motherhood as the noblest of all human activities was shared by many German feminists around the turn of the century and still lives on today among a minority of women within the contemporary women's movement. While the praise of motherhood has often served as an argument to support patriarchy, in that it sought to relegate women away from public life into the nursery, in the writings of Braun it supported the notion that it was women's *duty* to assume leading roles in public life. Similarly, Braun argued that all women, but especially mothers, had the capacity to become a revolutionary force able to fight heroically to end their oppression. In her agitational articles, particularly those addressed to mothers, she preached heroism, self-sacrifice, and militancy. Everything she wrote was infused with an unshakable belief in progress, with the certainty that it was possible to fashion a truly humane social order. "I would like to travel from place to place," she wrote in one of her earliest pamphlets, "and implant into the hearts of women that health-bringing discontent which is the mother of all reforms; and I would like to shake their conscience from its slumber so that it begins to be aware of its responsibility for all the wretchedness in the world. But there is one other strong sentiment that must become powerful in their hearts, a feeling that has animated all those who have rendered service to the human race: the faith that happiness for all human beings is a possibility."[1]

If this were the naive optimism of a Comte or a Spencer, it would surely make Braun a representative of the nineteenth century with its bland belief in the inevitability of progress, and this would diminish her relevance for our age. Yet her own faith in progress was tempered by a skepticism derived from Schopenhauer and by keen awareness of the immense obstacles to be overcome. Indeed, her Nietzschean stress on the need for heroism lends to much of her work an undertone of desperation that is more in tune with the mood of our own century. It surely makes her Marxism more modern than that of imperturbable determinists like Kautsky and Plekhanov.

Modern, and indeed quite up to date, also was her life-long attempt to see socialism and feminism as integrally related and mutually supportive elements of a broader movement toward our emancipation from all forms of alienation and oppression. In that attempt she is in fact the principal precursor of a most important strand in the women's movement of the last two decades. Her writings and activities should be compared to those of Clara Zetkin, who in the name of orthodox Marxism declared women's concerns to be a disruptive side issue; or those of Rosa Luxemburg, whose personal instincts, to be sure, were feminist, but who carefully protected her reputation among the patriarchs leading the Marxist movement by allowing those sentiments to remain in the closet: Luxemburg did not recognize the personal as being political. Or compare Lily Braun with Aleksandra Kollontai, who agreed with Braun that feminism and socialism ought to be regarded as an indivisible whole; she agreed with her also that the liberation of sexuality was an essential element of any women's emancipation. Yet in the end Kollontai was forced to knuckle under to Lenin and Stalin, in effect renouncing her feminism as well as her radical dissent on how to interpret and practice Marxism.

Braun never gave in. She waged a lonely struggle against many fronts, misunderstood, slandered, grossly overworked, and in continual financial distress, often despairing, often wounded, but never stooping to the level of her antagonists. It is time we rescued this brave pioneer of emancipatory ideology from oblivion.

The Feminism and Socialism of Lily Braun

I

EARLY LIFE

On July 2, 1865, in Halberstadt, a small town southwest of Magdeburg whose history goes back to the time of Charlemagne, the first
child of Jenny and Hans von Kretschman was born. Hans, almost
thirty-three years old at the time, was a Captain in the Prussian
Army. Later he was to rise to the rank of General of the Infantry.
The Kretschman family, originally from Bohemia, had settled in
Nuremberg in the fifteenth century and had attained noble title in
service to various princely houses in the eighteenth century, many of
them as military officers. Hans von Kretschman's father, too, had
had a brief military career before settling down on his small estate.
Jenny, Hans von Kretschman's wife, was descended from a baronial
family that traced its descent back to the tenth century; a long-
ruined fortress near Halberstadt had been the earliest family seat.
When the baby, whom they named Lily,[1] was born, they had been
married exactly fourteen months. It would be thirteen years before
they had another child.

Lily von Kretschman received the conventional upbringing of a
nineteenth-century aristocratic German female; she was taught
French and English, reading, writing, and reckoning, but got little
formal training of an academic sort. She took piano and drawing
lessons, and was introduced to literature and history by private tu-
tors. But her principal training was in being a future lady and housekeeper. Cooking, sewing, needlework, and related skills were
stressed. Sex education, of course, was not formally included in this
curriculum, although she did receive it, at age thirteen, from a

---

Portions of this chapter were previously published in John Fout, ed., *German
Women in the Nineteenth Century* (New York: Holmes & Meier, 1984).

chambermaid. Religious instruction was given sporadically by her
mother, and more systematically by a pastor in preparation for confirmation. Her mother's teachings seem to have consisted primarily
of the message that it is women's duty to serve, to suffer, and to be
silent. As a child of nobility, Lily was also taught the principle of
noblesse oblige, according to which aristocratic privilege carries obli-
gations. The early effects of this message were to make her incredibly
arrogant.

Lily was a sickly child and, perhaps because of this, often lonely.
A certain willfulness and rebelliousness, probably related to her arrogance, further contributed to her frequent withdrawal into fantasy
worlds of her own. All her life she would love fairy tales and myths,
and the first book she wrote, in her late teens, was a collection of
children's stories.[2]

She also displayed very early a philosophic disposition and a high
moral conscience. She took the ethical commands of Christianity
seriously but questioned some of its dogmas and already in her early
teens noticed that the behavior of confessed Christians by no means
always matched their professed beliefs. When she voiced these
doubts, she was scolded for her impious questions; this naturally
deepened her doubts. Precisely because she took the teachings of
Christianity seriously, she found hypocrisy abominable. At the age of
fourteen, when she was to be confirmed, she refused, arguing that
she could not perjure herself before God's altar. Her parents nonetheless made her go through with the ceremony in order to maintain
appearances.

The incident shows Lily to have been a person of high principles
who could nonetheless be persuaded to make compromises for the
sake of propriety. To her parents she appeared as a willful, capri-
cious, disobedient or at least difficult child. They must have
breathed a sigh of relief when she finally gave in on this issue. Yet
the bitterness with which many years later Lily related this event
shows that she never quite forgave her parents for forcing her to
simulate piety; nor did she forgive herself for making this obeisance
to convention.

In the years of her troubled adolescence, Lily's mother was close to
her, comforted her in moments when this or that flirtation had
turned into a disaster, and at times protected her from her father's

violent temper. Jenny von Kretschman was levelheaded, a model of sobriety and common sense, in many respects the real boss of the family.[3] In her younger days, Lily was drawn to her; and in her mother's last years, she provided her with solace and a refuge from the old general.[4] But in the end, finding her mother's attitudes about the relationship between men and women unacceptable, Lily was forced to repudiate her as a role model. Jenny obviously regarded sex and childbearing with distaste.[5] She saw herself and all women as victims and preached the virtues of meekness, submission, servitude, and silent suffering. This did not prevent her from expressing her contempt for men, or from trying to teach Lily—and, later, her younger daughter Mascha—the conventionally feminine arts of dominating and controlling men. In short, she was a highly intelligent and skilled practitioner of old-fashioned feminine wiles and, as such, played the role upper-class women had been playing for ages, enforcing and reproducing patriarchal culture. In Lily Braun's memoirs, her mother is portrayed as cold and stern, a killjoy who managed to repress everything gentle and humane and feminine in herself.[6]

In contrast, Lily's father seems to have been impulsive, charming, and warm at times. But within the family he was primarily the authoritarian patriarch, the dreaded disciplinarian whose wrath made Lily tremble and gave her nightmares long after his death.[7] Hans von Kretschman's conviction was that harsh military drill and discipline were good schooling for civic and human virtue,[8] and he treated his family as if they were troops under his command. As a military officer he seems to have been brilliant. He was also well informed in a variety of fields, and seems to have been eager to share some of his knowledge with his daughters. In her memoirs, Braun talks about his charming way of introducing her to the wonders of nature by sharing his wide knowledge of plants with her. In a private letter she relates that he acquainted her with the writings of Comte.[9] He is said to have been a witty conversationalist, and his letters to his wife during the wars of 1886 and 1870/71 confirm this. Kretschman was generous and courteous, but in that traditional, gentlemanly way that reveals a fundamental condescension: by the very act of showering his wife and daughters with presents he showed that he did not consider them his equals. No wonder, then, that his wife reacted with anger

rather than gratitude when he lavished expensive luxuries on her or
on Lily. She not only sensed the patriarchal dependency relationship
that such presents reinforced, but also knew that her husband could
not really afford them.

For all his brilliance as an officer, Kretschman—handicapped by his
strong aristocratic prejudices—found it difficult to adapt to the rapidly
changing world of the late nineteenth century. In money matters he
was altogether irresponsible, an eternal adolescent, according to his
sensible wife.[10] In addition to his predilection for overgenerous gift-
giving, he had expensive hobbies and speculated recklessly. His own
salary being insufficient for his needs, he quickly spent his wife's
generous dowry, then exhausted the even more generous inheritance
she was to receive from her mother, and finally borrowed from his
wife's older brother, Baron Werner von Gustedt, the owner of large
estates in East Prussia and an influential figure in the German Conservative Party. Uncle Werner wielded considerable influence in Lily's
family as well, even though he seems to have been an unpleasant,
crude martinet of limited intellect and narrow horizon.

To secure the loan from his brother-in-law, which in the end
amounted to the fantastic sum of 78,000 marks,[11] Kretschman mortgaged the inheritance that Lily was someday to receive from his older
sister, Clothilde, the wealthy widow of Baron Ulyss von Herman, in
whose home in Augsburg Lily was to receive her "finishing" as a
young lady. Because of her great wealth and the splendid people she
managed to attract to her home, this strong-willed woman was feared
and flattered by everyone in the Kretschman clan.

To the members of her family introduced so far we must add a few
more relatives or friends who played important roles in Lily's early
life. First there was cousin Tilly—Mathilde von Colomb—the
daughter of a lower court judge in Magdeburg, exactly one year older
than Lily and her closest confidante for many years. To be sure,
Tilly's replies to Lily's shocking confessions always represented the
voice of propriety, conformity, and conventionality, but at least she
was someone to whom the troubled girl could pour out her heart.
And both in Augsburg, during her two years with Aunt Clothilde,
and long after, there was her aunt's spiritual counselor, Pastor Julius
Hans of St. Anne's Church, humanist, liberal, and feminist,[12] who
always lent a willing ear to Lily's troubles and tried to intercede with

Lily von Kretschman in 1876 (Ullstein, Berlin)

her relatives on her behalf. Until his death in 1889, she found an
ally also in Arthur von Kretschman, one of her father's younger
brothers and like him a professional officer, but unlike him a free
spirit, rebel, and decided nonconformist who encouraged the tomboy
in Lily and treated her as a pal rather than as a fragile doll. In time,
Lily's sister, Maria ("Mascha"), thirteen years younger, also became
an admirer, friend, and ally.

But most important was Lily's maternal grandmother, Jenny von
Gustedt (*née* von Pappenheim), an illegitimate daughter of Jérome
Bonaparte, King of Westphalia. After the collapse of the Napoleonic
state, the young Jenny had moved to Weimar with her mother,
where at the age of fifteen she caught the eye of the aging Goethe,
became a member of his extended household, and was appointed
Hoffräulein at the Ducal court. Her association with the court and
the Goethe family lasted until her death, and the opportunities this
brought to Lily, the ideas it generated in her, were important shapers
of her mind. The grandmother was steeped in the spirit of Weimar—
cosmopolitan, tolerant, humane, and unconventional—and Lily
seems to have absorbed this spirit from her. If her mother and her
aunt Clothilde sought to make a proper young lady of her, someone
who would make an appropriate marriage, her grandmother provided
a thorough humanist education, as well as loyalty and support on
which Lily could always rely.

Even as a child, Lily was a voracious reader, not only of children's
books but of "adult" literature, including authors then considered
avant-garde or controversial. By the time she was thirteen she had
read Goethe's *Werther, Faust, Die Wahlverwandtschaften,* and *Iphigenie.* Within a few years she had sampled Ruskin, Browning, William
Morris, Shelley, Nietzsche, Ibsen, Wagner, and contemporary de-
fenders of Darwinism. Apparently as an antidote to all this, Lily's
parents found it necessary to send her to her aunt Clothilde in
Augsburg for two years of "finishing." In the salon of this rich and
powerful woman Lily mingled with the intellectual and aristocratic
elite of southern Germany and Austria.

The seventeen-year-old girl who returned home after two years of
rigid training by her aunt seemed to her delighted parents to be no
longer a rebellious teenager but a well-mannered young lady, skilled
in many gracious social arts, a witty conversationalist, radiant with

youth and slender beauty. She would quickly attract men with these attributes, but she would also puzzle them by qualities and habits that bordered on the unladylike: her arrogance and flirtatiousness; her strong opinions and interest in intellectual pursuits; her wild horsemanship; and her unconventional habits, such as smoking in public.

And inwardly, Lily harbored deep resentment against all the most important principles underlying her upbringing. She believed these principles to be pretense of the same kind she had detected in Christian practice: emphasis on proper form, polite phrases and manner to mask personal ambition, greed, and lust—this, it seemed to her, was the lesson all children were taught. Conventional child rearing, in short, was training children how to lie. Her letters written during her teens and early twenties are replete with condemnations of hypocrisy, which is also the prevalent theme in occasional verses she would write during carnival season in her early twenties; and the first serious work she tried to write (it remained unfinished) was a treatise on child rearing inspired by Nietzsche's philosophy; its title was, "In Opposition to the Lie" (*Wider die Lüge*).[13]

For the next eight years she was to play two principal roles. At home she was the dutiful daughter who relieved her mother of some of the household drudgery and child care (there was her younger sister Mascha). To be taken equally seriously was her duty to entertain and to be entertained, to cultivate an active social life with the young officers and the noble families of the garrison. This role had two purposes: first, her father, as regimental commander, considered it his duty to open his home to his officers; and as he explained to her, the presence of an attractive daughter would make this much easier for him, never noticing that this made her feel like a whore.[14] Second, and more important, the social games were designed to help her find a suitable husband, one whose nobility and wealth were sufficient to make him worthy of marriage. The social life in the garrison was, among other things, a marriage market for aristocratic daughters; and for these eight years Lily was indeed merchandise on display.

Daughters of the wealthy bourgeoisie and of rich estate owners might rely on their dowries to attract suitable men; and in the highest reaches of the nobility marriages may still have been arranged in conformity with dynastic politics. But a poor officer's daughter (and Hans von Kretschman was poor) who did not wish to end up as a spinsterish lady-in-waiting at some small court, or as an Evangelical deaconess caring for the sick or the insane, or to remain dependent on the charity of more or less distant relatives, had to use all her talents and skills to get a husband. Until she had succeeded in this, life for her would essentially be a market in which she was to display herself as eminently desirable merchandise.

In her memoirs, Braun tells us that she was seven or eight when older relatives first made her aware of the first rule of this marketing game: to be pretty, to be seductive, to dominate others through sexuality, and to learn that these love games are intriguing and enjoyable.[15] Rule number two commanded chastity. Women were to be seen but not touched, and to be seen only under controlled conditions. The code made clear when a woman might or might not be viewed by a man, and which parts of her were open to view. It allowed some slight and fleeting touch only under the most ceremonious circumstances. Violation of this code was a serious, often unpardonable, offense against respectability, since it was the woman who suffered the worst punishment even if the man had been the offender: she should not have given the man an opportunity to overstep the bounds of propriety.

The code of chastity also demanded that a young woman be equally charming, seductive, and unapproachable to all young gentlemen of her circle. The slightest deviation, the gentlest hint that she preferred one over all others would cause the gossip mill— an important social institution—to consider her as promised, engaged, a particular man's exclusive property. A young woman forced to issue a denial of such an engagement was considered compromised: she should not have allowed things to reach the gossip stage. The rules of conduct demanded sexual coolness until a woman had fully committed herself. A single kiss was enough to pledge her to a man.

The clothes women wore symbolized seduction as well as touch-me-not virginity. The formal ballroom wear bared the neck, the arms, and the upper part of the breasts, and by forcing the woman into an exaggerated hourglass shape it accentuated feminine curves. But the dresses also kept the lower extremities hidden, and the stiff corset functioned as an armor plate against lecherous hands during the dance. In short, the clothing of upper-class women symbolized the ambiguity of their situation. Moreover, women's formal attire was designed ingeniously so that they could not dress themselves. All the hooks and buttons were in the back, and the gowns fitted so tightly that a lady needed help getting into them. Upper-class clothing thus reminded the woman of her dependency on others, even if they only be servants.[16]

These two rules of behavior, of course, were incompatible. It was virtually impossible to be simultaneously seductive and chaste. The young ladies of the nobility tried to cope with this dilemma by flirting, behaving with a strange mixture of seductiveness and chastity which made coy pretense of both. Flirting conceived as a serious pursuit—and indeed it was the most serious one a woman could pursue under the circumstances—was a dangerous game. If the young woman was not seductive enough, she would remain an old maid, cheated of all conventional sexual experience and, much worse, doomed to economic dependence on a father, uncle, brother, or charitable institution, unless she found demeaning employment as a higher servant. If she seemed too seductive she might suffer the same fate because many serious suitors would not risk getting engaged to a woman who appeared to have sexual desires of her own; she might even slide down into the category of loose women and become a social outcast. Virgin, old maid, whore, and wife were in fact the only roles society reserved for women in this system which Frank Wedekind has called sexual feudalism. Lily von Kretschman found all four alternatives distasteful, even though for a long time she took it for granted that she would end up as some aristocrat's wife. It is clear from her correspondence, however, that every time this possibility threatened to become reality she saw to it that, by some unconventional behavior, she would turn the suitor away, usually by excessive flirtatiousness.[17]

What made this man-hunting game so devilish was that it demanded cool, dispassionate control over some of the most uncontrollable human urges—sexual desire, jealousy, ambition, rage, and the like—even while artfully arousing and feeding them in flirtation. The young woman's art was supposed to generate desire but not passion; for once passion flared up the game turned into disaster. In the final analysis, only a negative attitude toward sex, arising from fear, disgust, or disdain of the opposite gender, made it possible to play the game without breaking down under it. Lily von Kretsch man, however, was too sensual a woman to lapse into frigidity. Instead, she often was close to collapse, and many times she expressed envy of the whore or of the lower-class girl not caught up in this infernal code.[18]

She rebelled with equal stubbornness against the restrictions which conventions placed on her choice of career. She hated housework and had no wish to become either a governess or a lady-in-waiting. Intellectually she sensed her superiority to many men who were entering interesting careers in public life, and she envied them their opportunities. She wished to become *somebody,* to make her mark in the world, to assume a leadership position. Those were forbidden ambitions; even her purely intellectual and artistic interests, pursued as hobbies, tended to give her the reputation of a bluestocking.

Her unpublished papers contain a wealth of letters to her best friend and confidante, cousin Tilly. A number of conflicting themes recur in these letters: a love of flirting; burning sensuality; hedonism; delight in her power over men; a cult of youth and a dread of old age, when all these games would be over; deep resentment of the double moral code; and, as mentioned, envy of the lower-class women and prostitutes. "Every person," she wrote when she was twenty-one, "has a wild beast inside which will come to the fore sooner or later, and mine perhaps is the wildest of all; its name is sensuality. Almost since my childhood it has driven me from passion to passion; I have never been able to master it."[19] This sensuality, she suggested in the same letter, was the secret of her many successes with men.[20] "My feverish senses often are attracted by men whose minds and heart repel me; and conversely, my own mind and heart are often captivated where my physical senses almost feel disgust. *If I were ashamed of my instincts,* if I therefore were to cover them with the fig leaf of mendacious amorousness—how many unfortunate marriages I would already have allowed to bind me!"[21]

Lily von Kretschman deliberately rebuffed many men who in the eyes of her society would have been considered suitable husbands. She dreaded marriage, not only because she recognized it as a financial bargain from which considerations of love and affection were to be excluded, but also because it would spell out the end of youth.

Marriage, she knew, was forever, and she could not make peace with that fact. "I will," she wrote to her cousin, "be allowed only a marriage of convenience, so I probably won't marry at all. Because of this I am tired of life and poor of hope and have ceased to dream of happiness. I entered life with excessive expectations. . . ."[22]

Her expectations were, of course, shared by many other young women of her class. The ludicrous husband-catching business easily led a young woman to dream about her future husband as a Prince Charming with whom she would live happily ever after. Braun thus had described her future husband; he would be "beautiful as Apollo, intelligent as the Seven Wise Men, faithful as Toggenburg, brave as Alexander the Great, and rich as Croesus."[23] The fact that her educators warned her against such dreams apparently had no effect. And in fact Prince Charming did not arrive, at least not for a very long time; meanwhile, Lily turned down one eligible suitor after another.

This indecision, and the mixture of feelings in which it was grounded, her envy of men's social privileges, her fear of being crushed by conventions, her sexual ardor and her strong sense of propriety, her intellectual pursuits and her fear of becoming a bluestocking, her enjoyment of parties and balls together with her knowledge that these pleasures were empty—all this increased her tendency toward profound self-contempt. She felt herself to be useless, a parasite. "Most people," she wrote to Tilly, "complain because they are suffering; I probably am living much too well. I have no position to fill; no heavy burdens have been placed on my shoulders; everyone spoils me. I think of myself as a lap dog who does her tricks and gets petted for that, but is useful for nothing else. And I would have the strength to accomplish something. Or should it be some sort of duty to contribute to the amusement of others?"[24]

From early on, this rejection of herself as a useless parasite, as a doll, was mixed in with contempt for her entire class. When at the age of eleven she first ventured into the slums of Posen during a disastrous flood, she reacted to the sight and smell of poverty with disgust: poverty offended her aesthetic sense. But five years later, this had turned into shame over being privileged, and contempt for those, like her Augsburg aunt, who practiced charity only for self-indulgence and because they hoped it would woo the poor away from

Social Democracy. By the time she was twenty-four, her letters to her cousin began to contain criticisms of capitalism and the social problems it has created; [25] and in the wake of the Ruhr coal miners' strike of May 1889, which she observed from her father's then garrison in Münster, she expressed the hope that the nobility and the working class might form a coalition to defeat the bourgeoisie. "The power of capital must be broken. We will live to see the marvelous spectacle of nobility and workers marching together."[26]

From year to year her attempts at self-appraisal became more desperate and unmerciful, ending at last in almost incoherent outbursts of arrogance and self-contempt, shrewd self-analysis and shrewd self-deceptions—the desperate cries for help of a young woman totally at sea because her desire to become a personality came into ever-sharper conflict with the conventions of her society. Here is one of these outbursts, written on New Year's Eve 1889/90.

> . . .when I rise in the morning I see—well, what?—a face, pale, with tired veiled eyes which on rare occasions emit a strange flash, a deep furrow in the brow and, if I look quite sharply, a tiny crease around the mouth. That's me! There is a picture of me, a portrait of some time ago: a wooden figure, bony shoulders, the arms long and slim—all that no longer fits, though my waist is slim, 20-1/2 inches, impressive, isn't it! The shoulders have become full, the arms round, but, strange, the face has remained almost the same. A child's face it never was. But was I ever a child? A happy child? If so, it must have been a very long time ago, because I do not remember it. Nor do I wish to rummage in my memory because it shows only ugly pictures; to be sure, most of them are framed in gold and painted on ivory in the brightest colors, but take a closer look at these devil's tricks— was fate not a foolish and wasteful painter to take such precious colors for painting such—trash? Or was it anything better than that? What of all this has remained whole? Love, perhaps? You poor creature! There was a time when you dreamt of the future which you thought would bring you happiness and glamor and love. Where is happiness? It passed my by, I saw only enough of it to retain the feverish hot longing for it. And glamor? How quickly the excessively perceptive eye saw that there is nothing genuine about it—fool's gold, carnival mummery, fireworks, the rockets crackle and shine, and once they are burnt out it is much darker than it was before. But love? Once it freely flew to me, and I treated it the way children treat a new toy, it delights for a while and then is thrown away. And later? Later love entered my heart and wounded me deeply, and—

went away, the wounds healed, but there are times when the scars burn with pain. They say it is caused by change in the weather, that is true, for the closer autumn comes the more I feel them. . . . There was one who talked to me of love, of eternal love indeed, and what became of it? It went away or passed on to every—pretty face? Don't get the illusion that there is even one who loves you, your own self, your innermost personality which ceaselessly struggles to become better, ceaselessly works to become more intelligent—nobody knows anything about this, they love only with their bodies, their heart is not involved in this, it is only a muscle, the people say, but the body's senses are there, they are alive, yes indeed they are so alive they cannot be ignored! Stop yearning for love, it is a fairy tale from long ago. Do look at yourself carefully, soon no one will love you any more not even with that modern love. Then—people will respect you! Puh, I am shivering—you are talented, you have learned a lot, they will exploit that thoroughly, as much as they can. Then what will you have? You have pursued learning as if it were an illicit affair, otherwise the dear neighbors would have made fun of the "bluestocking"—that will stay with you! You have loved art, shyly, in order not to besmirch the noble Muse with your amateurish efforts, that also will stay with you. Is that enough? Learning is endless and yet so limited—there is a point beyond which we cannot go, and at that point we run against a wall and bloody our heads and hearts; and does science teach anything that goes beyond the human being? Everything carries the human stamp, everywhere you run into yourself, your own miserable little self. But art? Where is it pure and great, the real world looks all the more filthy, and the harmony of art glaringly reveals the disharmony of reality; but if it is like the world, what good is it? Or perhaps despite everything you will still have the future? You have sinned, more grievously than anyone has ever suspected, and you have been punished, not an atom of punishment was spared you, every punishment was murderously hard, and you took it because you considered it deserved. But what now? You know that you have become better, that you are worth more than many of those around, and yet darkness continues to envelope you while those others walk in the bright light. Are you remembering Biblical saying from previous habit? God punishes those whom he loves—is that just? What is the use of becoming better if life gets worse all the time? A nice image of the future! Then I would rather plunge into the wildest maelstrom of life and perish in ecstasy than carry a burdensome existence on my back and suffer hunger and thirst with the "elevating" idea of becoming better, hunger and thirst, those are the right words! Hunger and thirst for happiness and glamor and love—just as in previous times! When I was a child, it

was a wish which, in childish manner, carried the certainty of fulfill-
ment: the little Christ child will bring it. Later, in the religious
mind, a longing which clung to the hope: God is kind and will
reward those who are good, I want to earn it. By now, old Tantalus,
you know the score! Where is that sweet quiet happiness, the mild
sunlight, where is love—not that admiring slavish love, but a gentle,
compassionate one which softly presses me to its heart, saying, come
and rest, you poor tired child! For what purpose are you alive?
Would anyone miss you if you quietly went away? Your parents, your
sister, your friends. But for how long? You remained a stranger to
them after all, have caused a lot of trouble to all of them, they won't
miss you so very long, not even your little achievements. You have
looked around for those very painfully in order to kill time, in order
to be doing something. Who is going to be truly missed? A good
father, a faithful mother spreading her blessings!—Cut it out! Look
in the mirror—pfui, you have been crying, quickly put on the mask,
who these days shows her face? Without masks there would be too
many wrinkles, too many tears!

Several blows hit Lily von Kretschman in quick succession in her
mid-twenties and jolted her out of the passivity with which she had
endured her unendurable existence as a not-quite-proper young lady.
Her father was dismissed from military service; Arthur von Kretschman, her favorite uncle, committed suicide; her grandmother died,
leaving her a rich legacy of Goethiana; and the one great love of her
life, her own Prince Charming, came—and went.

General von Kretschman's retirement was ordered by the new
Emperor, Wilhelm II, effective at the end of 1889. Two years before,
at the Imperial maneuvers of 1887, the general had been in charge of
a mock army that had administered a decisive defeat to a division
ineptly led by the then Prince Wilhelm; worse still, at the Imperial
maneuvers of 1889 the general and his sovereign got into an argument about the relative importance of infantry as against cavalry.
The young emperor had no use for people who disagreed with him.
For the Kretschman family this was a disaster; the father's brilliant
career was destroyed, the family's finances seriously impaired—far
more than the general's wife and daughters could guess, because they
had no inkling of the fantastic debts he had incurred. They did know
that the situation was bad; and Lily tried dutifully to add to the
family's income by making and selling useless but pretty little arti-
facts in leather and textile—a commercial activity which only added
to her self-contempt.[27]

While the Kretschman family was preparing to move into a modest apartment in Berlin, Lily's grandmother died, and Lily inherited her collected papers and memorabilia: letters and poems written by Goethe; correspondence with his family and the Weimar court; the grandmother's own literary efforts; pictures; and presents she had received from Goethe. This inheritance gave Lily an opportunity to engage in some scholarly and editorial work, and she promptly set out to create a memorial to her grandmother by publishing selected papers and excerpts from these treasures.

Prince Charming arrived at that very same time, the one great, overwhelming love in Lily's life: a distant cousin, twenty years older than she, recently widowed, with two teenage daughters. Colonel Gottfried von Pappenheim, commander of a regiment of *chasseurs* (*Jäger*), whom she had known since her childhood, appeared to love her as deeply and passionately as she loved him. But the courtship ended abruptly after a very few months because his family objected to the match; Lily von Kretschman for some unknown reason was not considered good enough for Count von Pappenheim.[28] She never forgot nor forgave him; in various careful disguises he appears in her memoirs, in her novels, and in her bitter essays on the evil institution of marriage. And toward the end of her life, he was ironically reborn for her in the form of her only son, who joined a regiment of *chasseurs*, rose to officer's rank, and came home on furlough wearing the green tunic of a *Jägerleutnant*.

All of these events at last forced Lily von Kretschman to take her life into her own hands, educate herself, and establish her autonomy. She did this with determination and boldness, rapidly testing ideas and activities of ever-increasing unconventionality and radicalness, until five or six years later she broke uncompromisingly with her entire past and joined the Marxist movement.

Her self-education as a radical began with two projects that although unconventional were well within the bounds of aristocratic respectability. The first was the editing and publishing of her grandmother's papers. In order to do this properly, it was necessary to get in touch with the keepers of the Goethe archive in Weimar and with the Grand Ducal court; and, as the granddaughter of Jenny von Gustedt, she received red carpet treatment from both institutions. Her charm, wit, youth, and beauty soon won them over completely—the Grand Duke and his family as well as the Goethe

scholars. She was offered free access not only to the Goethe archive
but also to the secret archives of the Grand Ducal family. The
scholars invited her to join them permanently and suggested that she
undertake a major historical work on the history of Weimar society
during the last decade of Goethe's life. The Grand Duke offered her
a position as a lady-in-waiting.[29]

Between 1891 and 1893, she did indeed publish selections from
her grandmother's literary legacy and a number of monographs based
on research she had done in Weimar.[30] The royalties were dutifully
handed over to her family and to a young cousin who as a cadet
(Fähnrich) was living far beyond his income. As an associate of the
Goethe archive she would have been a member of one of the most
prestigious clubs in the German literary elite. Yet she turned the
offer down, and there is no indication that she ever regretted this
decision.[31] Scholarly life would have been too tame to suit her for
long.

While work as a Goethe specialist may seem a detour on the path
toward radicalization, the other project in Lily's early self-education
took a more direct route. In the summer of 1890, during her romance with Gottfried von Pappenheim, the latter introduced her to
a fellow cavalry officer, Major Moritz von Egidy. Egidy was just then
in the process of discovering and formulating his ideas about a humane and socially conscious practical Christianity (ideas for which
he was soon forced to leave the military service), and Lily von
Kretschman immediately recognized the similarity of their views.
They became friends and began to correspond with each other. The
correspondence culminated, about five years later, in an exchange of
"open letters" published in a journal of which she was coeditor. The
correspondence, private as well as open, shows that Egidy was the
more timid reformer, while Lily became increasingly radical, until it
became apparent that he aimed toward a society in which genuine
Christianity might be applied, while she had convinced herself that
Christianity must be overcome; her attitude toward the religion she
l.ad been taught had become thoroughly Nietzschean, and one could
say that it was partly through Nietzsche that she eventually found
her way to Marx.

I have suggested that Lily von Kretschman's work in the Goethe
archive may seem a detour on her road to radicalization. However, it

could be argued that it was not a detour at all. One effect of this work was that she began to move in the highest literary circles; another, that she took a very active interest in the arts and letters of her time. Berlin in the early 1890s was one of the centers of literary activity and literary controversy; censorship and stage gossip were in the news; and Lily threw herself into this world with enthusiasm. Soon she had befriended the leading lights of this world and had become involved in the literary disputes of the day. A series of about twenty articles she wrote on literary themes between 1893 and 1902 shows a determined trend toward the left.[32] In the conflict between the established writers and the young rebels—*Tendenz* writers and Naturalists—she increasingly sided with the young against the old, even while criticizing the young for excesses, immaturities, or rude manners; but just as often she criticized them for not going far enough in their denunciation of social evils. For indeed in her survey of literature, the stage, and arts in general, she focused more and more on social themes, especially poverty and capitalism, the hypocrisies of sexual morality, and the oppression of women.

Moreover, the circles in which she moved in Berlin took in the radical elite of the capital—religious reformers, controversial writers, radical Russian exiles, *Kathedersozialisten* (socialist academics). With many of these she became good friends, at least until she moved further to the left.

Among the *Kathedersozialisten* she befriended, one must be singled out: Georg von Giżycki, Associate Professor of Moral Philosophy at the University of Berlin. Paralyzed from the waist down as the result of a childhood illness, Giżycki was one of the most radical intellectuals outside the Marxist movement in Germany at the time. He preached religious skepticism and materialism, democratic socialism, absolute freedom of inquiry, and the emancipation of women, on the basis of a humanitarian philosophy that was a blend of Bentham and John Stuart Mill, Rousseau and Condorcet, Fourier and Marx, Goethe and Nietzsche, Wollstonecraft, Chernyshevsky, and Ibsen. He did so from his university lectern and in the organization he had helped create, the German Society for Ethical Culture, a branch of the Ethical Culture movement founded some years earlier in the United States. Together with Lily von Kretschman, whom he married in the summer of 1893, he owned and edited a weekly journal,

Ethische Kultur, which allowed her to publish her own contributions freely. Giżycki died in March 1895, but in the brief time that he and Lily had together, he became her tutor, introducing her not only to a wide range of works in history, economics, philosophy, and politics, but also training her in research methods, the use of libraries, and in statistics. Most important, he encouraged and helped her to make herself independent intellectually.

This independence more and more alienated her from her family, and her family from her. While her parents doubtless rejoiced in her ability to earn money by writing, they were alarmed and offended by where she published and what she wrote: criticism of Christianity, radical feminism, expressions of sympathy with the working class, issues concerning sexuality and prostitution, and increasingly uncon-cealed socialist rhetoric. They disapproved of her new friends and associates and strongly objected to the idea of marriage to a professed atheist and socialist, and an impotent wheelchair patient to boot. They would have preferred that she stay at home, be a dutiful daughter, and help her mother run the household. There were countless ugly scenes, and in the end, when her father in mindless rage ran at her with a pistol in his hand, she moved in with Giżycki even though they were not yet married.

One should not underestimate the difficulty with which the daughter made this break and the sincerity of her repeated attempts to smooth relations with her parents. What made the rupture so painful for her was not only genuine love for her family but also the knowledge that she was designated to inherit her Augsburg aunt's great wealth; a total break would mean forfeiting this comfortable cushion of financial security.

Yet, in response to Lily's radicalization, most of her relatives and old friends did break with her, not always irrevocably, but at first with such harshness that in effect she found herself cast out from her family. After she joined the Marxist movement and married Hein-rich Braun, her father officially disowned her, and her aunt, who surprisingly had agreed to meet Heinrich before the marriage,[33] eventually closed her houses to Lily. Cousin Tilly sometime around 1900 decided that she would not want to continue corresponding with a godless Communist and returned all of Lily's old letters to her—a cruel blow to Braun, but a fortunate turn of events for her biographers.

Meanwhile, in the course of her radicalization, Lily made and lost friends at a rapid rate. During her first years in Berlin (1890-1895) she made a splash among the radical intelligentsia, and many of them, in addition to the Christian reformer Moritz von Egidy, became close friends—social scientists such as Ferdinand Toennies (who proposed to her) and Werner Sombart; publicists such as Maximilian Harden and Albert Langen; prominent fiction writers such as Detlev von Lilienkron, Hermann Sudermann, Gerhart Hauptmann, and Thomas Mann; leaders of the socialist movement such as August Bebel, Kurt Eisner, Peter Struve, and the Bavarian SPD leader Georg von Vollmar; finally, virtually all the leading figures in the German, Austrian, and Scandinavian feminist movements. Further, during her stays in London (1896) and Paris (1900) she also befriended many outstanding British and French radicals, feminists, and socialists, including Léon Blum and Romain Rolland, George Bernard Shaw, the Webbs, and Alys Russell. Most of these friends turned against her once she had joined the SPD, or she in turn abandoned them, either because she considered them lukewarm politically or because the Party forbade all collaboration with bourgeois radicals. Braun was therefore, in the final analysis, compelled to seek friends, allies, and associates primarily within the German Marxist movement.

In this quest, however, she was bitterly disappointed. Although at first the SPD leadership hailed her conversion as a spectacular coup and gave her a warm welcome, the relationships of cooperation and friendship she had hoped to form did not develop, and the friendly reception she had received soon turned into reserve, coldness, and at last hostility. Intrigues, insults, slander, and even physical attacks were heaped on her, until it finally became obvious to her that virtually the entire party leadership had turned into enemies and would have liked to see her leave the movement.

While it is clear that by temperament, outward appearance, and conviction, she was at best marginal to the German Marxist movement, the root cause of her estrangement from it was her irreconcilable clash with Clara Zetkin, the acknowledged leader of the women's organization in the SPD. Although Zetkin clearly appreciated the bitter sacrifices Braun had made in joining the movement,[34] she seems never to have trusted her completely. She sensed Braun's boundless ambition to attain prominence in the Marxist movement and therefore saw her as a dangerous rival. She watched Braun's aristocratic manner and bearing and decided that in her heart this woman was not of the proletariat. She was totally out of sympathy with the humanist interpretation that Braun gave to Marxism, criticized her reform proposals as a betrayal of revolutionary principles, and regarded her feminist concerns as a harmful distraction designed to confuse and divide the working class.

Braun thus remained an outsider in the Marxist party. The attitude of outreach that had attracted her was decidedly onesided: while they seemed eager to acquaint her with the world of the female proletariat, she could not, of course, open up to them in analogous fashion about the glittering but empty life of the aristocratic lady. They would not understand why she had ever left such a life of privilege, could not recognize the emptiness beneath the glamor. Discussing her own past would only have further alienated Lily from her new comrades: and in fact she never overcame their suspicions that she was an intruder, a spoiled aristocrat who had contempt for workers and had come to assume leadership over them. In their essentially puritan culture, they could not understand her elegance; and because of the presents Heinrich lavished on her she acquired the reputation of a spendthrift who had dragged Heinrich to his doom. Similarly, her openness about sexual matters earned her the reputation of being sex-mad and shameless. Her very physiognomy, her speech, the simple elegance of her clothes, as well as the independence of her views—all these alienated her from the fanatically egalitarian group she had joined. In short, she encountered the same hostility met with by some men who have sought to join feminist causes or by white radicals who wanted to associate with black militants. In these and analogous cases, the primary victims of oppression seek to strengthen their own solidarity by drawing an absolute and impenetrable boundary between themselves and all members from the oppressor group. An article reviewing her memoirs puts it as follows:

> In order to compensate for the difference it is not enough if the individual who is more strongly developed culturally renounces the advantages he or she brings along: instead, he or she would have to acquire something positive, a totality of perceptions which might be summarized by the term proletarian conciousness. It is this acid test which deserters of both sexes from the bourgeois camp will almost

always fail. The Russians have a term for it: to go among the people: but those who decide to do this know that they take on martyrdom. It is possible to become a missionary, but that does not make one a Negro.[35]

In 1901 Braun published her major work, *Die Frauenfrage,* a milestone in the study of the political economy of the female work force. Under normal circumstances, having written such an important book would have made Braun a force to be reckoned with in feminist socialism. But for this very reason it intensified Zetkin's apprehensions that here was a dangerous rival, especially since she felt that the book had deliberately slighted her own contributions to the movement.[36] The publication of this work therefore deepened the rift between the two women.

In a very short time Zetkin managed to turn the SPD women's organization into a solid and bitterly hostile front against Braun; and, to isolate her in the party as a whole, she enlisted the aid of influential friends, especially Franz Mehring and Karl Kautsky, prominent party theorists and journalists and, for the time being, high priests of orthodoxy in the movement. In all these attempts to eliminate Braun as a rival and to belittle her contributions, her methods were so crude and the tone of her incentive so vile that even her close friend and political ally Rosa Luxemburg, seems to have recoiled from it,[37] and there were several instances when the party's governing board (*Vorstand*) or the major party newspaper, *Vorwärts,* rebuked Zetkin for her harassment of Braun.

The reason why the party nonetheless tolerated such harassment was, at least in part, that this conflict was dismissed by the leadership as a fight between two hysterical women. But much of it may also have been an indirect assault on Braun's husband, Heinrich, who was not very popular in the SPD, to put it mildly.

The son of a middle-class Jewish family, Heinrich Braun was born in 1854 and raised in Bohemia, obtained a doctorate in economics and so impressed his professors that they obtained an academic appointment for him, which he refused, however, because it was offered on condition that he be baptized. He turned to journalism instead and founded and edited a number of highly successful socialist periodicals.[38] An early and eager convert to Marxism, he joined forces with Wilhelm Liebknecht and Karl Kautsky to found the journal *Neue Zeit,* the theoretical mouthpiece of orthodox Marxism, and had for a while served on the editorial board of *Vorwärts.* He must be regarded as one of the principal inventors of orthodox Marxism.[39] A highly persuasive, restless activist, he was eager to recruit learned persons, intellectuals like himself, to the movement. One of the people whom he converted back to Marxism was Franz Mehring, who later turned into his bitterest enemy.

Heinrich Braun thus had high connections in the party. He had corresponded with Marx and, as editor of socialist journals of international reputation, was in touch with the intellectual elite of socialist parties throughout the world. His brother Adolf was a prominent leader in the socialist trade union movement; his sister Emma was the wife of Victor Adler, the leader of the Austrian Marxist party. Of imposing appearance and booming voice, Braun was a persuasive speaker and a restless activist whose life's aim was to widen the intellectual appeal of Marxism. He seems to have made friends easily, but lost as many as he made. The reason for this cannot have been merely his tendency toward Revisionist ideas. While outwardly the party made a show of unanimity, it did in fact harbor people of widely diverging views; and there were many far less orthodox than Braun who remained in good standing with the leadership. Hence the reasons for Braun's status as an outsider must at least in large part be sought in his personality. Assertive, argumentative, and easily offended, he liked to make other people look foolish. Also, he tended to be rather pedantic in his speech as well as his writing, all of which made him an easy target for party comrades with a desire to denounce intellectuals and academics within the movement.

In addition, Braun had the reputation of being financially unreliable and irresponsible, a ruthless and tricky negotiator. He was known also as a skillful and successful fund raiser, or, as some people from whom he had raised funds put it acidly, a genius at borrowing. This talent for mobilizing other people's money did not particularly endear him to many of his associates.[40] When asked about repayment he would haughtily declare himself to be above such grubby matters. He was generous, indeed lavish, forever ready to give his last penny to others; but this last penny had often come out of someone else's pocket. In his personal habits he was a crank, a health-food and physical-exercise faddist, overly fastidious in some respects and totally oblivious to the conventions in other matters, such as clothing. Once inflamed about some idea, he could not rest until he had imparted his enthusiasm to others and enlisted their support, which made him seem exploitative. The daughter of Paul Singer, a former friend turned enemy, thought that "Heinrich Braun had some sort of obsession which compelled him to exhaust others for his work."[41]

In short, Heinrich Braun was a perturbing presence, and a pattern developed in which the genuine admiration of party comrades, initially his collaborators, turned into intense dislike. Indeed, the entire party leadership seemed to belong to this category. One of the chief reasons for his unpopularity with the party leadership may have been his marital history, which was considered scandalous. On 5 January 1895 Braun had won custody of his two sons following a long and bitterly contested divorce suit against his first wife.[42] To take care of the boys he hired a young housekeeper whom friends in the party recommended. Within a very short time he proposed, and they were married on 21 March 1895.[43] Not long afterwards the recently widowed Lily von Giżycki came to him to ask for help in her financial distress, and the two immediately became deeply infatuated. They made an attempt to set up a *ménage à trois* with Heinrich's new bride,[44] but the latter soon balked at that. So less than a year after marrying her and shortly after she had given birth to a son, Heinrich Braun once again sued for divorce. After another bitter legal battle, the divorce was granted in June of 1896, and a few weeks later Heinrich and Lily were married. The SPD establishment, particularly old friends of the second Mrs. Braun, were scandalized. The Brauns never quite overcame the stigma of that scandal.

So much for Lily's early life. I hope to have given an adequate sketch of her origins and upbringing, the reasons for her break with her class and its conventions, and the circumstances that totally disappointed her ardent quest for comradeship with like-minded rebels. Henceforth she was to fight a terribly lonely fight for her ideas, and it is to these ideas that I intend to turn now. But these ideas in turn must be placed within their political and ideological background. I shall begin sketching this background by providing a summary of history of the German women's movement and Lily Braun's place in it.

II

GERMAN FEMINISM BEFORE 1895

When the Kretschman family moved to Berlin in 1890, feminism was in the air, and Lily took to it as if it had always been her natural element. Plays by Henrik Ibsen and his epigones were being performed on many stages; women's organizations were in the process of being founded or reorganized. A spate of female poets had begun to write about their specific pains and longings. In Reichstag committees, where drafts of the new imperial civil code was being discussed, questions were raised about the status that women were to be given in the new code. Prostitution was rampant, and sex scandals outraged public opinion. Lily von Kretschman eagerly followed these developments and soon found herself an activist in women's organizations. What was the nature of these organizations? How had they developed, and how did Lily fit into them?

As elsewhere in Europe, German feminism had begun as a feeble intellectual stirring in the eighteenth century, which received additional stimulus from the French revolution and liberal Christianity. It became a clearly discernible movement only toward the middle of the century as part of a growing *democratic* movement. Moreover, in Germany, as elsewhere, feminism suffered several severe setbacks, and after each such defeat the ideas and strivings for women's emancipation had to be reinvented.

A number of radical representatives of the German enlightenment advocated women's emancipation. The eminent eighteenth-century historian August Ludwig von Schlözer, wishing to prove that women were intellectually the equals of men, gave his daughter Dorothea (1770–1825) a thorough education, and at the age of seventeen she obtained a doctor's degree from the University of Göttingen. A well-known essayist of the time, Johan Georg Zimmermann, in a voluminous treatise on loneliness, emphasized the civilizing influence of well-educated women.[1] In their novels and plays Germany's leading writers presented heroines who personified the autonomous emancipated woman: for instance, Lessing's *Minna von Barnhelm* and Goethe's *Iphigenie*. Disappointed by the fact that the French revolution had not granted women equal status with men, T.G. von Hippel in 1792 (the same year in which Mary Wollstonecraft published her *A Vindication of the Rights of Woman*) devoted an entire book to the argument that women deserved equality of status in every area of public life.

The Napoleonic period subsequently encouraged a variety of nonconformist phenomena, among them the prominence of bright young women whose homes became salons in which the political and intellectual elite mingled freely. The best-known among these hostesses, Rachel Varnhagen, must be considered an important pioneer of feminist ideas in general. The Romantic movement of that time, among other things, encouraged the idea that women, like men, have a right to act freely in accordance with their emotions. This was most clearly expressed by Friedrich Schlegel in his novel *Lucinde,* published around 1800, which preached free love and the abolition of the double standard.

These and other radical notions, however, were silenced when, after 1815, political and intellectual repression descended on Germany. They reappeared (feebly, at first) in the writings of the Young Germany movement, which were probably inspired by the works of George Sand. Gutzkow's drama *Saul* presented a feminist heroine who was a sort of Joan of Arc among the Philistines; Hebbel's *Judith,* written in 1836, also focused on a woman wanting to liberate herself. If we add Kleist's earlier *Penthesileia* to this list of heroines, it may appear remarkable how often the image of the warrior woman dominates in these early feminist stirrings.

The Young Germany movement in its turn gave way to the broader democratic ground swell that led to the revolution of 1848. In 1844, Helene Marie Weber published a series of pamphlets on "Woman's Rights and Wrongs" dealing with a wide range of women's concerns, such as their equal intellectual potential, their claim to property rights, and the scandal of the institution of marriage, in which women were forced to merge their identity and their name with those of their husbands. Weber demanded citizen's rights for women, as well as their right to enter the ministry.[2] In the same year, 1844, Louise Otto-Peters, born around 1820, began to write feminist essays for Robert Blum's radical *Vaterlandsblätter*. During the revolution, in 1849, she founded a paper of her own, *Die Frauenzeitung*, which survived for three years; later, she continued to agitate for women's emancipation. In line with the democratic preoccupations of the period, she concentrated on agitation for equal rights, particularly political rights; indeed, she argued that participation in politics was women's *duty*—toward themselves as well as toward the community.

As a movement, feminism still did not exist, and the fight waged by Otto-Peters must have been terribly lonely. After brief revolutionary upheavels of 1848/9 there was a conservative reaction, and the unified Germany that emerged about twenty years later was shaped by the reactionary victors of the 1849 counterrevolution. The sovereign states which constituted Germany before that were undemocratic. Most of them did not acknowledge citizens' rights, but stressed the duties of subjects—not a suitable basis on which to found feminist agitation. Women's organizations did indeed exist, but they were either charitable endeavors based on an ideology which argued that women are the natural helpers of the needy, or literary circles that justified their existence by the argument that well-read females make better, or more valuable, housewives.

The creation of the North German Federation and of the German Reich, however, had a politicizing effect, as did the simultaneous burgeoning of corporate capitalism with its many societal changes—the rise of the bourgeoisie, the growth of independent professions and the white-collar stratum, urbanization, and the like. This politicization entailed a new beginning for the German women's movement. Several new organizations were created between 1865 and 1869, among them the *Frauenbildungsverein* (Women's Education Association), founded in 1865 by Otto-Peters and Auguste Schmidt; the Berlin *Verein für Erwerbsfähigkeit des weiblichen Geschlechts* (Association for the Earning Ability of the Female Sex), later known after its founder as the *Lette-Verein;* an Association of German Women Teachers; a German Women Workers' Association; and, in October 1865, the *Allgemeine Deutsche Frauenverein* (General German Women's Association), also created by Otto-Peters and Schmidt.

While the Women Workers' Association obviously tried to represent the interest of women employed in industry, the other organizations concerned themselves primarily with the fight for women's right to independent careers and to all the education and training necessary for them. These various associations tried in a wide variety of ways to prepare women for wage work and careers. They accumulated funds that could be spent on scholarships for promising young women, created schools and continuing education courses to teach home economics and many other useful skills, though mostly skills used in lines of work primarily dominated by women. They created libraries and day care centers or kindergartens run according to Fröbel's progressive educational theories. They agitated and petitioned for women's rights to independent careers, equal access to educational institutions, and equal wages for equal work. If at the time of the 1848 revolution German feminism had agitated for citizenship rights, the successor movement twenty years later argued that it was fighting for women's rights to develop their talent and energies freely and fully.

There were, however, other concerns which the women's movement of the 1860s made its own, particularly care for the least privileged among women. In this connection, these various organizations engaged in activities to rehabilitate female convicts, set up homes for aged single or widowed women, and for homeless girls, and protested against the system by which the states controlled prostitution. Prostitution in Germany at that time was a licensed profession controlled by the police. The sale of sexual services without a license was a serious offense; having a license made it legal. However, once registered, a woman was stigmatized as a whore, was subject to perpetual harassment and exploitation by the police as well as by pimps and madams, and was condemned to pariah status for the rest of her life. The literature of the time is replete with accounts of naive young job seekers from the countryside being trapped into the profession by unscrupulous exploiters.[3]

The leaders of feminist organizations created in the 1860s assumed that all genuine emancipation must be self-emancipation. Hence they were eager to mobilize women for action and to raise their consciousness. In this they were encouraged by some sympathetic men. At the founding congress of the Allgemeine Deutsche Frauenverein, Louise Otto-Peters asked Ludwig Eckardt, a veteran feminist, to open the proceedings; he declined by saying, "The women's congress must not begin with the inconsistency of being opened by a man. The women must manage their cause themselves, if it is not to be defeated from the very beginning."[4]

The organization took this to heart and in its bylaws specified, after heated controversy, that men could only become auxiliary members without vote. Its leaders were familiar also with the notion of networking. At its 1873 congress, Auguste Schmidt argued that a sisterly bond was being created among the members that was stronger than mere fellow-membership. This association, she said, was not only a means toward an end, but was in itself an important end. One year earlier, she had defined the essence of feminism by suggesting that the chief demand was the right to education and training, and the chief method was self-help. The women's question, she continued, was not a bread-and-butter question, but a question of equal status: women should share all rights and duties equally.[5]

On the other hand, the ideology of German feminism at this time was still based on the assumption that women had duties towards husbands, parents, or children which could preclude their pursuing a career. Similarly, these feminists took for granted that marriage and housekeeping, and particularly child rearing, were the "natural calling" of women, and that professional education which prepared them for these pursuits was most suitable for women.

In retrospect, the achievements of German feminism in the 1860s and 1870s appear to have been meager. A few promising students received scholarship stripends; membership in its organizations grew; their educational and library facilities served a growing number of users; and their journals had enough subscribers to keep alive. In time, liberal mayors in some German cities began to compete in offering to host the annual or biennial congresses of the General German Women's Association. Yet one cannot discern any major impact.

By the last decade of the nineteenth century, the situation of women in most German states was still one of total dependency on their husbands, fathers, brothers, or other males. Legally women were considered incompetent, on a par with children, criminals, and the insane. They had no right to dispose of their own property, and in many states they did not even have the right to know what their husbands did with their property. Their testimony in court was discounted as unreliable. They were barred from institutions of higher education and from most professions. In most states there were no female physicians, lawyers, secondary school teachers, or publishers. The Prussian law on associations provided that female persons were forbidden to belong to any political association; the mere presence of a woman at a political meeting was sufficient reason for the police to dissolve the meeting as illegal. For instance, in 1894, the city of Nürnberg agreed to host the SPD party congress only on condition that no women would be admitted to the meetings; the party then held its congress in the more liberal city of Frankfurt.[6] In addition, in Wilhelmine Germany, a middle- or upper-class woman could hardly go into the street alone without risking being treated as a whore, nor could she travel easily without an escort.

Beginning in the 1880s, however, the German women's movement became noticeably more radical, or at least it developed radical wings. The reasons for this probably lie in the rapid modernization of the country and its intensified contacts with the rest of the world. More women were drawn into work in the public sphere, often laboring under degrading and unhealthy conditions for pitiably low wages. Meanwhile, middle-class women were relieved of more household chores, because many of the things previously produced at home could now be purchased cheaply. The growing rationalization and bureaucratization of life, moreover, tended to erode the functions of the family as the focus of activities. Urbanization provided novel forms of social life and entertainment; it also meant the rapid growth of prostitution. A series of short but bloody wars lowered the male population, and thus increased the proportion of women who would remain single or widowed. Biological science convinced more and more women that the custom of tight lacing, which produced the fashionable hourglass figure, was destructive of their health. Also, there was the example of women's agitation in England and the United States. These and other developments made the time ripe for radical feminism to emerge.[7]

A volume of poetry, *Irdische und unirdische Träume* (Earthly and

unearthly dreams) was published in 1889 by Maria Janitschek. It
contained a poem, "A Modern Woman," which made the book a
scandal:

> A man offended once a woman in
> Such a way as no one possibly
> Could either pardon or forget.
>
> A long time passed. And then one evening
> The evildoer heard sharp knocking at his door.
> He called, "Come in," and was amazed to see
> Before him in deep mourning garb a woman.
>
> When she unveiled her face she let him see
> Into her eyes so large and stiff with pride,
> Into large eyes burnt out from pain. . . .
> He smiled, embarrassed, for a shudder
> Came over him. . . . "Sit down," he bade politely.
> But she declined and in a calm voice said,
> "You have committed grave offense against me,
> God only witnessed it. . . . Before this God, before you
> And before myself, I will erase
> This spot, this blemish on my honor
> Delivered by your hand.
>
>   Now listen!
> I only have one means to do this:
> I cannot possibly go to a stranger
> To tell him frankly what I hardly
> Dare tell myself. Hence there can be
> No judge for me except one blind, deaf, dumb
> (Telling about what's past would be exactly
> Redoing it, dishonoring me once more),
> Thus there is one way only: Here are weapons; choose!"
> She placed a little box upon the table,
> He opened it.—
>
>   For quite a while the two
> Stood silent. Then he peered into her face,
> She kept her glittering large eye directed
> Firmly at the guns.
>
>   And suddenly he burst
> Into loud laughter. But then a fiery red
> Rose up onto the pale white cheeks
> Of the young woman. What if this laughter
> Were all the answer he would give? She felt like screaming
> With rage and hurt. But she controlled herself

And mildly said, "Suppose some clumsy stranger
Stepped unintentionally upon your foot,
Not thinking twice you'd challenge him to duel
Without considering such reaction ludicrous.
Consider now: A man stepped, not upon my toes,
My heart he trod to pieces and my honor!
Am I demanding more than you would ask
For an incautious step? Do tell me,
Is this not fair?"

                    He smiled and had the gall to look
Into her glowing irate face. "Dear child," he said,
"You seem to have forgotten that a woman
Cannot engage in duel with a man.
If you go to a judge, dear child, and tell him
All that has happened, I will gladly
Accept his sentence. If you will not do this,
You simply should forget what you regard
As shameful injury. You see, my love,
Woman are made for suffering and for forgiveness."
And then she laughed. "My choice is self-dishonor
Or calmly tolerating my disgrace,
And *that,* that is the answer which a man
Dares give in this enlightened era
To women whom he has offended."
                         "None other
would be proper."
                 "Then you should know that women
Have grown up in the nineteenth century."
Said this with flashing eye and felled him with a shot.

The new feminist militancy expressed in this poem found various expressions around 1890. For one thing, a major political party, the Social Democratic party, which represented the Marxist movement, had taken up the cause of women's emancipation and written in into their party platform. Second, following the example of Ibsen's Nora, who walks out of her doll's house, a figure called the New Woman began to speak up—asserting herself and her right not only to a career, but also to her own sexuality, whatever form that might take. In the spirit of Strindberg and Nietzsche, a New Morality was being preached which demanded men's and women's liberation from all conventions and institutions, including the conventional sexual morality. "We want to be modern!" says such a New Woman in a novel, *Halb,* published by Käthe Schirrmacher in 1895. "That means a break with misunderstood Greek and Roman ideas—a break with orthodox religion—freedom, use of our energy, nature—independence, experimentation rather than abstraction and stereotype—a triumphant ego! In such a transition the weak may succumb, those transitional types that are no longer very old and not yet very new—but we, we will make it!"[8] In countless stage plays and novels this New Woman was portrayed, or, more often, caricatured; but she was also beginning to speak for herself, particularly in the form of poetry.[9] Further, a new civil code for the German Reich was being drafted in the 1890s; and much public debate focused on it, including agitation for provisions that would give women equal legal status with men.

A cursory survey of ideas advanced by Helene Lange (1848–1930) will show some of the trends of German feminism in the last decade of the nineteenth century. Lange was cofounder of the *Allgemeine Deutsche Lehrerinnenverein* (General Association of German Women Teachers), and editor of its journal, *Die Frau.* To judge by her writings, she appears to have been a person of considerable erudition, radical democratic convictions, and the courage to be unconventional. Her style is crisp, critical, and, within the German context, fairly unsentimental. While it is unfair to reduce her voluminous writings to a paragraph or two, one might nonetheless summarize her work by stating that she concentrated her attention on the conflict between women's private and public lives. Women, in her opinion, constituted the last protective bastion of the rapidly crumbling institution of the family, but they were nonetheless forcefully drawn into the public life of wage work and careers, and they should indeed be encouraged to participate in public life. Motherhood and careers were both proper callings, yet they were in conflict, and any women pursuing both would have to carry the well-known double burden.

Participation in public life, she suggested, was not only women's right, but also their duty. Women, she argued, have a specifically feminine culture to offer, which, if it were allowed to be activated in society, could significantly civilize the prevalent culture of masculinity. Yet the social and economic structure prevented women from pursuing careers, and this structure was sexist. Hence the systematic frustration of women's potentials for participation in public life impoverished humanity.

German feminism as expressed by Lange made ambitious demands. But almost always it carried the implicit conviction that women are different, and therefore that there is such a thing as feminine culture, equally as worthy as, and perhaps worthier than, the culture of masculinity. Bertha von Suttner, the first woman to win the Nobel Peace Prize, expressed this rather angrily when she wrote:

> *Free, Autonomous, Soft-hearted,* industrious, serene, independent, truthful, honorable, intelligent, moderate, morally clean, cultivating beauty, kind, resolute: These and quite a few others are the qualities which the human being of the future will have to possess if indeed the society of the future is to constitute itself as the kind of system which moralists and social reformers are striving to promote.
>
> Contemporary humanity—men as well as women—is still very far removed from this ideal; and the main reason for that is that the above-mentioned attributes have been divided, half of them given to the one half of humanity, the other half to the others, in the form of duties, and the vices opposed to the list of virtues have likewise been distributed among the sexes, though in the guise of privileges. For instance, independence, industriousness, intelligence, and resoluteness have remained the exclusive properties of men; but moral purity, soft-heartedness, and moderation have been entrusted only to the woman (i.e., to the "ideal" of the woman), and people of both sexes in contemporary society consist of one half which is permitted to manifest crudity, cruelty, and immorality, plus another half for which dependency, helplessness, ignorance, and unfreedom are not only permitted, but indeed seem obligatory: *This*, of course, cannot yield a totality in which we can attain that ennobled state of society enriched by freedom and happiness for which we are striving.
>
> The women's question therefore does not imply the question whether women should become what men are. Instead it asks whether all human beings, male and female, should have the obligation and the unhindered opportunity to strive toward an ideal which, once they reached it, would eradicate servitude and hatred, meanness, stupidity, and vice, from human society. The women's movement is not at all a struggle of women against men, rather it is a phase in the evolution of all humanity which strives upward in solidarity. Humanity wants to employ its total energies for the sake of making progress; it will not, it must not, let half of its intelligence lie fallow—or half of its earning power and and productive potential, half of its talents. . . . [10]

While one might interpret this passage as a protest against the stereotype which associates women with softness and compassion and men with enterprise, intellect, courage, and the like, the prevalent attitude among German feminists was that of Helene Lange, i.e., the conviction that women were by nature more caring, more ready for self-sacrifice and service.[11]

Lange and other late nineteenth-century German feminists minced no words in their indictment of sexism. Yet they were careful not to break the institutional framework of their society. That means specifically that they had no intention to destroy the existing political system, existing property relations, the Christian church, or the monogamous family. Indeed, they seemed frightened by feminists who attacked these institutions; they reacted with embarrassment to frank discussions of sexuality, prostitution, and venereal disease; and they fought bitterly against both the New Morality and the socialist movement. While radical feminists assailed modern marriage as a form of prostitution or dependency, one of Lange's associates in the women's movement, Marianne Weber, argued that the spread of monogamy had been a victory won by women over men's innate polygamous instincts.[12] And even innocuous reform like coeducation did not find favor with some of these activists in the feminist movement: might not some tender boys' souls be dented if girls in their class were smarter than they?[13] In short, this woman's radicalism was insufficient to let her question or challenge conventional gender roles. Meanwhile, her antagonism to Marxism caused her as late as 1914 to criticize Lily Braun's major work, Die Frauenfrage, as a one-sided application of economic determinism, and as arguing that the abolition of capitalism would solve all of women's problems. These criticisms reveal that after 1901, Lange had read nothing written by Braun; and this in turn demonstrates the deep gulf between "bourgeois" and "proletarian" feminism.

As a matter of political principle, Lange and her sisters in the liberal feminist movement believed in advocating and effecting reforms piecemeal, step by little step. If English women, she wrote in 1895, today sit in county councils and on school boards, if they can work with men in hospitals and colleges, then it is because they have always concentrated their attention on the next small step, and never wasted their energies on chasing after utopian goals.[14] Similar ideas were expressed by one of her colleagues who opposed women's agitation for the right to vote. Let us not set ourselves such an impossible goal, she wrote, let us not antagonize the establishment, let us not make radical demands while our numbers are still small; and let us not try to cooperate with the socialist movement or attack the family.[15]

On the left wing of the German feminist movement in the 1890s there were a few women who thought otherwise. They believed that gains are made only by those who set ambitious goals and make sweeping demands, and they were eager to bridge the gulf between liberal and socialist feminism. Among them was Hanna Bieber, founder of an organization which tried to abolish organized prostitution and to protect women against sexual harassment (Verein Jugendschutz), as well as Minna Cauer, who in 1890 set up an organization called Verein Frauenwohl (Women's Welfare Association), in which Lily von Giżycki became active and of which in 1895 she became Deputy Chairperson. Like other feminist organizations, Frauenwohl conducted a wide variety of courses in trade skills and secondary-level academic subjects. Like them, it fought against state-organized prostitution, and demanded equality for women under the law and in education. But it widened this demand to include the vote, full participation in politics, and an equal rights amendment to the constitution. It was more active than other organizations in trying to promote systematic research into the condition of women, and, in fact, tried to set up a special library for women's studies.[16] It sought to create wider opportunities for those women who ought to be seen as victims of special kinds of oppression, and created special organizations to serve them—legal aid associations for women, an employment agency for actresses and other theater personnel, an association for aid to female white-collar employees, and the like. Foremost, however, it differed from other feminist organizations by its systematic attempt to address women workers in industry, to discuss their problems and try to organize them, and by its attempt to unite all women's organizations, bourgeois and proletarian, under one comprehensive organization for concerted action.

For the Verein Frauenwohl Lily von Giżycki in the fall of 1894 started a press service, and a few months later she and Minna Cauer were able to publish the first issue of their journal, Die Frauenbewegung, which was to appear on the first and fifteenth of every month. The journal spoke not only for the Association but also for half a dozen other women's organizations in Berlin, Dresden, and Zürich.

Georg von Giżycki in 1890 (Friedrich-Ebert-Stiftung, Bonn)

Together with Cauer, Lily wrote the paper's statement of aims; she also contributed a biweekly column of news from the women's movement throughout the world, and during the first year (1895) contributed six lengthy articles. One of the first issues also featured an article by her husband arguing in favor of women's suffrage. Like the Association, the journal set itself the aim of uniting or integrating all the branches of the German women's movement and thereby encouraging the movement to make bolder demands.

It was this effort to unite all women's organizations that earned them condemnation from left and right. The leader of the proletarian women's organization affiliated with the SPD, Clara Zetkin, jeeringly denounced the editorial line of *Die Frauenbewegung* as "women's libbers' pipedreams about class harmony." Rebuked by the party paper, *Vorwärts*, about the rude tone of her attack, she defended herself by arguing that the appearance of a non-party feminist paper which had come out in favor of worker's rights had created confusion in the ranks of proletarian women. Most "bourgeois" feminists, meanwhile, rejected all and any collaboration with socialists. When in 1894 the roof organization Cauer had demanded was formed, this new organization, the *Bund Deutscher Frauenvereine* (League of German Women's Associations), claimed to represent all German women; but in the debates on whether or not socialists were to be admitted, a mere four, among them Cauer, Giżycki, and Bieber, voted in favor, and the proposal was roundly refeated.

One other preoccupation which the Association Frauenwohl sought to share with other feminist organizations in Germany was its conception of the women's movement as an international or cross-national movement in which the women of any country ought to learn from, and cooperate with, their sisters across the borders. This too appears to have annoyed the leaders of most other German feminist organizations greatly. When Frances Willard and Lady Isabel Somerset, speaking for the World Women's Christian Temperance Union, published an invitation to all German women's organizations to send delegates to the WWCTU's third biennial congress in London (14–21 June 1895), the only German women to heed this call and attend the congress were Lily von Giżycki and Minna Cauer.

Altogether, the line taken by the new radicals sounded too much

like a reproach to please the veterans of the German women's movement. Here is what Cauer and Giżycki wrote in the editorial with
which they introduced their new journal:

> The German women's movement has made gratifying progress in
> recent years. Even those opposed to the demands made by the female
> sex are beginning to take the women's question seriously. Nonethe-
> less, our English, American, and French sisters are ahead of us, not
> only in what they have achieved but also in the unity of their
> tactics. . . .
>
> The goal of the women's movement, equal rights for both sexes, will
> never be reached if women do not have a sense of belonging to-
> gether, however much they may uphold their special interests.
>
> We therefore create this journal, which is supposed to constitute a
> unification of all the separate endeavors for the benefit of the female
> sex.
>
> We want to give due attention both to woman's fight for equal access
> to higher education and to her fight for equal wages. Her intellectual
> as well as her material misery shall be described in these pages. At
> the same time, the victories won by women in all the civilized
> countries shall be discussed as fully as possible; for every success lifts
> the courage and hope of those still fighting their battle and is the
> most potent demonstration that their goals are attainable. . . .

The editors of the new journal then invited representatives of
every faction within the women's movement to contribute to its
pages. "We will make our columns accessible to all opinions being
voiced within the women's movement because we believe that only
full knowledge of these various opinions will be conducive to their
appreciation, and that mutual discussion of all views is the best
means to promote unity." This appeal did not find much of an echo.
From the point of view of most feminists, this willingness to cooperate with socialists made the journal suspect; from the point of view of
the women in the Marxist movement, it was a dangerous intrusion
into the territory of the proletariat. In the next chapter, we will take
a brief look at this movement, which in Germany was organized as
the Social Democratic party (SPD).

III

THE SPD IN THE EARLY 1890s

In Germany, in the middle of the nineteenth century, a workers' movement had begun in response to dislocations resulting from the industrial and commercial revolutions. It had grown out of the radical fringe of the revolutionary democratic movement. Its earliest activists were impoverished craftsmen—tailors, printers, weavers, carpenters, and the like—whose ideas derived from democratic rhetoric, from writings of some Utopian socialists, from Christian notions of justice, and from the memory of feudal freedoms and protections. As an organization, the workers' movement gradually coalesced out of disjointed and often competing political organizations and trade unions, formulating a variety of more or less socialist ideas. The party that Lily joined was the result of a merger in 1875 of two principal groups—one of them created by Ferdinand Lassalle, the other led by people who tended to espouse the ideas of Engels and Marx. What gave this party its most powerful impetus may well have been the Paris Commune of 1871, which came to serve as a role model for militant socialists everywhere, and which instilled an acute fear of the workers' movement into respectable people throughout the civilized world. Seven years later, memories of this scare enabled Bismarck to have the German Reichstag pass the famous anti-socialist law, which outlawed the party and all its auxiliary organizations, including its newspapers, leaving only the Social Democratic deputies to the Reichstag itself, who enjoyed immunity from prosecution.

Historians of Wilhelmine Germany have long taken it for granted that it was this restrictive law, renewed periodically for the next twelve years, that eventually made the Social Democratic movement strong. It gave the followers of the movement a sense of strength

39

through the common experience of persecution—a feeling of solidarity, comradeship, and mutual dependence. It strengthened the self-confidence of the party leadership and of the rank-and-file; it also reinforced their revolutionary rhetoric and gave them a sense of exclusiveness, which expressed itself not only in the invective they used in discussing non-members, but also in the resolve never to collaborate with anyone who was not a party comrade. The Social Democratic caucus in the Reichstag expressed these attitudes by occasionally introducing sweeping reform legislation, and by voting "nay" on virtually everything else. They also engaged in a good deal of symbolic politics, such as remaining seated when everyone stood up for some figure of high authority, or refusing to consider nominating one of their members for a Reichstag vice-presidency: horror of horrors, as Reichstag vice-president, a Social Democratic member of this steering committee would have to be received by the Emperor and make his obeisance.

Under its defiant front, however, the party was surprisingly tame, rendered ineffectual by its exclusiveness and attitude of absolute non-cooperation. While its ideologists covered this policy of *attentisme* by trumpeting out their confidence in the forthcoming victory of socialism, the party was in fact very much on the defensive. The period of illegal, subversive activity may have had a heroic ring, but it had also brought hardships, very bitter hardships at times; and there probably was no major socialist leader who wished to provoke another anti-socialist law. Hence, the party seemed anxiously concerned with doing everything legally; they did not want to do, say, or print anything that might bring about a new restrictive measure. While bravely talking about class exclusiveness, many Social Democratic leaders were in fact smarting under the political and social ostracism to which they were subject. In short, the party had a certain split personality, in which defiance and defensiveness coexisted uneasily; its leaders were proud to be revolutionaries and eager to show that they were not; they were against the system and very much part of it.[1]

A split personality suggests itself also to anyone examining the official ideology of the party, which was called Marxism. In chapter 7, I will discuss in some detail this system of ideas and the challenges it was to face from inside the party around 1900. The SPD's strong commitment to Marxist doctrine was a comparatively late phenomenon. The early programs of the workers' parties and movements had been an eclectic mix of socialist utopian ideas, with demands for improvements in work conditions and the extension of citizens' rights. Marx and Engels were far away in London or Manchester, unknown to most, highly respected by a few, feared by some, hated by others. Only a bare handful of socialist militants had ever read any of their writings. To the rank-and-file of the party in the mid-seventies, Lassalle was the founder, and Eugen Dühring was beginning to be regarded as the ideological spokesman. The party's affiliation with the First International—a moribund organization in any event—was not conducive to changing this situation.

What did change the ideological orientation of the German workers' movement was the publication in 1878 of a series of articles by Friedrich Engels, later published as a book, *Herr Eugen Dühring's Revolution in Science*, colloquially known as *Anti-Dühring*. In these articles, Engels, at the request of some of his German followers, sought to end the rising ideological influence of Dr. Dühring by proving him to be a fool. And while trying to demolish his rival, Engels also sought to lay out in systematic fashion the views he and Marx had jointly developed since their first ten-day meeting in 1844. It was this book which effectively introduced some understanding of Marxism into the German workers' movement, and, having given people an idea of its basic tenets, made large numbers of them into enthusiastic adherents of this doctrine. People like Kautsky and Bebel became Marxists only by reading *Anti-Dühring*. Engels's book then became the catechism of the movement. Anyone expressing an interest in Marxism was likely to be handed this work as the simplest and most comprehensive introduction.

Anti-Dühring is a relatively simple, popular presentation of a system of ideas so complex and opaque that Marx himself never managed to present it systematically or in understandable language. Among students of Marxism, controversy has been raging for fifty years or more about whether it is an adequate rendering of Marx's ideas. However, whether or not it represented the views of Marx, the book contained many statements which today appear naive, simple-minded, or based on ignorance or misinformation. As history, as philosophy, as anthropology, and as political science, it is easily dismissed, however valid and profound many of its insights. When this work became the ideological primer, something happened to the ideas of Marx and Engels, a process which is usually referred to as "vulgarization." What was called Marxism after the death of Engels (1895) was a strange mix of ideas, including simplified versions of the Marxian analysis of capitalism and his philosophy of history, but lacking in the original philosophic subtleties and the deep commitment to a humanist moral and aesthetic vision. As a social science, the new Marxism debilitated itself by a stupidly narrow interpretation of all phenomena in purely economic terms, i.e., with reference to the class struggle. In politics, it weakened its effectiveness by concentrating all its efforts on the coming seizure of power. And its philosophy was a hodgepodge of misunderstood Hegelian concepts, crude materialism, and Darwinian ideas of evolution, all of it frozen into rigid formulas.

The mass appeal of this ideology may have been rooted both in the simplicity and the dogmatic rigidity of its tenets. It became a set of slogans, a set of war cries—a litany intoned again and again, drummed into the listeners' heads at meetings and rallies. They always used the same phrases, fortified only by invective. It became language no longer for thinking, but for arousing. What is more, regardless of its doctrines, the Marxist movement attracted large masses of workers because it gave them an exciting feeling of self-liberation and self-education: it gave them pride in participation, solidarity in defying their bosses, and a great sense of camaraderie.

A number of people had become recognized in the party and in the entire International as the most competent interpreters and most learned masters of this ideological heritage; chief among them was Karl Kautsky, editor of the theoretical journal *Die Neue Zeit* and coexecutor (with Eduard Bernstein) of the literary estate of Marx and Engels.[2] Even if Kautsky's past personal connections with the two prophets of the movement had not given him high prestige, it would have been difficult to challenge him as the chief theoretician of the movement. For one thing, many members were reluctant to make trouble by raising painful theoretical dilemmas. In retrospect, the party, as a psychological collective, seems to have had a remarkably strong need to tell itself over and over again that it had the truth; and once such a conviction is well ingrained and widespread, those who challenge such dogma are labeled troublemakers and heretics. Even among comrades well established in the party, it was considered bad form to raise theoretical issues, because that would signal to the enemy—the bourgeoisie—that there was dissent within the workers' movement. This phobia against public airing of differences was reinforced by a lingering suspicion of intellectuals, of academically trained people from the ruling classes who had cast their lot with the workers' movement. It is ironic to note that all his life Lily's second husband, Heinrich Braun, himself an accomplished scholar with a doctor's degree in economics, tried to win intellectuals over to the party. Kautsky, his former associate, bitterly opposed this. "We are a *fighting* party much more than a scientific research party," Kautsky wrote. "We value loyalty and reliability over knowledge," he continued; and he capped this by asserting that "intellectuals are always unreliable."[3] His attitude was later to be espoused by Lenin and by Mao, who preferred "reds" to "experts." The phobia against intellectuals in the SPD suggests that even in political matters, militancy was prized above theoretical sophistication. (As a consequence, most party congresses were dull, uninspiring affairs.)[4]

Altogether, then, there was a marked reluctance within the SPD to raise big questions. But when they did debate, they did it in a petty and nasty fashion. The tone of discourse within the party was surprisingly rough, aggressive, and sarcastic. Anyone familiar with the life of Marx will be aware that the Old Man himself was a master of destructive invective; and it may well be that in their own style of argument people like Kautsky, Mehring, Zetkin, Plekhanov, Lenin, Trotski, and at times also Bebel, took Marx as their model. Of course, arguments within the party were not academic discussions airing subtle scholarly disagreements within the forms of gentlemanly discourse. They were disputes about political strategy and tactics, or differences in diagnosing and analyzing political situations. Hence, they were of immediate practical significance, and, at times, looked like questions that would decide the fate of civilization. No wonder the antagonists bitterly fought for victory, and sought to destroy their opponents—not just win an argument. Kautsky made this very clear in a lengthy exchange with the "Revisionist" Friedrich Stampfer, who had argued that a small clique of dogmatists was damaging the party because it treated comradely disagreements and loyal opposition as if they were treason. In his reply, Kautsky made it clear that one was either right or wrong, and if wrong, then one was, in effect, an enemy.[5] This arrogant assumption that they were right, scientifically right, and everyone else was a fool or a villain or both, came more and more to pervade "orthodox" Marxism. Everything the leaders of the movement discussed was argued with a supercilious smile of superiority, for which their enemies had a term, *Marxistenlächeln*. When provoked, these smirks of superiority turned into grimaces of hatred.

This anti-intellectual, self-righteous attitude is the precise analog of the position taken by those late nineteenth century scientists who basked in the certainty of their knowledge. When Max Planck, in 1875, wanted to enter the university to study physics, the professor whom he consulted discouraged him: We know everything there is to know, he said; there are no more important discoveries to be made, only details to be filled in.[6] The close relationship between the Kautskys and professors of this kind is revealed by the fact that both groups came to concentrate the fire of their dogmatism on Ernst Mach, the chief villain in Lenin's unfortunate attempt at defining and defending Marxist certainties. Mach, by challenging the concepts of absolute space and absolute time, opened the way for the Einsteinian revolution in physics.

Many of the orthodox Marxist leaders had not only been steeled by years of semi-legal struggle or exile; they had also been made nervous and thin-skinned by it. Some of them were insecure because they lacked academic credentials. Many of them were totally dependent on the journalistic positions they had created for themselves within the party. Should they be ousted from their editorial jobs, they might have no alternative employment possibilities.

This then was the intellectual tone reigning within the movement: dogmatism supported by a compulsive urge to *seem* united; intolerance of dissenters or independent spirits reinforced by the suspicion of academically trained comrades; and a nasty, backbiting tone in arguments, with free use of ad-hominem comments, in disputations which, in retrospect, often seem petty, talmudic, and nit-picking.[7] Rigid formulas were designed to conceal or camouflage real changes in view or policy. In the final analysis, all these attempts to create ideological unity came to naught; people highly placed in the party rebelled. And in the ensuing challenge to party orthodoxy, Lily Braun was to play a significant role; this will be examined in some detail in chapter 6.

If theorizing in the SPD and within the worldwide Marxist movement tended to make a mockery of open and honest discourse, the party's governance made similar mockery of the democratic principles to which, in theory, its members subscribed. The bureaucratization of the socialist movement, which Roberto Michels was later to analyze, had not yet completely run its course; nor had the party developed, as yet, all the auxiliary organizations which later were to make it a veritable society within German society. But it was a large, heterogeneous body of many groups pulling in different directions: regional organizations like the Bavarian party, whose policies differed from those of the central steering board; trade unions and women's auxiliaries; and influential journals and the Social Democratic caucus in the Reichstag. All this was complicated by personal friendships and antagonisms within the resulting cliques. What held this mixture of groups and interests together was the unbridgeable gulf separating all Social Democrats from respectable society, the common lip service they all paid to Marxism, and the tough, no-nonsense manner in which Bebel and an elite group around him managed to run the party. Members of this elite were free to speak up; non-members were well advised to keep their mouths shut.[8] And in party congresses, debate often was strangled skillfully so that congresses became rubber stamps for the decisions of the *Vorstand* (governing board). A party member whose articles were not printed in Kautsky's *Neue Zeit* or in leading party newspapers like *Vorwärts* or *Leipziger Volkszeitung* had little chance to be heard widely in the party. This governance naturally favored yea-sayers and disciplined time-servers, as well as intriguers and manipulators, especially if these were also ideological fanatics. It made the party an inhospitable place for people like Heinrich and Lily Braun.

Lily had joined the party in order to fight against everything that was wrong, in her eyes, with German society and politics. The ideas she had absorbed—Goethean and Nietzschean humanism, French and English theories of liberalism and socialism, and the muckraking tendencies of German Naturalism, placed her in opposition to the whole spirit of the Hohenzollern empire. Yet in many ways the SPD was a mirror image of Wilhelmine Germany. Its congresses were like the Reichstag—rendered impotent by a government responsible to none; its membership, like the German people, was cowed by the bigshots and surrendered willingly. Politics in the Reich, as in the party, were stage-managed to give the illusion of unity, unanimity, discipline, and solidarity. Helplessness and leaderlessness in both organizations were masked by saber- or revolution-rattling rhetoric. Critics of the systems were branded as traitors or renegades. Most dissenters did not, in any event, have the guts to rebel. Germans, as a whole, had the reputation of lacking *Zivilcourage* (the courage of one's convictions). The few who dared to speak out found themselves isolated. Most members meekly allowed William II or August Bebel to address them in almost the tone drill sergeants use to shout at their recruits. Prussian culture permeated both the SPD and the Reich. It was the authoritarian culture of impotent monoliths.

It was also victorian culture at its stuffiest—and here, too, the SPD can be seen as a mirror image of the order it sought to overthrow, "complete with its own 'high society' (the Kautskys, the Bebels, the Eisners), its time-serving mediocrities, predictable trajectories of advancement, exaggerated concern for rank and precedent, petty rivalries, jealousies and conspiracies." A woman entering this world faced dilemmas and decisions similar to those faced by a young woman daring to enter today's world of corporate business.[9]

IV

THE WOMEN'S ORGANIZATION OF THE SPD

Admittedly, the preceding portrait of the SPD is one-sided. In its leadership, as well as among its rank-and-file, the party had more than its share of decent, courageous, highly talented, and versatile people, who had joined the movement from entirely laudable motives and served it in a self-sacrificing manner. If in the heat of the political struggles they were ready to show their claws, then one might argue, with political philosophers from Machiavelli to Mao, that politics is no dinner party. Nonetheless, the portrait is pertinent here because it represents, by and large, the judgment that Lily Braun came to form of the party. Even before she joined, she was well aware of some of these features of the German Marxist movement, and she deplored them.[1] She despised everything that was Prussian and Victorian about it, having been steeped in Goethean humanism, and having taken Anglo-American radicals as her role models long before she read Engels and Marx.

That being the case, one might ask why she joined the SPD. One reason was that of all the parties in the German Reich, the SPD alone seemed hospitable to women; particularly for the growing army of women working in industry and other menial lines of work, the socialist movement seemed the appropriate association. The founder of the German Association of Working Women, Countess Gertrud von Guillaume-Schack, thought of herself as part of the international working-class movement, although in the long run her relations with Marx and Engels were disappointing to her.

The Marxist movement had committed itself to women's causes with a good deal of hesitation. Marxists had an easy time dismissing the struggle for political, economic, and educational rights as being primarily of interest to *bourgeois* women, hence of little concern to the proletariat. But they could less easily turn away from the interests of the female proletariat. Nonetheless, the first reaction of many socialists, in Germany as elsewhere, was to demand the removal of women from the labor force. Because as a rule women received lower wages, and also moved into and out of the labor force more often than men, men tended to see them as scab competition. Insistent demands for barring all women from work were made at the Eisenach Congress of the party in 1869, and these demands were repeated at many subsequent congresses. Often this tendency, which several writers have called "proletarian anti-feminism,"[2] expressed itself in the desire to protect women from the most arduous or the most unfeminine work, i.e., from work which most endangered their virginal morality (this definitely did not mean to include prostitution, a profession with which Marxist theory expressed only marginal concern). The Gotha program adopted in 1875 incorporated this demand. But fifteen years later, the party congress of Halle deleted it, arguing that there were no moral or physical differences between men and women.[3] Two years later, the congress of the Free Trade Unions (the socialist unions) voted to let women enter unions, and the Gotha party congress of 1896 demanded equal work *and* equal pay for women and men.

In fighting for the adoption of these and similar resolutions, advocates of women workers' interests not only had to combat the deeply ingrained antagonism against female competition, but to overcome the effects of a strongly rooted patriarchal culture, espoused not only by the German working class[4] but also by many of the Social Democratic leaders, from Karl Marx to many of his associates and disciples in the party leadership. Victor Adler once typically told Lily Braun, his sister-in-law, that "Politics consists in compromises. But you females don't understand anything about it. For that business you are either too good or too bad; so keep your hands out of it."[5] Indeed, an American feminist writer, Batya Weinbaum, has shown brilliantly and convincingly that Marxist theory itself has a profoundly patriarchal component.[6]

Nonetheless, from the very beginning of its political activity, the SPD endorsed the (liberal) demand for political and legal equality of both sexes—a demand which the liberal parties in Germany refused to make until the twentieth century. The leader of the SPD, August Bebel, published his *Women under Socialism* in 1879, in which he fully acknowledged the oppressions to which women were subject, including even the sexism still reigning in the workers' movement. He urged women to liberate themselves from these oppressions, and sketched the image of a future socialist society in which women and men would work jointly and equally to build and preserve a world free from oppression and exploitation. The book was very popular, went through several editions quickly, and mobilized large numbers of working women for political action. It has been asserted that Bellamy's even more successful socialist utopia, *Looking Backward,* is based largely on Bebel's book. A few years later, Engels also endorsed the principle of sexual equality in his *The Origin of the Family, Private Property and the State.*

By the late 1880s, many women were active as organizers of and agitators among, working women. Prominent among them were Emma Ihrer, Ottilie Baader, and Clara Zetkin in Germany; Eleanor (Tussy) Marx and Luise Freyberger in England; Henriette Roland-Holst in the Netherlands; Laura Marx Lafargue in France; and Adelheid Dworak Popp in Austria. By the early 1890s, women were a noticeable force in the party and in the International—a force that could not be ignored. At the same time, their importance is easily overestimated, partly because, as women, they were conspicuous, and partly because women, once they became mobilized for politics, tended to be more radical. If success in organization is measured by the numbers of workers actually organized, the unionization of women in Germany in the late 1890s was not extremely effective. In 1894, 9.36 percent of all working men were in unions, but only 1.1 percent of all working women were unionized.[7] According to Evans, one year later the percentages had risen to 12.86 and 2.58, respectively; the figures given at the Breslau congress of the SPD indicate that the proportion of women in industry who were organized in unions was still below 1 percent (5,251 out of 692,066), and this does not even include women working outside industry—women whom the SPD did not care to mobilize for union membership.[8] These figures also correspond with a statistical table published by the union movement in 1897, which shows a German working force, in fifty-one different trades, of about five million men and about one million women. Of these, roughly 317,000 men, or 6.37 percent, were organized in unions, as against a mere 12,000 women, or 1.2 percent. Whatever the correct figures, this is a poor showing, especially when compared to the relatively much more impressive participation of women in strikes,[9] and also when compared to the proportion of women in France, England, and Denmark who by that time were organized in trade unions.[10]

Nonetheless, German Marxism welcomed women activists and tended to endorse the demands of women workers, despite many lingering reservations held by many male members. These reservations occasionally surfaced at party congresses and in party resolutions. One has to be sensitive to the context in which the resolution was passed at the 1889 congress of the Socialist International that demanded "equal pay for equal work"—and one must suspect similar demands made in the SPD, because these demands were based on the silent assumption that women's productivity was lower. Hence, they amounted to a call for lower pay for women. An uncharitable doctoral dissertation written in 1904 explains the male workers' sympathy with women's demands on the basis of purely Machiavellian motives:

> It is by no means altruism or cultural enlightenment which drives the majority of the workers to feminism; instead, naked, barest interest, purely selfish motives, constitute the driving force. For social democracy, the woman still is no more than the means for the great cause of the proletariat.[11]

In other words, women allegedly were recruited merely to serve as an obedient and subordinate auxiliary force in the proletarian class struggle.

Oddly, the evidence for this alleged falsity and brittleness of feminism in the socialist movement could have been gathered most conveniently from the writings of the SPD women themselves. By the early 1890s, a women's section had been formed as an autonomous group affiliated with the SPD.[12] The fiction (if fiction it was) of its separateness as an organization was necessary because Prussian law forbade women to enter political parties, and the law was enforced harshly.[13] But the separateness also was real. The women's organization was linked to the party through several devices, but it prided itself on its autonomy. One of these devices was the election of spokespersons (*Vertrauenspersonen*) by the local women's organizations to provide liaison with the party. Women also were allotted quotas of delegates they might elect to party congresses, although the men in their local organizations also could, and sometimes did, delegate women to party congresses and conferences.

Because Prussian legislation forbade women's participation in politics, the women's organization led a semi-underground existence, each meeting being somewhat of a conspiratorial act, which may have added a certain romantic touch for some women, although it must also have been a source of aggravation. The most important group of SPD women was the Berlin organization, which, informally, was recognized widely as speaking for all socialist women. It became the model for women's organizations in other parties affiliated with the Second International. The Berlin group, which even at its height had no more than about a dozen members (indicating the token nature of female participation in the party as a whole), was directed and dominated from afar by a woman who stood out among SPD leaders by her intelligence, eloquence, vigor, and fanaticism. This was Clara Zetkin, who, as the undisputed leader of this model organization of socialist women, became, *ex officio,* the world's foremost Marxist-feminist.

Born in 1857, eight years before Lily Braun, to a middle-class family, Zetkin was trained as a teacher and became a feminist as a disciple of Auguste Schmidt. Her common-law husband, a Russian named Osip Zetkin, converted her to Marxism; and in the SPD and the Second International, she began to speak vigorously about the exploitation of female labor, and to exhort all working women to join the cause of the proletariat. She did this in her journal, *Die Gleichheit,* and in her brief book, *Die Arbeiterinnen- und Frauenfrage der Gegenwart.* Her point of view was one of most rigorous orthodox Marxism. Briefly, Zetkin argued that the problems of working women could be understood and solved only as parts of the problems faced by all proletarians. There is no such thing as a special *women* workers' question, she argued, nor a special women's question at all. "In contrast to the character of the bourgeois women's libbers' movement, the proletarian woman's struggle for her right to fully become a human being is not primarily a women's movement at all, but is a socialist workers' movement. It does not fight against male privileges but against the power position of the capitalist class. The proletarian woman cannot attain her highest ideals through a movement for the quality of the female sex, she attains salvation only through the fight for the emancipation of labor."[14]

To be sure, Zetkin recognized that women were exploited not only as workers but also as housekeepers, mothers, and members of an allegedly inferior sex. But even this multiple exploitation, which made them proletarians even within the nuclear family, was to be explained as a consequence of capitalism, so that proletarian women had only one option, that of joining their male, fellow proletarians in a concerted, unrelenting revolutionary struggle to overthrow the capitalist system. Once that had been accomplished, women's special concerns would solve themselves. In the meantime, to attribute any importance to them, or to waste any energy trying to ease the burden under which women were laboring, would be a reformist heresy designed to wreck the movement and to sabotage its efforts. Zetkin even chided Bebel for being excessively feminist in his book *Women under Socialism.*[15]

Zetkin's conviction that the working woman's cause was a fight against class exploitation, not against sex oppression, was the basis for her unyielding opposition to any cooperation whatsoever with feminist groups outside the party. Her slogan was "reinliche Scheidung," meaning a clean and clear separation between the proletarian movement and any other political movement. Moreover, her very narrow definiton of the term "proletarian" (as comprising only the direct producers in modern industry) rendered her hostile to those who sought to mobilize and recruit into the Marxist (or feminist) movement groups hitherto rejected or neglected, such as rural laborers, household servants, and sexual workers (prostitutes and related professions). With the last of these she had no sympathy whatsoever, not only because they did not in her opinion constitute part of the proletariat, but also because, despite all her radical views about capitalism, she and most of her female comrades held conventional views concerning the sanctity of the family, the virtue of chastity, the commonly accepted sexual division of labor, and the reticence with which one should treat—or rather not treat—the entire subject of sexuality. Bedroom matters, she wrote, should not be discussed in public.[16] For Zetkin, too, the intimately personal was not political.

As mentioned, Zetkin's interpretation of Marxism defined the political aim of the movement strictly as the seizure of power by the proletariat and its party, and the subsequent establishment of the dictatorship of the working class. This meant that she rejected all work for improvement of workers' or anyone else's lives as dangerous reformism: If the movement successfully agitated for reforms, that might give the workers illusions about possible improvement of the system, and thereby lessen their revolutionary elan. Zetkin propounded this rigid interpretation with the fanatic zeal of the convert. She was always on the furthest left wing of the movement, and her invective was feared by many comrades, female and male. *Die Gleichheit* was notorious within German Marxism for its combative tone and its coarse language, for which it was often criticized by other party papers. It was criticized also for its absolute refusal to make concessions to the less than highly literate reader; in response, Zetkin, in her editorials, proudly proclaimed that she did not write for the masses, but for the initiated.[17] This too may have added to her dominance within the small circle of party-affiliated women, the majority of whom were work-hardened, tough, fanatical proletarians. An Austrian socialist woman has described this group as follows:

> Admittedly, these first Social Democratic women were not easy to deal with. Beginners in the class struggle, they were anxious to maintain their prestige vis-à-vis their male comrades. Nervous and insecure in their new and unaccustomed role, forever afraid of doing something foolish or of being jeered at, they had little empathy for new faces, and thus they constituted a limited circle in the double meaning of the word. And deep inside, perhaps, they still were a little bit women of yesterday, tending much more to belittle each other than to develop a new feminine solidarity.[18]

That seems to have been an apt description of the group of Social Democratic women Lily Braun joined when she became an active member of the Marxist movement.

V

THERE IS NO DIRECTION
BUT FORWARD

Whatever its shortcomings, the women's group in the SPD was the only organization in Germany that appeared committed to fighting actively for the goals of female emancipation. This, however, was only one of several reasons why Lily von Giżycki joined the party. Her total web of motives is relevant to an understanding of her overall ideology and personality and therefore is worth disentangling here.

Some of her reasons for joining were purely personal, as I have suggested already. After Georg von Giżycki's death, virtually the only people who showed her kindness and compassion, who encouraged her to go her independent way and tried to help her make herself financially autonomous were some of the top leaders of the SPD, including, of course, Heinrich Braun, who was to be her second husband. The marriage would be, among other things, an intellectual and political partnership, so that one could say that in marrying Heinrich she also married the party. As suggested in chapter 1, Heinrich Braun's relations with the party were troubled, and that inevitably affected her situation within it also.

The help and compassion that the highest party leaders showed her must have been due in part to her personal magnetism. A few months after she joined, a sketch, its author identified as G. von Beaulieu, appeared in the 8 April 1896 issue of *Die Zukunft*, a left-wing journal of opinion notorious for its irreverence toward authority and respectability, but hated also on the far left because it dared criticize the narrow-minded bureaucrats who ran the SPD. The sketch was a portrait of Lily Braun:

Tall and slim, the fine, narrow, aristocratic face raised proudly—thus she strides through the large numbers of proletarians. We realize how young she is only once she is standing on the brightly lit speaker's platform. She wears her light-colored hair cut short so that it frames her face in springy curls resembling captured rays of sunshine; she is clad in black, but quite fashionably; a bunch of freshly cut aromatic lilies-of-the-valley decorates her belt. Even though she is a mass agitator she has not ceased being a charming woman; indeed, she does not disdain making herself look festive and pretty for the comrades.

In rather sophomoric style, the sketch then describes some people in the audience—a brawny worker and his lover, a wise old union militant, an intellectual in playboy garb who glibly mouths radical phrases—and then gives a sympathetic impression of her speaking style, her clear alto voice, her crisp and incisive sentences, her indictment of patriarchal and capitalist relations of oppression, and the stirring effect of her oratory:

"A splendid woman," said the agitator with the playboy mannerisms. Then he remembered that for the sake of his reputation he ought to be critical and added, "but she is ambitious! She is consumed with ambition; she is not doing this out of love for us. I guess she will play a leading role once things start popping here."

The blonde young speaker stopped talking. Only the flowers on her breast were trembling, otherwise the pale woman did not show any excitement. She gathered her black dress and strode through the yelling, noisy, jubilant crowd toward the exit, lone as she had come, the fine, narrow, aristocratic face raised proudly.

Is she really going to play a leading role some day?

That she might be allowed to play a leading role in the party surely was one of Lily's expectations. Long before she joined the SPD, the party had tried to entice the Giżyckis to enter its ranks; and both clearly leaned toward socialism. For the party to convert two such high-born, well-connected, and well-known people would have been a major political coup; and when after Georg's death Lily did join, the party leadership openly expressed its elation.

This is how it happened: Zetkin's women's organization sent one of its veterans to speak up at one of the meetings of the Ethical Culture society, which Lily chaired. The woman was Ottilie Baader, a worker who had gone through the hell of the home-industry sweatshop system as a garment maker, then became a union organizer and

an SPD activist. At the meeting, Baader argued that while the
Social Democratic Party did not work toward the violent overthrow
of the system, timid reforms and ethical preaching alone would
change nothing—a contradictory statement that neatly reflected a
serious unresolved problem in Marxist ideology of the time.[1] Lily was
impressed by Baader's forthright and simple presentation, and she
befriended her. Baader subsequently took her on guided tours
through the poorest proletarian quarters of Berlin, introduced her to
other women workers, and told her about the activists of the party's
women's organization.

Meanwhile, sensing that the Giżyckis might be ready to join, the
party leadership lavished courtesies on them. Even the arch-doctri-
naire Kautsky conceded their potential usefulness, arguing that their
fuzzy-minded writings could make converts to socialism among people
who would otherwise remain inaccessible to the movement. Orthodox
Marxists rarely held such opinions about people who were not totally
committed to their own theories (except proletarians); and Kautsky's
grudging praise is a measure of the Giżyckis' radicalism and persuasiveness. In the summer of 1893, Bebel went out of his way to be courteous to them. The aging Friedrich Engels, after attending the Zürich
congress of the Second International, came to Berlin for a visit; Bebel
not only invited the Giżyckis to the gala banquet that the party gave
in his honor, but he seated them on the dais, and he also asked them
to come for an intimate dinner party at his house afterwards, with
Engels and the Paul Singer family as the only other guests.[2] If they
wanted Georg for his persuasiveness, it is likely that some of these men
wished to recruit Lily into the party as a counterweight against Zetkin,
whom many of them feared and detested.

Privately, Lily Braun had already called herself a socialist for several years.[3] She had come to it partly as a result of her aristocratic
disdain for the bourgeoisie, fortified by the noble service ideology
that she had been taught as a child. In May of 1889 she had wit-
nessed a major skirmish in the battle between bourgeoisie and proletariat, the strike of the Ruhr miners. The rapid growth of corporate
capitalism was about to sweep away many ancient miners' rights;
these changes were sanctioned in the new civil code about to be
adopted. The miners protested against this process of proletarization.
We have here a neat illustration of the revolutionary dialectic in

which the traditional and the radical, nostalgia for the past and pioneering for the future, may subtly merge with and feed each other. It also explains why Marxism had by that time not yet made significant inroads among the miners, and why the Westphalian aristocracy, including guests among them like Lily von Kretschman, tended to side with the miners and against the despised mine owners. She seems to have expressed the feelings of many of her fellow aristocrats when she wrote to her cousin Tilly, "The power of capital must be broken. We will live to see the marvelous spectacle of nobility and workers marching together."[4]

She then projected her own idealism onto the Marxist leaders she met. Again, from a letter to her cousin: "We are deliberately given as untrue an image of the social-democratic movement as of its materialism; only through my own investigation of both have I found that true idealism, i.e., an idealism based on a solid foundation, is to be found on their side alone."[5]

Intricately mixed in with this idealism, and indeed part of it, was her burning ambition. She wanted to serve, but she wanted to serve with distinction—the way she thought her noble and royal ancestors had served. She seems to have thought that here was an opportunity to establish herself as a leader in public life and to make her mark in history. Moreover, a typical representative of her generation, she was deeply committed to the religion of progress; and as she observed the political scene in Wilhelmine Germany, she convinced herself more and more that the party which in its ideology and actions represented progress was the SPD. More and more the word "forward" appeared in her writings; and that was the name—*Vorwärts*—of the SPD's principal newspaper.

She considered the socialist women's movement progressive. The women's movement as a whole, she wrote early in 1894, is divided into two camps in Germany, one a solid army of thousands of proletarian women fighting side by side with their men for equal rights; the other a small group of isolated women, supported by a handful of men, fighting for equal access to education. While in her article she deplored the rude tone in which Zetkin attacked any and all feminists, she showed how impressed she was by the fact that the proletarian women's demands were backed up by a large party. Proletarian women, she concluded, had the potential of being politically effective; bourgeois women did not. Nor, apparently, did they have the wish to be effective. While the leaders of the Marxist party rose in the Reichstag to demand the right to vote for women, bourgeois feminists, she thought, were faction-ridden, lacked clear or great aims, and indeed deliberately refused to think big. As a result, after almost fifty years, the German women's movement was where it had started. It had achieved nothing.[6]

Moreover, in October 1895, when the SPD congress debated resolutions supporting equal rights for women as well as the rights of single mothers and illegitimate children, Lily noted once more that here was a party which backed up women's demands, and she added that these demands were by no means specifically socialist ones. They were, instead, true to the principles of liberalism. "Yet will even one of these demands receive solid support from the liberal parties?" she asked.[7] At the congress, Zetkin had said the very same thing: Equality of the sexes is a bourgeois-liberal demand, but in Germany bourgeois liberals so fear the proletariat that they become especially reactionary. Hence the solution of liberal problems, including equality for women, becomes the task of the proletariat.[8] Evidently Lily agreed with this.

And so she gradually persuaded herself that the Marxist movement stood for everything she herself believed in: radical liberalism, feminism, compassion for the exploited and the rejected, and self-sacrificing idealism. Marxism, to her, was the movement that represented progress; anyone believing in progress would have to identify with it. It implied a commitment to action, whereas the Ethical Culture movement, in which she had thought she could be active, was moving in the direction of Tolstoyan pacifism, which she thought too tame.[9]

Yet for a long time she hesitated to join. It is easy to see why. Joining the Marxist movement in the 1890s meant a total break with one's class and one's family. It meant foregoing not only all former associations, but also all hopes for a respectable career and indeed, for respectability. Self-confessed socialists in Wilhelmine Germany were pariahs. Considered traitors, and so labeled by the emperor himself, they were subject to police surveillance and harassment, and to public insult of various kinds. One instance will suffice to illustrate this situation: After his daughter joined the SPD, General von Kretschman, already in retirement, put on his dress uniform and made a formal call on the Chief of the Imperial General Staff, General von Hanake, in order to let him know that he no longer considered Lily his daughter. However, once he became reconciled with her, that made *him* an outcast, and when he died the Emperor pointedly omitted all the customary courtesies a decent sovereign would have shown to the body of one of his senior generals or to his widow, an affront so gross that one must read about it in Lily's letter to her cousin Tilly; for in her memoirs she made it appear much less blatant.

Furthermore, it was precisely her doubts about her possible effectiveness as a fighter for the party's aims that made her hesitate to enter it. In reply to the urgings of the socialist leaders that her natural place was in the party, Lily pointed out that people like herself would be much more useful to it if they did not join it openly, and that indeed, once she had joined, her usefulness to the party would be over.[10] Meanwhile, she made a number of proposals for political action in which the left wing of the women's movement might collaborate with the women's section of the SPD: draft proposals for a new law on associations; an ambitious plan for the creation of an organization for the study of working women; and others. She also submitted an article containing a social critique of contemporary art to Kautsky's theoretical journal, *Neue Zeit.* Kautsky rejected it, arguing it contained too little about class warfare. Similarly, even though the newspaper *Vorwärts* received some of her proposals favorably, the hard-liners in the party rejected all collaboration with her.[11] In short, as long as she was not in the party, they would not work with her. In order to be effective, she would have to take the plunge.

What may have persuaded her that it was proper to join was her experience at the 1895 WWCTU congress in London. There she met and made friends with many leading English socialists, trade union leaders, social workers, feminists, and other radicals: John Burns, Tom Mann, Keir Hardie, and Herbert Burrows; Fabians like the Webbs and G. B. Shaw; the anarchist Peter Kropotkin; and the radical journalist William Stead, a promoter of feminist causes, who had written a series of articles for the *Pall Mall Gazette* in which he exposed the white slave traffic.[12] The liveliness, practical political sense, and seeming effectiveness of British socialism and feminism greatly impressed her. Moreover, London impressed her as a highly sophisticated city; there she felt she was in a genuinely *modern* society. By knowing only Germany, she wrote to her cousin, one does not know the modern world.[13] Foremost, however, she may have been fascinated and encouraged to see that in the milieu of British radical politics workers and peers, poor and rich, professors and self-educated people mixed with grace and ease, and that a confession of socialist or anarchist beliefs was quite compatible with being a prince or a dowager duchess. Fear of social-ism, she wrote, had made the German women's movement into a negligible side show; the readiness to embrace socialism had given the women's movement of England strength and had made it successful. She was deeply impressed by the mix of practicality and idealism that she saw in many of the people she met, and by the radical thrust of their attempts at consciousness-raising: "Our aim is to generate dissat-isfaction among working women," she quotes a Christian missionary to the poor (probably a Salvation Army officer) as saying. In the final analysis, it was this combination of radical idealism with the readiness to work within the system that made others take women in Britain seriously, whereas in Germany, women were still being patronized.[14]

In December 1895, at a mass meeting organized by the socialist party organization in Vienna and chaired by Adelheid Popp, the young, scrappy leader of Austria's Marxist women, Lily von Giżycki announced her allegiance to the Social Democratic movement.[15]

VI

AN ORTHODOX MARXIST WITH A FEW IDEAS OF HER OWN

Lily's usefulness to the SPD as a spectacular "catch" was indeed over almost as soon as she had joined; and the party did not intend to use her for other purposes—Zetkin and her women's organization certainly did not. To be sure, Zetkin appreciated Lily's effectiveness as a speaker, and wrote to her friend Kautsky that she was "very happy" with her.[1] Moreover, in her journal, she devoted an entire article to welcoming her to the party, including warm words of appreciation for the sacrifice and courage her conversion must have entailed.[2] Indeed, for the next four years, Lily (who was soon to become Mrs. Heinrich Braun) worked with Zetkin on the journal, although her assignment there was relatively menial—editing the News and Notes section. Even that ended in 1900.

In retrospect, Lily Braun was never made to feel genuinely welcome in the party. Instead, she was treated with suspicion, as an alien intruder, and, within a few years, was insulted, slandered, and literally spat upon. Yet she did not leave the party until a few weeks before her death. She continued to consider herself a revolutionary socialist, and often asserted this in her publications. Moreover, much of what she spoke and wrote, particularly in the first few years of her membership, was clearly in line with orthodox Marxism. This applies particularly to her major work on the condition of the female proletariat, *Die Frauenfrage*, which will be discussed at the end of this chapter.

Immediately after joining the party, she used a number of public lectures and articles to defiantly dissociate herself from the liberal women's movement. However well-meaning they might be, she ex-

plained at an international women's congress meeting in Berlin in
September 1896, bourgeois reformers cannot solve the women's question; and it was time to show the entire world that they did not
represent all German women. Nor was the fight for admission to
universities or the fight against prostitution the total of women's
concerns. Instead,

> it is the problem of women workers that touches the greatest num-
> bers of the female sex. These are women who mourn their wasted
> youth behind factory walls or as toilers in the cottage industry,
> women who carry out the much extolled 'sole woman's calling' of
> wife and mother, exhausted from their hard work and yet putting
> children into the world to whom most often they cannot even give
> the care and attention which every animal offers to its young.[3]

Two days later, on 25 September 1896, at a socialist mass rally,
she denounced bourgeois feminists for dominating the women's
movement and thereby preventing working women from developing
their autonomy. Bourgeois feminism, she argued, was incapable of
liberating women, and only socialist feminism would be adequate to
the task, for the solution of women's problems could only be provided once the class state, with capitalism, gives way to the people's
state with a communal economy. All other proposed solutions, she
continued, merely perpetuate the exploitative relations prevailing
now. This is an inhuman society and an irrational one. Those who
produce have no control over their product; stores are full of merchandise while those who have created it go cold and hungry.

> Not to understand this, to speak about justice and Christian love in
> the face of this fact without sensing what mockery is being made of
> justice and love—that is possible only in a society whose heart had
> turned to stone on account of the curse-laden glistening gold of the
> Nibelungen hoard; whose eye has lost its power of sight; whose mind
> has been deranged.[4]

The welcome mat in the Marxist movement, she added, was not out
for bourgeois sympathizers; their motives were suspect; they lacked
vigor; they were lukewarm, whereas the proletarian movement
needed people who were hot and cold. Again, she reiterated that the
real solution of the women's question could come only once the class
state, with capitalism, had given way to a people's state with a
communal economy.[5]

Lily Braun now found herself spurned by her liberal, former friends;[6] and in many ways, she had begun to sound like Clara Zetkin. Yet from the very beginning of Braun's entry into the party the two women clashed, as Braun continued to raise issues or advance positions that Zetkin and her colleagues considered inappropriate.

One such issue was Braun's proposal, made formally at the 1899 party congress in Hanover, that the party demand the inclusion of domestic servants among those to be covered by the new labor legislation (Gewerbeordnung) then being discussed in the Reichstag. The German housemaid (in her various roles—cook, nanny, washer woman, chambermaid, and wet nurse), was a patriarchal institution still semifeudal in culture. Her conditions of employment were either left unlegislated or were covered by semifeudal *Gesindeordnung,* i.e., the body of law regulating the relations between a noble lord and his peasants. The work force in the urban household consisted primarily of young women from the country, often illiterate. (One of Braun's first maids could not read recipes.) Maids' pay was so low it can only be called pocket money. They often ate the leavings from the master's table, lived in cramped garret chambers without plumbing, heating, or other modern facilities. They worked from dawn deep into the night. Their lives were fully controlled, the employers taking for granted that they were to act *in loco parentum.* They could not, of course, receive visitors, and were told when to be back home on their weekly night out. Sexual harassment by the master of the house or his adolescent son(s) was often taken for granted; it is one of the typical situations in the novels and comedies of the period.

Household workers were organized in a union of their own which was dominated by the male servants, and which was very conservative. But Braun believed that maids could be drawn away from this union and recruited into the Social Democratic movement. Her party comrades discouraged her, arguing that maids were not genuine proletarians. Braun then attempted to do some mobilizing and recruiting on her own,[7] and she seems to have kept the discussion in the party alive. In the end, the party leadership suggested that domestic workers be regarded as the same as wage labor, hence that they should demand the same work and wage conditions as industrial workers. In a series of articles, Braun tried to show that this solution was unrealistic, given the special conditions of live-in work which

cooks and maids were performing, and that therefore the party line
was nothing more than a way to define the problem out of existence.

Her own solution was that, while indeed the party should strive to
give household workers parity with the industrial proletariat, the
problems of this part of the work force could, in fact, only be solved
by the destruction of the patriarchal household, and by establishing
cooperative housekeeping in its place. Only in such housekeeping
communes would the cook and the cleaning person be able to receive decent pay for regularized hours.[8] For turning her attention to a
group which at best seemed marginal to the industrial proletariat,
Braun was accused of deflecting the working class from its struggle for
power. The fact that there were many thousands of oppressed and
exploited young women did not seem to impress her Social Democratic comrades.

A very different proposal of Braun's met similar resistance. Braun
was convinced that there are some modes of oppression which all
women suffer, regardless of their class, and therefore that some collaboration with women not in the party was desirable—at least communication and sharing information. Guided by this argument, she
revived her idea of creating a nonpartisan central committee for the
study of women at work; and she formally submitted this proposal to
the Social Democratic women's organization for discussion.[9] A series
of articles, pro and con, appeared in the journal during the subsequent weeks.[10] Even though a few comrades supported the proposal
or some modification of it, it ultimately was defeated. The arguments
against it suggested that this kind of work would not educate for
socialism and would, in fact, interfere with the party's agitational
work; that there were neither human nor financial resources which
might make it possible; and that the very proposal, by suggesting that
the party had been remiss in its work so far, cast aspersions on the
movement. Besides, some of this research had already been done by
the unions or by bourgeois economists, and much of the German and
foreign legislation was already being discussed in various journals.
Ottilie Baader suggested that the proposal was condescending because it implied that the workers themselves were not intelligent
enough to know what ailed them or how to become competent
agitators.[11]

By the time of the Social Democratic women's congress in Munich, which met just prior to the party congress of 1902, Braun supported a much tamer variant of her proposal; this was a resolution calling for the appointment of a paid secretary for the Social Democratic women's movement. This too was defeated.[12] Also, she continued to suggest that the Social Democratic women cooperate with non-socialist women's organizations on other matters. She argued for this both at the women's conference meeting prior to the 1900 party congress in Mainz, and at the 1902 conference in Munich; and after she had ceased attending these conferences, she argued for it in print. In essence, what she advocated was a policy similar to what (some decades later) became known as the popular front tactic, a political tactic based on the realization that Marxists and left-of-center reformers share many interests, that the movement can make significant gains by mobilizing like-minded reformers outside the movement, and that in fact it might recruit valuable new members by demonstrating to these outsiders the commonality of their goals.[13]

Like many other prominent members of the SPD, Braun herself continued her membership in some reform organizations which were not social democratic. I assume, without having real knowledge, that just because she joined the party she did not relinquish her membership in the League against Anti-Semitism; and I doubt that the league excluded her for having become a socialist. There is at least one non-party organization which she joined after entering the SPD: that is the League for the Protection of Mothers (*Bund für Mutterschutz*), an organization caring primarily for unwed mothers. August Bebel too was a member of this organization. Again, like many other prominent members of the party, Lily wrote for journals which were not strictly party organs. Her husband's own *Archiv,* though socialist in orientation, published articles by socialists and non-socialists, and nobody raised an eyebrow. Similarly Maximilian Harden's radical *Zukunft* was a journal in which prominent socialists, including Braun, published gladly and frequently, at least until 1903. She did this partly because Harden paid good honoraria, but also because she very much believed in keeping the lines of communication open to non-socialist radicals. She genuinely thought that airing her views in such radical journals would promote the cause of socialism, whereas her critics considered such communications with the class enemy to be treason. Did they not know that Marx and Engels, too, had published in bourgeois journals and kept lines of communication open to people and groups not sharing their views? But then, the people who ran the SPD notoriously engaged in the corrupt practice of measuring various comrades with different yardsticks, or enforcing arbitrarily defined standards of behavior selectively, according to the Latin proverb, *Quod licet Iovi non licet bovi*—what Jupiter is allowed to do an ox is not. The abuses of what later came to be called Democratic Centralism obviously were not an invention of Lenin or any other Russian.

Yet another issue over which Braun clashed with the party leadership and with the Social Democratic women's organization was her concern for the protection of working mothers. Existing legislation and practices allowed pregnant women to perform arduous work until they actually gave birth, and allowed for no furlough after delivery. Note that as late as 1891, the *minimal* work week for women over sixteen in industry, including pregnant ones, was fixed at sixty-five hours![14] Pregnant women worked until they gave birth, and, if economic need made them dependent on the work, they simply had to come back as soon as possible. The results were disastrous: The proportion of miscarriages and premature births to total pregnancies was six to seven times higher among working mothers than among those who did not work outside the home. And, regardless of wage work, miscarriages and infant deaths, as against births, were between 50 and 51 percent for working-class families, as against 18 percent for middle-class families. These statistics make quite clear the high cost of female wage work.[15]

From the very beginning of her agitational work as a socialist feminist, Braun expressed her indignation at the cruel treatment of pregnant women, and she demanded that they and new mothers be protected from health-endangering work. To do this would require granting them furloughs of considerable length both before and after delivery; during such furloughs they should continue to receive their regular wages, and their continued employment in their old jobs should be guaranteed. She called her proposed scheme maternity insurance, and argued that such a scheme, which would be expensive, be made into a new branch or category of existing social security legislation, to be financed by a progressive income tax.[16]

Clara Zetkin vehemently opposed this scheme; many people in the party supported her arguments that women were not in need of any special protection, and that asking for such special protection was a violation of socialist egalitarian principles.[17] Moreover, she argued that the kind of protection it envisioned would be possible only under socialism. To suggest that a capitalist system would institute such an insurance scheme was utopian dreaming based on a misunderstanding of Marxism. Indeed, even radical feminists outside the socialist movement, such as Helene Lange, Marianne Weber, and Henriette Fürth, wrote in opposition to the proposal for maternity insurance, arguing that the scheme was too expensive, hence utopian. Utopian dreams, Braun's party comrades argued, are dangerous, because fighting for such impossible reforms deflects the proletariat from its real aim, which is the seizure of power. Watered-down versions of Braun's proposals were nonetheless adopted. Already at its Hannover Congress of 1899 the party, after heated debate, passed a resolution demanding that women be granted maternity furloughs both before and after delivery, demands which at the Mainz and Munich congresses (1900 and 1902) were repeated; and the women's conferences of Munich and Mannheim (1902 and 1906) endorsed a demand for a four-week furlough before delivery. These resolutions did not even come close to what Braun had envisaged. In fact, it was not until 1927 that the German Reichstag passed a maternity insurance law which she would have approved.[18]

Maternity insurance, incidentally, was but part of a package of measures that Braun proposed at party congresses for the protection of working women. Other parts of the package included the prohibition of night work and of any work harmful to the female body; free Saturday afternoons; the appointment of female factory inspectors; and others.[19] Some of her positions were supported, both inside and outside the party.[20] But in most cases Braun's position tended to be more radical than that of others. For instance, she not only demanded that women be barred from unhealthy work, but she argued that all health-destroying work should be outlawed, and that the manufacture or use of any health-impairing materials be forbidden by law. Such a rigorous ecological position was far ahead of her time.[21]

Yet another bitter argument ensued over the following: Braun shared with her comrades in the socialist women's organization the conviction that work liberates, that meaningful, creative labor is essential for human self-fulfillment, and that therefore women must, without question, be part of the labor force. But she also was aware, as were they, that women still carried a double or triple load as wage worker, housekeepers, and mothers. Unlike her comrades, she proposed that the party should try to do something about this, not only because the movement owed its female members all the support it could give, but also for the sake of the children, who under present circumstances were woefully neglected. The solution she proposed was communal living, with shared household and child-rearing chores which would release spouses and parents for work and for more leisure time. In a pamphlet she published in 1902, Braun argued for such a scheme by first providing a vivid and devastating description of how living in nuclear families, or singly, wastes time, money and talents, wrecks marriages, ruins health, and encourages child neglect. The communal dwellings she advocated would enable the sharing of meal preparation and many other domestic chores. Utilizing up-to-date technology, it could also provide for the communal sharing of expensive tools such as sewing machines; it might furthermore free the commune members for their own work by hiring service personnel on a fixed salary, with overpay for additional work. Meals prepared for all could be consumed either in the communal dining room or in the private apartments. Day care centers would be an integral part of the commune. The entire plan presupposed relative equality of incomes, so that, at the beginning, it could not cut across classes. Nonetheless, such communes could be founded by worker families as well as by middle-class people. The entire scheme was modeled after existing living cooperatives in various countries, especially the United States.[22] It had also been discussed for some years already in radical circles in Berlin.

Braun not only advocated this scheme in theory but tried for several years to get a group of interested friends together who might create a model commune of this kind.[23] These efforts failed. Most people found the scheme much too radical and communistic. Many feminists outside the movement saw it as a plot to destroy domesticity, and, as indicated in chapter 2, many "bourgeois" feminists in Germany sought to preserve and strengthen the family, not to jeopardize it. Helene Lange, while recognizing that, in theory, communal housekeeping would help relieve the double burden, thought that communal living simply went against people's instincts.[24] Heinrich

Herkner, the professor of economics under whom Rosa Luxemburg had obtained her doctorate, suggested that it would lead to the bureaucratization of activities that should remain personal and intimate.[25] Among Marxists, reactions were equally sharp. Zetkin devoted four separate articles to denouncing the scheme.[26] Her argument once again was that this was a reformist scheme. Braun, she argued, was trying to create socialist enclaves within the capitalist system, and this was an abandonment of the movement's political goal, hence amounted to an acceptance of capitalism.

One can, of course, note in the history of Marxism that similar proposals, at other times, and in other places, were accepted more readily. One might argue that Mao's islands of liberated territory also were enclaves within a capitalist society. Or one might point out that in the first draft of *The Communist Manifesto* Engels had suggested something similar when he demanded communal child rearing facilities.[27] Indeed, Braun's proposal was little more than an elaboration of statements by Engels and Marx that women would not be liberated until the monogamous family ceased functioning as an economic unit.[28] But, among "orthodox" Marxists of the time, communes, as an idea, were suspect, partly because a "bourgeois" sociologist, Franz Oppenheimer, a few years before had suggested communes as a positive alternative to combat communism.[29] Any kind of cooperative was suspect to orthodox Marxists precisely because it seemed to be an alternative to the proletarian revolution, hence a bourgeois scheme.

Still other areas of great concern to Braun, concerns which simply did not interest her comrades in the women's organization of the SPD, were her activities for educational reform—part of her broader concern with children's rights against their parents and their teachers; her attempts to cure the workers' movement of its members' habit of treating female comrades with condescension,[30] of its undemocratic structure and administration, and its uncomradely conduct of meetings and discussions; her keen interest in making the rich cultural heritage of Western civilization accessible to the working class, rather than destroying it as the product of old ruling classes; and her effort to make the socialist movement a joyous dance, not a dreary Puritan pilgrimage, into a new society fit for human beings. We will deal with these and similar issues in chapter 8.

She further antagonized her new comrades by criticizing them for their own inconsistencies as socialist women, as in their demand for both equality and special treatment in organizational questions. The women within the party, as suggested before, had been given special privileges in response to Prussian legislation barring them from membership in the party—special representatives and provisions for the election of delegates to party congresses by women's organizations. But they enjoyed these privileges also in those federal states where such discriminatory laws did not exist, and they insisted on keeping them. In this connection, Braun repeatedly argued that such segregation and favorable treatment were incompatible with the spirit of equality between the sexes, and that by continuing such demands the women were demeaning themselves: "Where there is no compelling reason for its existence, every exclusively female organization within the women workers' movement is of evil," she wrote.[31]

Further, Braun was ready, on occasions, to sacrifice women's concerns for the sake of the party's larger interests, according to the rule that one must fight for what one can get, not for what is unattainable. For instance, for the sake of obtaining universal male suffrage, she was ready to drop the demand for women's suffrage temporarily, a position sharply criticized by Zetkin's group, but endorsed by the International Socialist Women's Conference of 1907.[32] One might assume (perhaps correctly) that Zetkin's arguments on these matters were more feminist, and Braun's were anti-feminist. But in fact, it was Braun's feminism which made her insist that women's dignity forbade their enjoyment of privileges which circumstances did not make necessary, and that to block male voters in the party, who might possibly make significant gains, would be wrong. Can we perhaps explain all this ideological sparring as a struggle for power between these two women? In that case, Braun's arguments were simply attempts to weaken the power of Zetkin's women's organization within the party. It would not matter greatly. (Most political ideas are generated by a mix of motives that ranges from idealism and abstract reasoning to ambition, envy, resentment, and other personal stimuli; it is once they have been written down, that they acquire an existence independent of their origin.)

In any event, contemporary students of Marxism are likely to agree that there was little in any of these proposals made by Braun to which a committed Marxist would object. Even though she used the esoteric vocabulary of Dialectical Materialism less readily than some more fastidious comrades, most of what she proposed could well be accommodated within fairly narrowly defined Marxist frameworks of political action and social analysis. That is particularly true of the major scholarly work Braun produced during the first five years of her party membership, the aforementioned *Die Frauenfrage, ihre geschichtliche Entwicklung und ihre wirtschaftliche Seite*. This comprehensive survey of women in the world of work became famous at once. More than twenty editions were published within a few years after publication, and it was translated into several foreign languages. For many women in the Marxist movement, such as Aleksandra M. Kollontai, it became the fundamental treatise on socialist feminism.

It is indeed tempting to argue that *Die Frauenfrage* does for socialist feminism what *Das Kapital* did for socialism, i.e., provide a basic description of the system that is to be overthrown and some glimpses into a better alternative. But such a claim must be hedged in with reservations; the similarities are balanced by dissimilarities. Both are incomplete works, first volumes of larger projects which remained incomplete. An early outline that Braun made projects a book with the following structure:

Part I — *Development of the Women's Question up to the Nineteenth Century*
    ch. 1—The Women's Question in Antiquity
    ch. 2—Christianity and Women
    ch. 3—Women's Economic Position
    ch. 4—Women's Relation to Intellectual Life
    ch. 5—Women in the Age of the French Revolution

Part II — *Economic Aspects of the Women's Question*
    ch. 1—The Fight for the Right to Work in the Bourgeois Women's Movement
    ch. 2—Moving Forces of the Bourgeois Women's Movement
    ch. 3—Basic Principles for Evaluating Women's Professional Work
    ch. 4—The Development of Proletarian Women's Work
    ch. 5—Women Workers in Their Several Branches of Industry
    ch. 6—Society and Law Concerning the Women Workers' Question
    ch. 7—Prostitution

Part III— *Legal Aspects of the Women's Question*
    ch. 1—The Struggle for Legal Equality in the Nineteenth Century

ch. 2—Women and Private Law
ch. 3—Women and Public Law

Part IV— Moral-Psychological Aspects of the Women's Question
ch. 1—The Evolution of Femininity
ch. 2—The Problem of Marriage
ch. 3—Family Life and Communal Life
ch. 4—The Moral Liberation of Women [33]

Of this ambitious outline, Braun, in time, managed to cover almost every issue, but she was never able to compile all of this in her major work. The contents of Part I were treated in two lengthy articles which appeared in her husband's *Archiv* before *Die Frauenfrage* was finished and were then incorporated, with alterations, in the book.[34] In addition, the book covers Part II, chapters 1–6, leaving the remainder for a second volume. Thus *Die Frauenfrage* treats the women's question from the point of view of women's roles in successive economic systems. To put it in Marxist terminology: it discusses the economic base for the oppression of women, while the second volume was to deal with the legal, moral, ideological, and psychological ramifications, i.e., with the superstructure of women's oppression. To return to the comparison between Braun's and Marx's works, the most important difference between them is the fact that *Das Kapital* was a theoretical breakthrough—a fundamental critique, rejection, and inversion of nineteenth-century political economy, and its replacement by a new system of concepts; whereas *Die Frauenfrage* is based on the *acceptance* of a theory, namely, Marxism. One might argue that at times this was an uncritical acceptance of Marxism. This is apparent especially in the use Braun makes of the ideas on ancient matriarchy developed by Bachofen, Morgan, and Engels. Instead of inverting Marxism, *Die Frauenfrage* extends it to the analysis of the oppression of women. It is therefore far less theoretical, far more descriptive, and far less profound than *Das Kapital.* It is also more readable, and it uses more up-to-date statistical information, even though if anything makes the book obsolete today, it is the specific information on which it is based.

The work assumes history to be a series of different modes of production, and it sees the oppression of women (including their culture, their education, their self-image, their freedoms and unfreedoms, and their manner of coping with their lot) as functions of the kind of work they are allowed or forced to do, and the kind of leisure they may or must enjoy. If offers a summary history of male-female relations from ancient matriarchy to monogamy. It has an interesting chapter on women's lot in ancient Greece and Rome, and their relation to early Christianity, a religion which, according to Braun, exalted women in theory but degraded them in practice. Women in antiquity, she pointed out, were almost exclusively without rights, hence there could be no such thing as a women's movement, despite occasional voices that recognized their oppression. Nor were the Germanic women so admired by Tacitus much better off, she claims.[35]

A lengthy section dealing with women in Western society from Carolingian times to the French revolution emphasized the kinds of work they were allowed or compelled to perform in various eras, the countless losing battles they fought against discrimination and degradation, and the many valiant, but futile, efforts they made to gain equality. She also pays tribute to pioneers of female emancipation, especially Condorcet, Wollstonecraft, and Th. G. von Hippel; she also included Rousseau, whose theories of personal authenticity and femininity she interpreted as having feminist implications. Emphasizing the importance of women in the French revolution, she describes the relation between revolutionary women and male Jacobins in terms that give a foretaste of what was to happen to feminists in the Marxist movement and the Russian revolution. Here too, much of the material in the book had been published before.[36]

The bulk of the work deals with women's work under capitalism. It accepts the Marxian definition of capitalism as the exploitation of free wage labor for the extraction of surplus value, and the Marxian notion that capitalist relationships can be traced not only through the economy but also in politics and culture, including the family. It echoes Engels in condemning the bourgeois family as a business deal that victimizes the woman, but goes far beyond Engels (to say nothing of Marx) in emphasizing the emotional and sexual destruction of those women who lose out in the marriage market. Throughout her life, Braun offered empathy and compassion to that figure of universal ridicule, the old maid. In Marxist fashion, she had earlier argued that a solution to the women's problem could become possible only after the industrial revolution and the development of capitalism had

drawn masses of women back into the labor force and evoked a
socialist workers' movement that promises to create a social order in
which women and men can for the first time lead fulfilling lives.

> While male and female were equal at the stage of primitive culture,
> the distance between them widened more and more with progressive
> economic development. The interests, the struggles, the aims of the
> man, who was physically stronger and less tied down by the condi-
> tions of sexual life, as against those of the woman who was tied to
> home and children, became the cause of an intellectual and legal
> separation which the woman at first could not even sense, because
> her domestic work claimed all her time and attention, and because of
> the general societal conditions she was unable to see beyond the
> narrow confines drawn around her sex. She became conscious of her
> oppressed state only after the many different chores of the housewife
> were taken over increasingly by craft and industry, so that the
> woman, at least when as a member of the possessing classes she
> gained leisure, came to feel herself superfluous, sensed the emptiness
> of her internal and external life, or as a member of the dispossessed
> classes, she was forced to transform her domestic activity into wage
> labor outside the house and away from the family. Not only was she
> stuck on a stage of intellectual retardation corresponding to cultural
> eras long past; she also saw herself made unfit for the struggle for
> survival, which she had to fight just like the man—made unfit by
> economic, legal, and political fetters. These contradictions caused a
> profound discontent which grew steadily and reached its culmination
> in the women's movement of the French revolution. The right to an
> education, the right to work, the right to equality before the law—
> these were the aims proclaimed by the revolution, and argued theo-
> retically by its literary representatives.
>
> New problems of the women's question were not posed after that
> by the nineteenth century. All that was left to do was to elaborate
> them more profoundly, formulate them more sharply, and then
> evoke a social movement spreading through all civilized countries
> which are now preparing the definitive solution.[37]

The remainder of Die Frauenfrage (and its bulk) is a guided tour
through hell, the hell of women working in the capitalist economy.
Carefully distinguishing between the situations and interests of bourgeois and proletarian women, she painted a horrifying picture of
exploitation, discrimination, and miseducation of women in general,
but waxed most eloquent when she described the lot of female proletarians, agricultural workers, saleswomen, waitresses, and domestic
servants. Chapter by chapter, she relentlessly guides the reader from

one branch of industry to another; and each branch turns into a different circle of the inferno.

> In this best of all worlds, poverty is a crime punished by life-long forced labor; and children's children still carry the Cain's mark of their ancestors. True, the rod and the whip have disappeared when the slaves were driven to work; but out of the gold which the poor have torn from the womb of the earth bourgeois society has forged a weapon more terrible than all instruments of torture. With it, it dominates and subjects those without possessions and forces them to dig further and further for gold, with bent backs and callused hands, for the rulers' benefits. . . .
>
> Whereas the bourgeois woman seeks work as the great liberator, for the proletarian woman it has become a means of enslavement; and though the right to work is one of the noblest human rights, to be condemned to work is a source of demoralization. But a social order based on this, a social order built on the dehumanization of labor and the enslavement of those who work, is condemned to death.[38]

The book ends in a final vision of an order of things

> in which her work will not damage or demean the woman but will elevate her to be the man's free comrade; work will be an activity in which she will be able to fulfill her highest and noblest potentials as never before, and a healthy and happy generation will testify that it never lacked a mother.
>
> Without women's work the capitalist economic order cannot continue to exist and will be less and less able to continue in existence. But women's work undermines the old form of the family, shakes the ethical conceptions on which the moral code of bourgeois society is built, and endangers the existence of the human race, for which healthy mothers are an essential precondition. If the human species does not, in the end, give up on itself, it will have to give up the capitalist economic order.[39]

True to her convictions, Braun in her book emphasized the deep gulf separating proletarian feminism from the bourgeois women's movement, and she even quoted Zetkin and the resolutions she had introduced at the Gotha congress of 1896.[40] But in the same breath, she also repeated most of the heretical positions over which she had clashed with her comrades in the women's organization—the demand for a scheme for communal living; the need to educate socialist men away from sexism; the abolition of health-endangering work for women and men; and the need for additional propaganda among women. Socialist feminism, she boldy stated, has, so far, made only *minimal* achievements. Further, she came out in favor of reforms of all kinds. Reforms, she argued, clear the path to socialism even if they are proposed by people not aiming for it; for reforms enable working men and women to become conscious of their solidarity and their community of interests, even while they ease the conditions of their lives.[41]

Thus even when she tried to stay strictly within the framework of Marxist theory, she continued advancing ideas of her own; and for that, her status in the party was insufficiently secure.

VII

REVISIONISM AS THE
LIBERALIZATION OF MARXISM

In chapter 8 I intend to show that Braun's ideas anticipated much of what today is called Neo-Marxism or Western Marxism. In order to demonstrate this, I shall argue that all of her writings can be interpreted as an extension or elaboration of the Marxist theory of alienation. Elaborations or extensions of Marxist doctrine, however, were not readily tolerated in the Marxist movement in her time; anyone daring to suggest that something was missing in the holy writ of the movement, or that the founding fathers had neglected to treat some issue, was likely to be denounced as an opportunist or a revisionist. And Braun was so labeled. But even if she had done no more than restate the Marxist theory of alienation as Marx had formulated it in his early essays, she would have found herself branded a heretic, because during her life time, the theory of alienation was not recognized as part of Marxist doctrine. The early essays, published and unpublished, were still gathering dust in the party's archives. What was known as Marxism was a set of ideas derived, instead, from fragmentary knowledge of the classical writings—the *Communist Manifesto*, the *Critique of Political Economy*, *Capital*, *Anti-Dühring*, *The Origins of the Family*, Engels's essay on Ludwig Feuerbach, and a host of writings by both Engels and Marx on the revolution of 1848, the German peasant war of 1525, and the Paris Commune of 1871.

What the party ideologists took from these writings was a system of ideas which accepted as valid only one side of what Marx and Engels had developed. One can define Marxism in a variety of ways; let me do it here by arguing that it is a method of examining human relations, human institutions, and human interactions by focusing on the dialectic of productive forces and production relations. All history is the progressive and cumulative development of the productive forces slumbering in the human species (production here being defined as the purposeful attempt to control and master the forces of nature with the aim of transforming or recreating the entire universe in conformity with human needs); Marx referred to this as the appropriation of nature, suggesting that the human species is endowed with the ability to remake the world in its image. The productive forces we have developed obviously include science and technology, but also organizations and institutions and, indeed, attitudes and predispositions, chief among them the spirit of enterprise and the urge to accumulate, which under capitalism has dominated all or most other human instincts. In turn, this preoccupation with amassing possessions was linked historically to the institution of private property in the means of production. Thus private property must be recognized as key to understanding the productive forces of capitalism.

Private property is also key to understanding the production relations of capitalism. Under the rubric of production relations, Marx and Engels comprehended all the relationships, organizations, and institutions that form the framework for the social production process. Each society and each mode of production generates such a framework, which is an elaboration and institutionalization of the social division of labor, including the class structure, the patterns of authority and deference, of service and benefits, duties and privileges, rule and obedience. While the productive forces are continually growing, the production relations have a static, conservative effect; they are the system-maintenance devices by which any given society seeks to perpetuate itself, by which any given beneficiaries of that society seek to guarantee the continuation of their favored status. Hence, when Engels and Marx argue that the production relations inevitably come into conflict with the productive forces, they are suggesting that the former seek to retard or repress all further development, while the latter aim toward continued expansion. The resulting strain will be relieved by the next revolution, in which the burgeoning productive forces will shatter the superannuated productive relations. And when they discuss capitalism, in which private property in the means of production is at once the most powerfully liberating productive force and an intolerable fetter on the further development of the productive forces, they are merely arguing that private property, having fulfilled its liberating function, becomes a hindrance to further progress. Thus at the heart of the Marxist analysis of capitalism lies the view of private property as a profoundly contradictory principle of social organization—a principle fundamentally at odds with itself.

When Marx and Engels focused on the productive forces, they dealt with all that they considered rational and purposive in the history of humanity. When they wrote about the production relations, they were eyeing institutions and relationships they considered irrational and counterproductive. In discussing history as a rational process, they used the language of social scientists: one studies rational purposes in objective, detached, amoral, positivist fashion. The irrational, the counterproductive, the obstreperous features of human history, however, are predominantly the concern of the moralist; one cannot easily remain detached about them. And while the study of the productive forces suggests a deterministic philosophy, the concern with the obstacles still to be overcome in the quest of progress compels us to stress the importance of freedom.

In the philosophy of Hegel, reality was comprehended as an ongoing argument: the absolute spirit was continually generating statements and counterstatements (theses and antitheses), which it transcended on a higher level. The structure of reality was therefore analogous to the structure of sentences and arguments, so that, in Hegelian philosophy, logic and ontology became one—much to the horror of more conventional schools of philosophy. A similar statement can be made about Marxism. But the substance of reality for Marx and Engels no longer was the absolute spirit, but productive, creative human activity. This human activity, however, can be viewed both objectively and morally, as a determined process as well as an obstacle to the full flourishing of all human potentials. The objective and the moral—inevitable progress as well as the human cost of progress—are part of the same dialectic. Hence the puzzling merger, in the writings of the two founding fathers, of detached, objective language and scientific pretensions with the flaming moral indignation that pervades every statement they made. From the point of view of conventional philosophy, such a merger of objective science with moral judgement is as objectionable or questionable as

Hegel's merger of ontology with logic. In fact, both Hegel and Marx can be understood only as a merger of social science with poetry, or, if that is too strong an expression, as the rigorous study of human relations informed by the artist's vision.

But the dialectical philosophy which expresses this merger of scientific rigor with poetic imagination was too profound and complex for the first generation of Marxists following the death of Engels. If classical Marxism was a synthesis of the Enlightenment theory of progress-through-science with the Romantic lament over the price we paid for it, then one might assert that Romanticism had gone out of fashion around 1900, at least in left-wing politics. Romanticism was regarded as an expression of reactionary views; and moral arguments smacked of the church. Positivism was in the air, as was deterministic, reductionist thinking. Established Marxism around the turn of the century prided itself on its hard-nosed amoralism, and also on its unsentimental approach to the study of history as a process governed by objective laws that made the ultimate coming of socialism inevitable. The basis of their entire world view was the doctrine concerning base and superstructure as Marx had outlined it in the Introduction to his *Critique of Political Economy*. According to this doctrine, all social life is the function of the mode of production, which ultimately is reducible to the state of technological and scientific development. Each stage of technology generates a corresponding social division of labor, a class structure and related property arrangements. All human activities correspond to this class structure. The state is the steering committee of the ruling class; all culture—art, religion, and philosophy—serves the ruling class as a set of system-maintenance devices.

Capitalism, in this world view, was the economic system in which all dependency relationships prevalent under feudalism had been dissolved. Free people now faced each other in a competitive market society. Only one thing differentiated them from each other: some possessed surplus wealth which could be used to produce even more goods, while the majority were without substantial property and had only their labor power and skills, which, for survival, they were compelled to sell to the owners of the material means of production. Because labor power, when applied in the production process with modern technology, produced more than its own value, those who could purchase it were able to extract surplus value, exploiting the labor of their workers. While this system had accomplished marvels of productivity, which had led humanity to the threshold of abundance and close to mastery over the forces of nature, it had outlived its usefulness. The very same laws of development that had caused it to flourish were now causing it to become less and less efficient, less and less capable of functioning. The business cycle was vivid proof of the impending collapse of capitalism. Meanwhile, in the working class, the system had created its own gravediggers—a well-organized group of men and women destined to constitute the vast majority of people, who, because of systematic sufferings, would learn to recognize the nature of the system. Having nothing but their chains to lose, the workers would make revolution, establish their own dictatorship, and lead society to socialism. Such a revolutionary scenario, for Marxists, was not a dream, a hope, or a moral resolve; it was a scientific certainty, an unshakable conviction. Any doubt in its inevitability was in itself denounced as reactionary, harmful, and treasonous. There was no room for doubters in the movement.

In thus denouncing anyone who would challenge the adequacy of Marxism as an objective description of current reality and of future developments, the ideologists of official Marxism let morality in by the back door: doubt was morally suspect. To have faith was treated as if it were a categorical imperative. Nonetheless the party continued to profess a supposedly amoral philosophy, displaying its own real moral convictions covertly, thus they could not be discussed or built into the party's actual world view.

Note, too, what served as criterion of moral approval: Not a person's behavior nor even his or her professed principles of behavior, but, instead, an attitude most antithetical to positive science, namely, faith. Faith in the eventual reality of the Marxist predictions concerning the collapse of capitalism and the coming of socialism was the acid test of being a genuine Marxist. Marxism thus became a religion, reversing the resolve of its founders to strip political philosophy of all religious residues. Marx, following Feuerbach, had rejected the habit of positing an abstraction (God, the state, the absolute idea, Reason) as the ultimate demiurge of history and of the universe. Instead, the demiurge that Marx and Engels recognized was the human species. But their successors substituted historicism for this humanism. They forgot or did not recognize that human action and human interaction, human needs and human freedom were the root causes of all history. By looking instead for historic laws of development as the ultimate reality, they made Marxism into a new religion, and the political movement into a church. This new religion not only was based on dogmatic faith in a demiurge standing outside of human beings; it also betrayed its affinity with other religions in its attachment to a holy writ, in its puritanic humorlessness, in its disapproval of any individual search for joy, and, finally, in its vindictive, gloating anticipation of the day of reckoning, when the last would be first and the first last. One must go back to the *Book of Revelation* in order to see the earliest example of such vindictiveness expressed by an ecstatic and charismatic rabble-rouser; it is possible that the popularity of Marxism among its working-class following may have been based on this expectation of a reversal of the social order.

Marxists, of course, did not think of their ideology as a charismatic religion; they considered it science. Nor did they think of the party as analogous to a church. But what, then, was the SPD? Formally, of course, it was a political party, but one should call it that only with some hesitation. Parties in European politics developed as parliaments (or other representative assemblies) became organs of national self-government. The origins and history of parties are linked with the development of liberal and constitutional democracy. The German Reichstag, however, was a comparatively ineffectual body; the Reich was not governed on liberal or democratic principles. Moreover, the SPD was uncertain in its attitude toward constitutionalism and parliamentary government. The party was deeply divided over the role its elected delegates should play in the Reichstag and in the state diets, and over which position they should take on the various issues that came up for debate. In significant respects the SPD saw itself as an anti-party, as an organization or movement intent on destroying government by parties, just as Marx and Engels had seen the proletariat as an anti-class, a class which by coming to power would eliminate the division of society into classes. Nonetheless, this anti-party took elections very seriously, treated its own deputies in the Reichstag as party leaders, and in many ways showed a keen interest in having a strong Reichstag caucus.

The chronic disagreement over the functions of this caucus' originated in a more general uncertainty over the broad goals, strategies, and tactics of the Marxist movement. As faithful followers of Marx and Engels, the leaders of the party accepted not only the founding fathers' explanation of capitalism and its origins, but also their scenario for its replacement by socialism—the Marxist theory of revolution, the proletarian dictatorship, and the withering away of the state. Acceptance of this scenario also implied acceptance of the strategies and tactics they had worked out for the working class and its party.

Marx's analysis of capitalism suggested to his followers that the system was about to break down and that a militant, organized working class was standing in the wings, ready to wrest power and property from the faltering bourgeoisie. Various pronouncements made by Marx and Engels also suggested to them that the movement needed to wait patiently for this propitious moment. Premature militancy smacked of Jacobinism and would only spoil things. No system disappears, Marx had argued, before it has reached its full flowering (i.e., developed all its productive potential). The image of capitalist society they projected (in their most abstract statements) was that of a relatively simple system dominated by the conflict between the two principal classes, bourgeoisie and proletariat, with the continued existence of a land-owning aristocracy a complicating factor bound to disappear. The political form corresponding to this bourgeois society was the democratic republic.

The event of 1848/9 demonstrated to Marx and Engels that reality was far less simple than this abstract image. The class structure of Germany and France was infinitely more complex, hence political alliances, movements, and outcomes were less predictable; and bonapartism appeared as a form of bourgeois rule more prevalent perhaps than constitutional democracy. Altogether, reality had taken turns which Engels and Marx had neither foreseen nor desired. As a result, they became more than ever preoccupied with problems of strategy; and if before 1848 they had thought that theirs was a revolutionary strategy, after 1848 it subtly changed into a strategy *toward* revolution, i.e., policies designed to bring about, not utilize, revolutionary situations.

Ever since the first men and women recognized the superior political acumen of the two founding fathers, they went to them for political advice; and at times they received such advice without asking for it. When the SPD was in its formative stages, both Marx and Engels played this role; Marx until his death in 1883, Engels until his death twelve years later in 1895. Their advice was not always heeded; some of their memos and letters were filed away without being discussed at all. Still, during the last two decades of the nineteenth century, the party increasingly took it for granted that its policies, tactics, and strategies were those that the founding fathers had elaborated. In defending party practices, it was customary for the leadership to assert that the party was pursuing a *Marxist* course of action. Once Engels had died, such claims could be supported either by reference to some pronouncements he or Marx had made, or by showing that at one time or another the founding fathers had pursued the same policy.

Careful examination of all this supporting evidence, however, yields advice and precedents that are contradictory. Based on pronouncements made or policies pursued by the founding fathers, it appears equally Marxist to wait for the inevitable collapse of capitalism and to organize a revolution for its overthrow; to work within the system or to refuse any participation in it; to seek an alliance with all progressive forces and to keep clear of any such alliances; and to impose vigorous leadership and careful guidance on the workers and to leave them alone, arguing that the only effective liberation is self-liberation. In their theory of the proletariat, Marx and Engels suggest that the exploited masses are the salt of the earth; but they describe the *Lumpenproletariat* as the scum of the earth. In the former case alienation, when driven to its ultimate point, raises the consciousness of the exploited; in the latter case it corrupts and de-humanizes. They wrote about the peasantry with boundless contempt, and in other places, demanded a coalition between workers and peasants. They suggested that the nation-state is obsolete, and that the proletariat is an international class, but they also accepted nationalism as an existing reality, and did not hesitate to take sides in the conflicts between nation states.

Marx and Engels wrote about the French revolution both as a model and as a counter-model for the coming proletarian revolution. Depending on the text one reads, the Jacobins have either shown the proletariat how to do it or how not to do it. Similarly, they praised the Paris Commune as the first socialist revolution, and they also denounced it as the last pre-socialist one. One could heap example upon example in order to show that behind such vague phrases as the "proletarian dictatorship" or the "democratic republic," there is no satisfactory Marxist theory about the transition from capitalism to socialism, hence no firm political guidelines for the workers' movement. Let us note that, ultimately, this failing is immanent in the dialectical philosophy which merges the objective study of reality with the moral judgement of it. Where ontology and ethics coincide, the philosophy is unlikely, if not unable, to recognize the famous problem of the relationship between means and ends.[2]

Thus the SPD, in claiming to be the repository of Marxist orthodoxy, subscribed to an interpretation of reality which it misunderstood, and to a program of action which did not, in fact, exist. That the policies it actually pursued were muddled and contradictory should therefore not astonish anyone. Yet the conflict and zigzag maneuvers are much more obvious to the historian today than they were to those involved, because at the time the conflicts were hidden under dogmatism and the felt need to make an outward show of party solidarity. To be sure, the SPD was not a church; but in many respects it behaved like a church, labeling those who questioned accepted dogmas as heretics or, in a more benign mood, suggesting that they had not sufficiently mastered Marxist theory,[3] and in general relying on discipline and obedience for its continued existence as a militant movement.

In becoming dogmas, moreover, the vibrant, imaginative, picturesque language of Engels and Marx had fossilized into a set of fixed terms and formulas, in which the very sequence of words within the sentence often was prescribed. While the party theoreticians may have compared their writings with the stiff language of science textbooks, a more apt comparison would be one with prayer books. This was not a language which stimulated thinking or the exploration of reality, although it may often have done it; rather it was a set of empty formulas designed to instil self-confidence, loyalty, and other proletarian virtues, repeated compulsively and endlessly like a litany; and, since it was designed to arouse feelings rather than the intellect, it was supplemented increasingly by invective. The journals edited by Kautsky, Mehring, but especially Zetkin, were criticized at times for this language, which made them boring to many readers. Thus a sociologist sympathetic to Zetkin said about the style of *Die Gleichheit*:

> It annoys by the constant repetition of similes or parables that once were effective, by exaggeration, cynicism and cheap phrases. . . . The baiting jargon of *Die Gleichheit* produces a language culture of slogans and a rich store of class-war invective. Brutality of expression is adopted as an easy tactical device.[4]

Peter Gay in his biography of Eduard Bernstein has argued that Revisionism, as an intellectual movement, was the result of the bureaucratization of the party. What he means to suggest is that the waning of revolutionary radicalism, which to him is the essence of Revisionism, occurred because the party leadership succumbed to the bureaucratic imperative, which gives administrators a stake in the existing system, making them timid, conservative routineers. But this is a misleading statement. It was precisely the bureaucratic managers of the movement who were radical hard-line, orthodox dogmatists, while many Revisionists were rebels against the organization. To be sure, some trade union leaders sympathized with Revisionism, or at least with reformist tactics which many Revisionists advocated; but among other things, Revisionism was a rebellion against the bureaucratization of the party. The ideological bedrock of the orthodox, of the so-called Radicals, was built on the value they placed in their political machine—their organizational fetishism. Just as, for a believer, the Church is the indispensable human organization which alone can guarantee salvation, so for the high priests of the SPD, the party was the guarantee of success in the coming proletarian revolution and collapse of capitalism. As long as the party existed, the coming cataclysm could be awaited calmly and steadfastly, because an organized political movement was waiting in the wings ready to take control over society. The destruction of the party, conversely, would be the greatest disaster that could hit the proletariat, and anxiety over such a possibility was the psychological basis for orthodoxy, dogmatism, and the fossilization of the language.[5]

This story of the organization becoming an aim in itself, and how anxiety over its preservation turned the leaders into dictators and censors—this transformation of a mass movement into a hierarchi-

Heinrich Braun ca. 1895 (International Institute for Social
History, Amsterdam)

cally run political church—is familiar to all students of Russian Bolshevism. A study of the SPD shows that Democratic Centralism—
the principle by which the Bolshevik Party was managed—was no
invention of Lenin, but was pioneered by the German Marxist movement around the turn of the century. What Rosa Luxemburg said
about Lenin, Braun thought about Bebel: "He concentrates mostly
on *controlling* the party, not on *fertilizing* it, on *narrowing* it down, not
developing it, on *regimenting* not on *unifying* it."[6] If Carl Schorske
could call Friedrich Ebert the Stalin of the SPD,[7] then surely
Bebel—one of whose nicknames was August the Strong—was its
Lenin.

Underneath the brave front of solidarity and unanimity which
Bebel and his comrades eagerly tried to maintain, the party from its
very inception was torn by factionalism and dissent; in discussing its
conflicts, it is customary to divide the contestants into hard-line,
orthodox Marxists (also called Radicals) on the one hand, and the
moderate, pragmatic, reformist critics of orthodoxy on the other.
The latter were also called opportunists and other names of contempt. By 1900, they were called Revisionists, and I will use that
term in this chapter. In doing so, I will try to show that the understanding of Revisionism in much of the literature on the subject may
be incomplete or inaccurate, if only because previous scholarship has
given too much attention to the ideas of Eduard Bernstein, who
should, in fact, be recognized as one of the lesser contributors to
Revisionist theory. Incidentally, the fact that for many years Bernstein was one of the leading hard-liners or radicals in the party
illustrates the fact that many party leaders switched from one side to
another at various times; moreover, since several issues were involved in the debate, it is not always clear who belonged to which
faction.

At issue were questions of policy, organization, and philosophy.
Policy questions ultimately revolved around the issue of revolution
versus reform: whether or not the workers' party should promote
constitutional democracy, or liberalize the system in any fashion.
Should the party's representatives participate in the legislative process, perhaps even making deals with other parties, or should they
use their parliamentary seats only for propaganda purposes to raise
the revolutionary consciousness of the voters? Should they function
as a party within the system or as a tightly separated sect outside it?

The organizational problem concerned the conflict between centralizing, authoritarian, and bureaucratic tendencies, on the one hand, and democratic principles, on the other. It involved questions concerning the role of leaders and followers in the party, the amount of open discussion that might be tolerated or encouraged, the kind of people the party ought to attract, and many other related questions. Ultimately, the organizational problems were closely related to the basic policy question concerning revolutionary strategy. Openness of discussion, participation for the rank-and-file, and similar democratic forms were advocated by those who believed the party should participate in politics like other parties. Those who wanted the party to be a militant striking force, gathering the proletariat for class warfare and, ultimately, the revolutionary takeover, by and large preferred forms of organization and habits of discipline and obedience that are usually associated with military units.

The philosophical debates revolved around the adequacy or inadequacy of dialectical and historical materialism as interpreted by the party's leading theoreticians. These official interpreters took it for granted that the philosophy presented in their texts, the theory of history, politics, economics, and social relations, and indeed, the method of analyzing art and literature they were advancing were true, and all others false. Revisionists voiced their doubts on these issues.

The dispute over these and related issues is difficult to summarize precisely because much of it went on beneath the surface. As I have already suggested, while the theory propounded by the party followed a hard-line orthodoxy, its practical politics included a great deal of reformism and parliamentary maneuvering. Orthodoxy often was no more than a desperate attempt to stem the reformist trend or to conceal it from the party. Conversely, classical Revisionism, i.e., the heresies of Bernstein, began as an attempt to realign the theory of the party with its practice. After defending the orthodox line for many years, Bernstein at last concluded that it was no longer realistic, and in his famous book, *Die Voraussetzungen des Sozialismus und die Aufgaben der Sozialdemokratie,* he subjected the orthodox line to fundamental criticism. He rejected the laws of capitalist development outlined by Marx, demonstrating that the life of workers was improving, not worsening, that the business cycle was abating, and that capitalism was, if anything, becoming more profitable and stable. This, in turn, implied that the breakdown of capitalism and the proletarian revolution were by no means inevitable. Nor was such a revolution desirable. Instead, a step-by-step transformation of capitalism into socialism, without violence or catastrophes of any kind, was to be preferred. Socialism should not be imagined as a decisive break with the old order, but a gradual improvement of conditions and a process of democratization. Indeed, democratization was the key to Bernstein's program; democracy would guarantee an equitable society. If it had not yet been attained, that was due not only to the greed of the exploiter class, but also to the political immaturity of the proletariat.

In his criticism of orthodox philosophy, Bernstein was equally harsh. He dismissed the dialectic as meaningless mumbo-jumbo, materialism and economic determinism as naive, and the amoral theory of inevitable progress as morally untenable. In suggesting that the party should go back to Kant, he was actually suggesting a new and sharp separation between a truly objective sociology and a morally inspired action program.

I have summarized all this as briefly as possible to provide the essential background for understanding the nature of Lily Braun's Revisionism. What I will try to show is that she was in general agreement with the positions advanced by Bernstein, but that her criticism of orthodoxy was infinitely more trenchant. In comparison to Braun and many of her friends in the party, Bernstein was a second-rate theorist; his ideas were shallow, and, from the point of view of the party hierarchy, relatively harmless. Hence the gentleness, comparatively speaking, with which his "radical" comrades treated him.

I will try to show also that Bernsteinian Revisionism represented a *liberalization* of orthodox Marxism, hence, as it were, a softening, a retreat from militancy, whereas Braun's Revisionism contained elements of increased militancy; it was an attempt to *radicalize* the workers' movement, with the word "radical" here used both in the conventional sense and in the specific sense which Marx gave it. While Bernstein and others sought to temper the Marxism of Kautsky, Mehring, and Zetkin with ideas taken from Kant, Comte, and John Stuart Mill, Braun's Revisionism was a replication of the ideas advanced by Marx and Engels, which their orthodox followers did not know, had misunderstood, or were misrepresenting. Like Marx, she rebelled against Christianity in the name, not of materialism, but of humanism.[8] Further, while Bernstein countered Kautsky's philosophic monism with Kantian dualism, Braun's philosophy must be regarded as a dialectical rejection of both those positions. In calling herself a revolutionary, she insisted that this implied continual self-criticism, continual readiness to test and reject yesterday's truths, while dogmatism of any kind, to her, was a betrayal of the spirit of revolution.[9] Like Georg von Vollmar, she said, she would have voted against the resolution against Revisionism which the Dresden congress passed in 1903, "for is not the condemnation of my Revisionism essentially a denial of our most important party principles? We are, after all, not dogmatists, but perpetual revisionists if indeed we want to stay alive at all."[10] And in another letter to her husband she wrote, "Thanks, but no thanks for a so-called party unity which is nothing else than lack of character!"[11]

What I am suggesting in all this is that Braun enriched Marxist theory while Bernstein watered it down. The fact that their antagonists called both of them Revisionists obscures this crucial difference. Church hierarchs often lump all heretics together; it makes it easier for the faithful to explain all dissent as part of the same Satanic conspiracy.

To be sure, many of Braun's views coincided with those of Bernstein. Like him, she preferred evolution to revolution, and, in any event, believed that the party should participate vigorously in day-to-day politics, fighting for improvements in the workers' political, economic, and cultural conditions. Like him, she was in favor of broadening the party's base of support among the voters, and improving democratic relations within its own organization. While she never shied away from conflict and struggle, even violent confrontations, she never forgot the price in human misery and material destruction paid for violence, be it in a major strike or in a revolution. Hence, if sufficiently thoroughgoing reforms could be won by negotiation or other peaceful means, she preferred it.[12] While orthodox Marxists like Zetkin and Lenin always expressed the fear that successful reforms would satisfy the workers and thereby lessen their revolutionary ardor, Braun believed that, on the contrary, they would raise, not lower, the workers' revolutionary consciousness.

Precisely those reforms that really work, she argued, show vividly what *could* be done, and therefore increase revolutionary dissatisfaction with what exists.[13] Bebel and Zetkin sharply distinguished between policies that were effective and those that were true to principle; Braun, with equal sharpness, rejected such a dichotomy: if effectiveness and fidelity to principle were truly opposed to each other, she asked, what concrete gains could the party ever make?[14] "After all," she wrote to her husband, "we want to emphasize constructive change, not mere criticism."[15] What Bebel and Zetkin obviously meant in making this remark at the Mannheim women's conference was that the SPD could pursue only one single goal—the conquest of power. Both Bernstein and Braun, as well as other Revisionists, continued to remind the party that, in fact, it was pursuing a host of more immediate and less ambitious tasks, and suggested that all members might as well think positively of them.

Since practical aims short of the proletarian dictatorship could be obtained only through cooperation and coalition with others, Braun, like Bernstein, was in favor of tactical alliances and deals with parties to the left of center—a tactic which Lenin and Stalin adopted at various times, calling it the Popular Front. Nonpartisan reform efforts, Braun always believed, need not be a betrayal of one's principles.[16] Like Bernstein, she was eager to force the party out of its isolation from practical politics. Negotiating with other parties would be one device; another would be the attempt to attract as many supporters as possible, even if they did not agree with the party on every issue. After the election victory of 1903, Bebel and his comrades in the *Vorstand* had voiced apprehensions at gaining so many unreliable fellow travelers. Braun rejected this vanguard theory in favor of democratic notions, just as she objected to the esoteric language of the orthodox journals for deliberately addressing themselves to a small circle of those initiated in it. If we really want to come to power, she argued, if we really want to make revolutionary changes, we need as many fellow travelers as we can get. Such fellow travelers could be attracted only by systematic efforts to communicate with them and to work with them.[17] They would be attracted also to genuine radicalism, a radicalism of deeds, not phrases. Deeds here meant meaningful practical reforms; she wished to substitute deeper philosophic ideas for the phrases, the radical rhetoric of the orthodox.[18] As a socialist, her aim was to introduce socialist notions into circles which did not know them or fought against them; and to do this these notions would have to be clothed in the language of the people who were resisting them.[19] She explained in her memoirs:

> The best elements of the bourgeoisie were politically homeless. Their rudderless ship was unintentionally coming closer and closer to socialism. . . . The number of modern snobs who construct a whole ideology out of the recognition that clean underwear and neat fingernails are necessary, and who had accepted Romberg's (her thin disguise for Werner Sombart) pronouncement that the possession of higher learning and participation in politics are irreconcilable, was shrinking visibly.[20]

In short, the progressive elements in the bourgeoisie were astir, showing their radicalism in politics, education, art, religion, and sexual morality. All that was needed was a political force to unite and mobilize them. The only party which could and should do this was the party of the workers, of socialism, of the future. In attracting people from the radical bourgeoisie, the party should judge these sympathizers by the practical work they were accomplishing, by their actions, and not by their philosophy, especially since the faithful party members' own philosophy often was no more than a litany chanted obediently but stupidly. Had not Kautsky himself acknowledged the benefit his party derived from a philosophical dissenter like Georg von Giżycki? But no: Braun's perennial attempts to make converts in bourgeois or aristocratic circles were condemned as breeches of discipline. She commented: "Another one of our contradictions: We so much stress the value of person-to-person propaganda work, and yet we condemn that person as a deserter who does not exclusively move within a circle of like-minded people!"[21] Obviously, and perhaps correctly, the party suspected her of seeking to attract people from her own background so that she might have some like-minded allies.

To these broad areas of agreement between Braun's and Bernstein's Revisionism, another agreement must be noted: their shared concern over the political immaturity of the proletariat. In diagnosing the reasons why socialism had not as yet come, despite the confidence expressed by Engels and Marx, Bernstein had singled out the workers' poorly developed political maturity as a chief cause. Braun seems to have agreed with him. She maintained that the party's policy of sulking on the side lines while waiting for capitalism to collapse was the cause of this immaturity. Instead, the party should engage in practical political work within the system and thereby teach the workers confidence and self-respect. Only thus would they ever be able to free themselves from capitalist oppression—and self-liberation, for her as for Marx, was the only genuine liberation. Comparing social welfare legislation in England with that in Germany, she once wrote that the measures adopted in England were not as advanced as those put into effect by Bismarck, "but whereas our laws resulted from the bourgeois parties' fear of the Social Democrats, the English ones will be the work of the socialists themselves."[22] With this, finally, we have touched on another point of agreement between them—their respect for the achievements of the socialist movements in Britain and France, which, with their undogmatic, flexible tactics and their tolerance for dissent, their ease of mingling with the establishment and their emphasis on immediate tasks of reform, seemed to have more inner strength than the SPD with its Prussian discipline.[23] Revisionism, in a profound sense, represents the attempt to de-Prussianize and de-Russianize Marxism. In Braun's case, it is part of a much broader rejection of Prussian and Russian cultures. In many respects, indeed, the Revisionists around the turn of the century were the genuine internationalists of the Marxist movement, people with international experiences, interests and contacts, and a genuine practical interest for promoting international understanding and democratic foreign policies. In contrast, the internationalism of the German and Russian Orthodox was abstract, at least until 1914; and in their personal lives their discomfort at being away from their home soil showed in the habit, especially of Russian exiles, to segregate themselves into little ghettos. Lily and Heinrich Braun very early developed a special antipathy toward the high priests of orthodoxy from Poland and Russia—especially Luxemburg and Plekhanov. One wonders how they would have reacted to the knowledge that Luxemburg, in her turn, loathed most Germans.

What I have tried to show in this chapter is the extent to which Lily Braun's ideas concerning tactics, strategy, and organization coincided with the ideas of Eduard Bernstein. In the next chapter I shall qualify this by suggesting that the conventional definition of Revisionism does not in fact fit her overall ideology and that therefore her Revisionism must be distinguished clearly from that of Bernstein.

VIII

REVISIONISM AS THE RADICALIZATION OF MARXISM

Let me begin my attempt to differentiate between the two kinds of Revisionism by pointing out that, unlike Bernstein, Braun was not a Kantian in her philosophy, but a Nietzschean; and while Kant, when applied to twentieth-century politics, yields liberal implications, Nietzsche's ideas can be given a much more radical twist. Politically, despite what was stressed in the preceding chapter, she was not a reformist; indeed, in some significant respects she was, if anything, more revolutionary than the orthodox Marxists. In fact, I shall try to show that she, more than either the Kautskys or the Bernsteins, came close to the political philosophy of Marx and Engels. An examination of Lily Braun's political philosophy will reveal her to have been a precursor of contemporary Western Marxists.

While Bernsteinian Revisionism implied a return to Kant, and also to Comte and Mill, one could easily name other intellectual precursors, all of whom would symbolize a suspicion of dogma, a healthy skepticism which we associate with the Enlightenment. While Braun admired these same intellectual heroes, she also found them wanting, and with them their admirers, including not only Bernstein, but also her husband Heinrich. Writing about these friends of hers, she argued,

> Revisionism possessed the intellect and the insight of old age, but on account of this had lost the fire of youth. But whoever wants to gain the future, must keep this fire, must nourish it with his love, his hatred and his hopes, so that it goes on spending light and warmth, and so that the torches of those that follow him can be lit with its flames. [1]

In short, she believed in the necessity for charisma in the socialist movement. When she was in Paris, doing research for her book on the women's question, she attended a soirée at the house of some socialists. Everyone there, with one exception, was attacking Jean Jaurès, criticizing him for his oratorical talent: "They all argued that it was neither socialistic nor democratic to sway meetings with oratorical accomplishments; instead, one would have to convince them by objective reasoning. I and [Romain] Rolland disagreed, and I was sorry I could not do it effectively enough with my French."[2]

To be sure, this endorsement of charisma was hedged in with reservations. She was aware that charisma often is no more than lunacy, rage, or some other destructive emotion shared between speaker and audience, "that hypnotic connection which makes the speaker appear as nothing more than the mouthpiece of the masses, while the masses, in turn, are under the speaker's suggestive spell."[3] (Here she is trying to characterize Clara Zetkin's speaking style.) She also was sufficiently suspicious of mere charisma to think that Heinrich's rational argument was more valuable than the passion she or Jaurès might be able to display. Discussing the election campaign of 1903, she wrote about Heinrich:

> He addressed the intellect; he sought to convince where I would appeal to feelings. He spoke the language of the professor, not that of the agitator. Whomever he won for socialism became a genuine adherent [Bekenner]. Whatever I kindled may all too often have been no more than fireworks.[4]

In the final analysis, what she rejected in the orthodox was not the appeal to reason, but their shallow reasoning and their substitution of dogma and organization for both reason and passion. Like today's Neo-Marxists of the Frankfurt School, she wanted to deepen both our intellectual comprehension and our passionate concerns; she believed as they did that this should involve the spinning of utopias, and like them, she went back to Hegel for inspiration. She tells us in her memoirs:

> Yesterday, in a letter written by Hegel, I read a sentence which engraved itself into my memory, "Theoretical work accomplishes more in this world than practical work; once the realm of the imagination has been revolutionized, reality can no longer maintain itself." We revisionists in particular have almost forgotten this pro-

found truth. . . . If we had a program that left aside all the theories that have become dubious, left all practical demands to day-to-day decisions and made definitive statements only about the point of departure (the class struggle) and the final goal (the abolition of private property in the means of production), we would have fewer destructive conflicts in our own ranks, and millions now standing outside would become, not fellow travelers but party comrades.[5]

This certainly does not sound like Bernstein's admonition to forget about the final goal.

Like Hegel, Braun saw the master-slave relationship as pervading all human intercourse, and she tried to understand its dialectic. Like him, she recognized the alienating results of all dependency relations, their dehumanizing effect on both the slave and the master: "Where the judge forgets the humanness of the accused, he himself ceases to be human," she wrote in a commentary on some scandalous judgment.[6] Consequently, like Hegel, she assumed that the slave, in casting off his chains, would also be liberating his master—indeed, that only thus could the master ever be liberated.

I fear—yes, I do fear—that "the liberation of the workers can only be the work of the working class itself"; but the liberation of the descendents of the masters of the old world from the past will also have to be the work of the working class itself. To tear oneself loose hurts terribly, and yet the road into the army of the workers for those born far from them goes only through this pain.[7]

This suggests that she believed in the necessity of a painful expropriation of those now enjoying privilege and wealth. She was suspicious of what today is called radical chic, the profession of socialist convictions by the rich. During her stay in England in 1906, she renewed her acquaintance with many of the radicals she had met there eleven years before, including an immensely wealthy duchess who was active in the socialist movement. About her she wrote:

Whoever can feel comfortable under such a load of diamonds can hardly be a convinced socialist. To be sure, the combination of highest artistic and personal culture with socialist convictions is not only possible and self-evident—in fact, it is one of the goals toward which we strive for all. But the barbaric luxury of London's upper ten thousand is incompatible with it. I really cannot understand the state of mind of those women who, that evening, discussed the misery of the cottage industry workers with me, and all that time had the

nerve to carry hundreds of thousands in pearls and precious stones on
their bodies. Sport—that is all it is for them![8]

Of course, this sentiment did not make her commit the opposite
offense of sporting proletarian garb; on the contrary, by always dress-
ing with simple elegance even in proletarian gatherings, she voiced,
with silent eloquence, her continual protest against the drab uniformity which the levelers in the party expected to introduce into the
society of the future.[9]

Still, by protesting against the vulgarities of radical chic, Braun
showed that she accepted and shared the workers' hatred of capitalism and the bourgeoisie, their warlike conception of politics as a
zero-sum game. In that, too, her Revisionism differed from that of
Bernstein. And yet at the same time she rejected the possiblity that
the end result of this class war might be no more than a reversal of
the roles of oppressor and oppressed.

> For us the goal of the struggle is not the changed rule of human
> beings over human beings but the absolute rule of humanity over
> nature. The earth it is which we want to conquer, in order to create
> equal conditions of development for all, not enemy country which is
> to be tilled by conquered peoples. . . . [10]

To be sure, she knew very well that many workers thought this was
the goal of the movement; Marxism, she realized, was fed by resentment and envy among the exploited, emotions which, in their turn,
fed the fanaticism, narrowness, and vindictiveness of the orthodox
leadership, who, she thought, were a discredit to the socialist
movement.[11]

Similarly, she denounced as a betrayal of socialist ideals any definition of socialism as a mere redistribution of wealth. In his biography of
Bernstein, Peter Gay suggests that this was in fact the goal of Revisionism, and he argues that this redefinition of socialism was a consequence of the growing prosperity which raised even the workers' living
standards significantly. It may be correct to argue that many Revisionists, including Bernstein, may have visualized socialism as nothing else
than a more equitable distribution of material wealth; Braun, on the
contrary, decried the ease with which material gains seemed to satisfy
some socialists. To her, socialism was more than full stomachs and a
change of clothing in the closet. Her definition of socialism, in fact,

envisaged our liberation *from* material concerns through their universal satisfaction, and the freedom to pursue the worthier goal of self-improvement. If she had written in the jargon of contemporary Neo-Marxism, Lily might have argued that her idea of socialism revolved around the goal of self-transcendence through revolutionary praxis—the same aim which Engels suggests at the end of his *The Condition of the Working Class in England,* and Marx in such works as *The Poverty of Philosophy,* the *Theses on Feuerbach,* and the essay on communism in the 1844 manuscripts. In Braun's time, this side of Marxism, however, had been forgotten; and she herself derived her humanist definition of socialism from Goethe, Nietzsche, Hegel, and others.

Self-transcendance, for Braun as for Engels, was not a distant goal to be attained at the very end of a chain of transitional stages but an aspect of revolutionary praxis, a transformation needed now, because in revolutionary praxis, means and ends, the methods and the goals of the struggle, coincide. The journal published by the Brauns, *Neue Gesellschaft,* printed an interesting article by Franz Laufkoetter about the tactics of the proletariat in its fight against capitalism—when to make a stand, when to give in, and when to honor or not to honor agreements made. The writer argued that the workers must always honor agreements, for dishonesty, sneakiness, and the like are the weapons of weak and base people. Applying Nietzschean ideas to the class struggle, the writer urged the working class always to fight honorably; why? Because the proletariat wishes to create a higher, nobler culture; and noble behavior (the behavior of the strong) promotes nobility, while base behavior (the behavior of the weak) undermines nobility.[12] There is no hint in sentiments such as these that the proletariat or its party should be less militant. Even as a Revisionist, Lily Braun always identified with the class struggle and was able to say, "whoever is not with us is against us."[13] And years after she ceased being active in the party, she was looking for opportunities to prove to the public that she had never ceased being a convinced socialist.[14]

Braun knew that the rank-and-file workers could behave rudely and inconsiderately. She knew they liked fanatics because they hated fanatically, that they were drawn to the orthodox because they, too, had a deep psychological need for ideological certainty, and that they distrusted the educated and well-bred.[15] She was only too painfully aware of the deep gulf separating the philosopher from the proletarian. Philosophers, she pointed out, preach high ideals and may, for instance, talk about the ennobling effect of suffering; and rightly so, she added. But how could an exploited worker possibly understand that some individuals of high intellectual sensibilities might curse a life without suffering? And how great was the distance still to be traveled before such an understanding could be created?[16] Like Marx, Engels, and Lenin, moreover, she was convinced that those most oppressed—whether proletarians or women—could not become conscious of their oppression. About radical women, she wrote:

> Those who first became conscious of the misery and oppression of their sex and formulate this insight in words could not, of course, be the most severely maltreated; they had to have attained a certain level of education and understanding. For the most abject misery dulls our sensibilities; it destroys all our capability to act; it even prevents the feeling of discontent with the own misery from arising.[17]

Yet ultimately she always expressed faith in the workers' inherent nobility and capacity for understanding. Only these inherent virtues needed to be fostered. Hence the education of the working class was the most pressing task. The first duty of the socialist movement was to raise the consciousness of the masses of the masses. Marx had urged this, and Braun echoed him. "Rousseau depicted the virtue and happiness of a coming world," an eighteenth-century character in one of her novels argues; "others will have to come who will hold a pitiless mirror up to the face of society, a face disfigured by gruesome ailments."[18] But, equally as important as instilling radical class consciousness, or perhaps more important to Braun, would be to teach them socialist morality—nobility even in the bitter class struggle, consideration for others, the ability to treat all people, even enemies, as human beings, in politics as well as in private lives.[19]

Ultimately, this concern with the deficiencies of working-class culture flowed out of her overall conception of the socialist utopia. In her memoirs she sketched the outlines of this utopia as follows: equal rights for all, male and female; freedom of conviction and expression; a secured existence—freedom from economic want and economic dependency; nationalization of all land and industry; work as a universal duty; art, science, and nature belonging to all and accessible to all; the free development of the personality, regardless of caste, race, sex, or property.[20] Note the following: first, that her concern was not only with political economy, but also with cultural goods, and second, that she emphasized freedom. While she insisted on equality of rights, opportunities, and benefits, Braun decidedly did not believe that all people are equal. Indeed, her insistence on individual freedom within the socialist society presupposes inequalities. For her, the aim of socialism was to develop the full creative potential in every individual—what Isaiah Berlin has attributed to John Stuart Mill's notion of liberty: "neither rationality nor contentment, but diversity, versatility, fullness of life, the unaccountable leap of individual genius."[21] While Mill believed this could be achieved in bourgeois society, Braun thought bourgeois society would have to be overcome. Bourgeois society afforded primarily the freedom to accumulate, to own, and to consume; and it made greed careerism, and the hunt for profit the driving motives. To Braun, these freedoms, while necessary, were fundamentally contemptible, and to the extent that Bernsteinian Revisionism extolled them, she considered it a betrayal of socialism. The freedoms she demanded were the freedom to develop as individuals; freedom to develop morally, intellectually, and physically; and freedom to participate, to contribute, to create. To a friend she wrote:

> I would abandon socialism if anyone could prove to me that it will make people lazy or that, what would be worse, it would tear down the protective wall between individuality and mediocrity. I am convinced that the drive for material gain will be replaced by ambition, by the need to unfold all one's talents in order to let them be effective. Marvelous to the core, the drive today often is totally repressed by the compulsion to make money. . . . Socialism in my opinion is the only healthy basis on which individualism can flourish. If I am wrong—well, I have enough confidence in the healthy instincts of human beings that I am convinced they will then overcome socialism just as they must overcome capitalism.[22]

Note that this conception of socialism implies a rejection of equality, of uniformity, and of unrelieved collectivity. We are not equal either in our potentials or in our tastes, she insisted, and we do not all understand or get along with one another. Hence we need privacy as much as we need collectivity.

> As if nature, which differentiates every blade of grass from all others, should not make it possible for human beings to develop a far richer diversity;—as if true fraternity were not becoming rarer and rarer, but also deeper and deeper, the more we develop! To respect natural boundaries, not tear them down—to recognize distances instead of trying to bridge them with phrases—in short, to act in conformity with evolution, which always progresses from uniformity to multiformity,—that would be our task! Instead, under the mask of fraternity we are promoting arrogance and eradicate all reverence for the heroes of intellect, so that in the end every Tom Fool will call Goethe his brother. Only one among the trinity of demands which the Revolution took over from Christianity will remain valid: liberty![23]

Again, this is liberty for the aim of self-transcendence. In the final analysis, her socialist utopia was a Nietzschean dream of a society of superior human beings, as was Ibsen's vision. In his lecture to the workers of Tronthjem, 14 June 1885, Ibsen argued that liberal democracy was inadequate to solve existing social inequities and oppression. What was needed was an aristocratic element—not an aristocracy of birth, money, science, or talent, but an aristocracy of character, will, and ideas. Where would this aristocracy come from? It would come from women and workers.[24] Orthodox Marxists condemned such talk as unscientific and harmful petit-bourgeois dreams; but Braun would have been in full agreement.

Here we have a rejection of egalitarianism, a rejection which does not seek to keep people in their places, but, on the contrary, seeks to revolutionize society. It regards present inequalities as unnatural, because they derive from inequalities in property, not from innate personal differences, and therefore, they are degrading as well as harmful. Perpetuating unnatural inequalities alienates individuals and destroys society; fostering natural inequalities, in contrast, will enrich the species. "Socialism," she wrote, "is the necessary precondition for individualism just as much as individualism must be the necessary complement to socialism."[25]

But, she asked herself in another article, are we not, as socialists, supposed to practice solidarity? Are we not a party in which the individual must subordinate her will, her wishes, her interests to the party? She answered this question:

> It seems to me that if we continue going along this road thoughtlessly we will be well on our way from a great truth to a monstrous

error. The final goal of any work for the well-being of the community, for the liberation of humanity from every form of intellectual and personal slavery, can be nothing else than the freedom of development for the individual, the right of everyone to his or her own personality. But whoever is engaged in the struggle for these goals must be doubly careful not to lose his own ego in this struggle, but must preserve it.[26]

Again, this is a merger of Nietzschean ideas with Marxism, in which Marxism becomes Romantic, aesthetic, and humanist, while Nietzsche turns into a revolutionary. Nietzschean was her burning hatred of Christianity, and her understanding of the Renaissance as an age which gloried in humankind and in the human capacity for knowledge and achievement, an age which cultivated great individuals afraid of nothing, who thought big thoughts in politics, and regarded the state as a work of aesthetic creativity. Her long-standing admiration of the lonely philosopher was greatly boosted by conversations with George Bernard Shaw during her second visit to England. In her memoirs, she summarizes these conversations in a revealing passage:

The will to power, the highest possible development of the personality as the goal for the individual, the superior human being as the goal of humanity: the tones that had met me in England this time suddenly united into one single full chord. My heart beat almost to bursting like that of a prisoner whose leg chains are being taken off, and whose prison door is opening so the he can roam freely. He sees nothing else than the old familiar world of his youth, and yet it appears to him miraculously new. I was still half a child when I heard the first call to personal liberation out of Nietzsche's *Fröhliche Wissenschaft*: "Life says: Do not follow me, but yourself! Your own self!" Was not this same summons today addressed to all humanity?[27]

Nietzschean, too, was her preoccupation with the aesthetic dimensions of the coming revolution. Her definition of socialism we have seen, stressed the aim of making culture the property of all. To her, the enjoyment of beauty, both in nature and in works of art, and the playful exercise of the mind in conversation with the great classics of literature and philosophy were essential elements of a full life.

Not he is the holiest among us who most effectively deadens his senses, but he whose eyes are clearest, whose ears most sensitive to the perception of all the beauty of the world. And not he can claim

a place in our heavenly realm who suffers and endures, but he who
acts and enjoys. Enduring and suffering is something everyone can
do, but only the son of a ripe culture knows how to enjoy, and only
the knowing one is able to act.[28]

Her statement reminds me of a sentence in Kleist's *Penthesileia*
(Scene 14):

Der Mensch kann gross, ein Held, im Leiden sein. Doch göttlich ist
er, wenn er selig ist.[29]

In Braun's eyes, the exploitation of the workers and, incidentally,
the discrimination against women consisted not only in their economic dependency and their political oppression, but also in their
being deprived, systematically, of intellectual stimulation and aesthetic joys. Hence her frequent demand that the world of art, science, and philosophy be made accessible to the masses through an
aggressive program; that their cultural level be raised by the party;
and that rays of beauty be brought into their drab lives, be it through
inexpensive exhibits and stage productions, reading clubs, adult education programs, cheap editions of the classics, or whatever.[30] In
short, Braun anticipated Bogdanov and Gramsci in her discovery
that the political struggle of the proletariat must be accompanied by
a cultural transformation of the workers. She was convinced that the
workers would be eagerly receptive of such a program.[31]

No less important a part of the planned socialist revolution than
the seizure of power, the cultural revolution that Braun demanded
would nonetheless be fundamentally different from it; for while the
political overthrow and the expropriation of the bourgeoisie would
be acts of destruction, she saw the cultural revolution as a process of
preservation—preserving the classics for the people, taking art out
of the hands of the commercial exploiters and the rich, and handing
it to the nation, thereby making the underprivileged receptive to the
accumulated cultural wealth of our civilization. Such a task would be
based, not on hatred and resentment, but on reverence for the classics; and in stressing this, Braun voiced her anger at the cultural
Philistines in the party who treated them with contempt. In her
journal she printed a double distich by Count von Platen which says,
in effect, "The mob rules, not where Sophocles once wore laurel
wreaths, but where the dabbler wins the laurel. Mob and tyranny are

intimately linked; freedom lifts an ennobled people above the mob."[32] In turn, her own arguments were easily dismissed as indications that she had not managed to shed the prejudices of her aristocratic upbringing.

In her concern with proletarian culture she anticipated others who advocated a special proletarian culture; she advanced notions we associate with Adorno, Jameson, and other contemporary critical theorists. I have in mind her insistence on the revolutionary or progressive role of art and the artist. Here too she placed herself in sharp opposition to party ideologists who insisted that the scientific method of dialectical and historical materialism was the only valid way of gaining insight into social reality. In contrast, Braun stressed the significance of the artist as analyst of the present, rouser of consciousness, and seer of the future.[33] To be sure, even among the orthodox there were some who recognized the potential role artists might play in describing the dark reality of capitalism; but they tended to specify quite narrowly whom they might or might not recognize as progressive. The tone here was set by Franz Mehring and George Plekhanov, who can fittingly be described as precursors of Andrei Zhdanov and György Lukács in the cavalier manner with which they decided which writers a class-conscious proletarian might or might not read with profit. Braun, in contrast, anticipated contemporary Western Marxists by recognizing the revolutionary potential in works of art that were in no ways inspired by Marxism. "It is not essential that our painters and poets be convinced Marxists, but that they be great artists," she wrote;[34] and she paid close attention to avant-garde movements of all kinds, trying very carefully to weigh the uselessness of their aesthetic escapism against their value as expressors of unfulfilled longing, social malaise, and alienation.[35] The only demand she tended to make of artists—and here she not only echoed Engels but also anticipates such contemporary Marxists as Adorno and Jameson—was for them not to lapse into pessimism and despair.[36]

In her opinion, the aesthetic experience itelf was something she believed to be a means for consciousness-raising, if only because glimpses of beauty and moments of joy were likely to remind us forcefully of the ugly present, and stir us into action. This is the reason why she objected vehemently to the puritanism of feminists and Marxists who believed it to be immoral to be joyful or indulge in aesthetic pleasures in this world of suffering. On the contrary, said Braun: With so much misery afflicting the world, every spark of beauty, every pleasurable experience ought to be treasured, and if at the same time we can remove some of the aesthetically repulsive features from the lives of proletarians, that too is part of the revolutionary praxis.[37]

Every year in one of the December issues of *Die Gleichheit*, Clara Zetkin would publish an article denouncing Christmas as a fraud and an abomination, a device of the capitalists to benumb the mind of the exploited. However, this did not prevent her from celebrating Christmas as a family feast like other people, even though in almost the same breath she expressed her loathing of the duplicity of those comrades who in their personal lives did not live up to their socialist ideas.[38] Lily Braun replied to some of these articles in her own journal, urging even the poorest proletarian to celebrate Christmas. She exclaimed:

> Go ahead and light your Christmas candles! Let the star of the magi shine on top of the tree! What paralyzes our will and our readiness to fight are not festivals in which devout tradition is irradiated with the light of energetic hopes for the future. Instead, what robs our souls of its elan is the gray emptiness of uninterrupted everyday life with its senile reasonableness, and the icy coldness of its purist lack of faith which freezes the blood in our veins![39]

Obviously Lily Braun decried what Max Weber has called the *Entzauberung* of the world—that process by which modernization robs the world of myth, mystery, and magic. She told an audience, at one of her lectures on the great courtesans in history, that the twentieth century is ruled by cold, calculating intellect, by practical reasoning. This represses our emotional life. But our emotions want to come into the open. There is a universal longing for the lost paradise of love, joy, beauty, great passion, and, indeed, even religion.[40] Capitalism, she was arguing in effect, was not only alienated labor and alienated citizenship, but also alienated beauty and alienated joy. For the rich, beauty turned into pretentious display, and joy into degeneracy; among the poor they were prostituted or absent altogether.[41]

Against orthodox Marxism, which insisted that the enjoyment of

beauty and other pleasures would accrue to the proletariat once socialism had been achieved, Braun demanded that the proletariat
fight for them now. Moreover, the struggle for socialism should have
an aesthetic dimension in yet another way: the movement itself
needed festivals, celebrations, rites, and ceremonies. Festivals and
rites are part of being human; they create and strengthen the spirit of
community. Braun had a fine eye for political symbols. As a child
and an adolescent she had experienced the magic of massive displays
of flags and uniforms. She appreciated the importance of the ceremo-
nial in tying simple people to the Catholic church; and she wished
the socialist movement were smart enough to learn from armies and
churches and tap the emotions of its followers in this fashion.

> When an old nag which has long been panting in front of heavily
> laden wagons hears the sound of the trumpet, it pricks up its ears,
> lifts its tired head and tries to make its stiff legs do graceful gaits; and
> when a person, who has long ago decided that the nation's play at
> soldiers is a crime, hears the old military marches, he has to restrain
> himself in order not to fall in step; and once the troops themselves
> appear before his eyes, . . . his heart begins to beat faster, however
> much he would want to keep it calm. . . .
>   Do these sounds awaken lost memories of our dim barbaric past?
> Does the sight of armed troops whip up that drop of blood which
> rolled through the veins of our ancestors, for whom fighting was a
> pleasure and their life? Or is it not merely the suggestion of the
> masses, the music, the colors, which inebriates our senses? Would it
> not give us just the same excitement if these soldiers were men of
> labor, their weapons, shining tools, their uniforms, festive garments,
> and the entire brilliant and colorful picture a mighty review of
> labor?[42]

After observing a magnificent Catholic rite in a small Bavarian
village, she wrote to her husband: "This may have been the single
'big' day in the life of these people! But how cleverly the Catholic
church knows how to tie these folk to it even with these things! We
could learn a great deal there!"[43] Would it be unfair to her to point
out that the fascists and National Socialists did learn these lessons
about converting politics into public spectacles?

If her delight in celebrations and festivals went against the puritan
spirit of orthodox Marxism, so did the ecological dimension of her
socialism. Like much of our own contemporary ecological move-

ment, her concern over the frighteningly rapid despoliation of nature through the machine age sprang from aesthetic considerations, and it was also linked to a Goethean lament over the alienation of human beauty.[44] But there was in it also a yearning for the allegedly unspoilt life of our savage ancestors; hence her delight in any and all residues of heathen nature cults, which for her symbolized a closeness to nature and an affirmation of life. She wrote:

> The mechanization of labor enriches our external cultural life, but it smothers primordial spontaneity and leads to inner emptiness and impoverishment of the human race.
>   Liberation from the smothering slavery of labor will reverse this! In the individual creativity of the thousand hands we will have to become like the Negro again. This is a problem for socialist education.[45]

Still, her ecological concerns were based also on her dim awareness of the coming shortages in energy and raw materials.[46]

Braun's revisionism also implied a decisive rejection of one set of ideas concerning the coming revolution that was central to orthodox Marxism. She rejected the historical scenario of the step-by-step development from capitalism to socialism in well-defined stages, none of which could be skipped.

This is not the place to investigate whether either Marx or Engels ever held this view or, if they did, whether they managed to identify the discrete stages. That they had done so, however, was taken for granted by orthodox Marxists then; and the belief in such a rigid timetable, in allegedly scientific laws of revolutionary development, was closely linked to the identification of "economics" as the determinating feature of societal development (economics here means the structure of capitalism and the resulting class struggle between workers and bourgeoisie). Its allegedly central place among all issues implied that, in the final analysis, the only political question which mattered was the struggle for power.

By her insistence that there were many modes of oppression, hence many issues, all important, Lily rejected the exclusive stress on the proletarian struggle for power as delusory. By implication, she also repudiated the suggestion that the discrete stages of the revolution could be defined in advance. Instead, she insisted that fights were to be fought on many fronts simultaneously, that revolutionary leaders must do this with their eyes open for unforeseen opportunities; that small gains ("reforms") should never be disdained; and that no one issue could ever be preeminent over all others. This is the attitude which the orthodox called "opportunism," ignoring the fact that their own Engels had, at times, given similar advice. Contemporary Marxists are beginning to call this "revolutionary praxis," especially when it is linked with a conscious attempt on the part of the individual to apply revolutionary morality even in her or his individual life. For revolutionary praxis means nothing more or less than the infusion of revolutionary attitudes, revolutionary views of the world, and revolutionary behavior models into the total life of the individual, hence an attempt to change the world by changing one's self and the people one knows. In the most abstract terms, the rules of revolutionary praxis are suggested in Marx's eleven *Theses on Feuerbach*. Braun herself, who had not read these *Theses*, derived them (as noted already) from Nietzsche's philosophy of heroism and self-transcendence. Whatever the derivation, Braun's entire life can be seen as an example of revolutionary praxis. In the final analysis, that was the quintessence of her revisionism.

Like Herbert Marcuse, Braun defined the guiding principle of all her thoughts and actions as the spirit of total negation. The spirit of negation, she wrote, must fill the nation if it is to revolutionize it. As long as it animates only limited sections of the people, compromises with the past will sooner or later be made: The people of the Renaissance built churches; the French revolution adopted Christian phrases; and we too, in our slothful unwillingness to be consistent, are pouring new wine into old skins by modernizing the churches or mobilizing Kant for socialism. The consistent spirit of negation, however, must be Nietzschean, not Kantian or Christian. Nietzsche's philosophy is the ethical basis for socialism; in contrast, the ideal of the greatest happiness for the greatest number will create a society of portly petit bourgeois. It is a moral revolution which must lend wings to the idea of the coming economic transformation.[47]

Lily Braun expressed all these heretical ideas in a language which was entirely her own, even though its roots in Rousseau, Goethe, and Nietzsche are unmistakable; and this language, too, is an essential element of her revisionism. In the writings of the orthodox, the language of Marx had been fossilized into a tired jargon, no longer

serving to open eyes and minds, but functioning rather as a set of
ideological blinders, ostensibly to mobilize and revolutionize, but
often designed instead to maintain order. Braun's writings were a
restatement of revolutionary socialism in fresh imagery and a new
vocabulary. In pleasant contrast to the arid scholasticism of the
orthodox, her style was polished as well as elevating; it avoided the
vulgarities of the agitational tone of the orthodox; disdaining to
descend to the masses even as a speaker at mass rallies, she sought,
instead, to raise them to her level. One party paper said of her, in
her obituary,

> She came to social democracy from noblest motives, her heart full of
> ideals, and sought to serve the party to the best of her abilities, even
> though her aristocratic origins and a heap of illusions rendered her
> rather unfit for petty day-to-day conflicts. Her efforts to remedy this
> deficiency did not always find the proper support, even though Lily
> Braun, who had always remained a *woman*, often made much deeper
> impression as representative of our doctrine, and could register far
> more success than those female agitators who only aped the male
> propagandists and were far less able to appeal to female souls with
> their purely theoretical sermons.[48]

Another obituary, however, suggests that in fact she did not manage
to reach the masses with this style. Zetkin, it implied, with her
biting invective, appealed to feelings of hatred and resentment,
while Lily's lofty but militant idealism was wasted on the rank-and-
file:

> . . . even as an agitator, she always deliberately sought to avoid
> common and popular vulgarities of style and expression. She did not
> go to the masses, but she allowed the masses to come to her. Even as
> an agitator she was always, as it were, wearing her black silk robe.[49]

Her writings abound in vivid imagery from nature, her favorite
metaphors being those of growth—birth and death, blossoms and
fruit, sunshine, soil, and gentle rain. It is a language also of aesthetic
sensibility, which sees beauty in justice, and injustice in ugliness.
Hers is, moreover, a language of liberation, in which defiance re-
places not only conformity and conventions, but also the orthodox
insistence on the iron laws of historical determinism. Again, it is
Nietzschean in its insistence on brutal honesty, even when the truth
is painful. Most importantly, perhaps—and this may be the essence

of Lily Braun's revisionism—hers was always the language of feminism. All her adult life, she strove to rebel against the prevailing language of learned and artistic discourse, which she thought had been fashioned by men. Her resolve was to write as a woman and like a woman, and, by doing so, to project femininity, to infuse the socialist movement with the healing spirit of revolutionary feminism. *She wanted to humanize Marxism by feminizing it.*

This undertaking, with its refusal to talk in formulas, and its determination to employ her artistic imagination and her feminine pride for a redefinition of revolutionary socialism may, in the end, have been her most significant contribution.

I hope I have demonstrated the fundamental differences between Braun's Goethean-Nietzschean humanist Marxism and the neo-liberal conceptions of people like Bernstein—differences were obscured when both of them were called Revisionists. In fact, "Revisionism" is little more than a hate word with which dogmatists in the movement have, ever since the 1890s, tried to rid themselves of those who ask questions. The questions Braun raised differed fundamentally from those posed by Bernstein. To be sure, these two "Revisionists" did agree on many points of practical reform work. But in her philosophy and overall conception of revolutionary politics, Braun was in many ways closer to Rosa Luxemburg. The same radical spirit, thirst for action, and total condemnation of contemporary society drove both women. Both fought against organizational fetishism, urged the party to dip into the masses of the working people for active support, and stressed the need to educate the workers and their leaders to consciousness. Both, finally, injected a deep concern for humanist values, and admiration for the classics of art and literature, into their conception of politics. Carl Schorske, in his excellent history of the German Marxist movement, describes Luxemburg as having a penetrating, analytical mind, combined with imaginative warmth; a sharp rapier of wit used in intellectual combat, but never as the bludgeon of character assassination; as having a cold hatred of injustice and oppression, and a genuine love of humanity. For her, he writes, the question was not reform or revolution. Instead, she thought that reform work must be carried on with the aim of leading to revolution.[50] All these statements, and several more he could have made about Rosa Luxemburg, well describe Lily Braun.

Orthodox Marxists would not necessarily quarrel with this observation. In their eyes, the difference between the Bernsteinian "dilution" of Marxism and a humanist "intensification" of it is slight. Both the right and the left deviations, in their opinion, amount to one and the same thing—a denial of the Marxist laws of development, and, therefore, a repudiation of Marxism. Both of them also constitute an abdication of politics; for the only politics which the orthodox recognize as effective is that based on organization. If Luxemburg rose in the party while Braun was shoved to the sidelines, it was because Luxemburg was much more self-consciously Marxist in her language, and much more one-dimensional in her insistence that problems of political economy crowded out all other problems. In that sense, Luxemburg herself was in the camp of the orthodox, while Braun, with her insistence on the interdependence of various issues, was not orthodox, but radical.

IX

THE ALIENATION OF
FEMININITY

Toward the end of the preceding chapter, I defined the thrust of Braun's Revisionism by asserting that she wanted to radicalize Marxism by feminizing it. It should be obvious from everything written so far in this book that this statement could also be reversed. In fact, her own intellectual and political development can be summarized by stating that she had radicalized her feminism by joining the Marxist movement. I have also shown that by keeping to her feminist convictions, her comrades in the SPD thought that she had not understood Marxism, or that she was not faithful to it. Meanwhile, her former associates in the women's movement believed that by embracing Marxism, she had abandoned the women's movement. Today Braun's attempt to create a synthesis of both is very much on the agenda of both movements.

To show how much Braun anticipated contemporary feminist thinking and vocabulary, I shall begin this discussion of her theories concerning the oppression of women, by reproducing in its entirety a vignette she wrote around 1905 entitled "Fair Game."[1]

> A young woman is standing on a suburban railroad platform. She obviously is waiting for her train—an entirely ordinary situation, one would think. Her figure and her face are of that ordinary prettiness which one can observe daily in hundreds of variations on young women of all classes. So here too there is really nothing remarkable. Nor is there anything provocative in her eyes or her attitude or her clothing. She is simply standing there waiting for her train.
>
> So why is every man that passes giving her the eye? Why do some of them go close by her, questioning her with ambiguous, or rather unambiguous leers? Why does one of the group of unwashed fifteen-

year-old punks have the nerve to make a filthy remark at her under
his breath?

Simply because she is a young *female*, and because the average
male of all social classes evaluates the female only as a sex object,
even in the so-called "age of the women." From the raw lad barely
out of school to the noble gentleman, they all show, and use with
brutal thoughtlessness, their seigneurial right of control over female
sexuality.

It will be good medicine for women clearly to realize over and over
again the revolting nature of the actual relationship between male
and female, as it is revealed in the praxis of daily life. In the depth
and in the breadth of our time, there is as yet no women's
liberation.[2]

A summary of Braun's ideas on women's oppression and women's
emancipation would have to begin with her assumption that women
have been oppressed in all but the most primitive societies. In discussing why sexist oppression is so universal, she, like Engels, argued
that women were oppressed because men wished to secure for their
children the inheritance of their property. But she laid greater stress
on the oppressive results of the sexual division of labor that freed
men to gather food or hunt, while the women, tied down by their
reproductive functions, became the "natural" home workers, preparing food and clothing and caring for the small children. In classical
antiquity, Braun argued, this sexual division of labor had been developed to such a degree that in effect, all women were slaves, confined
to the home so strictly that it was prison. The only liberated women
in ancient Greece, she suggested, were those who became famous
concubines or whores attached to the temples of various love god-
desses. That kind of dependency was a far cry from liberation, but
nonetheless, Braun made clear that she herself would have preferred
the freedom and respect enjoyed by Aspasia or Diotima, or the
pleasures enjoyed by the love slaves in a temple of Isis, to the
confinement of the Greek married woman.[3] I will return to this
theme shortly.

According to Braun, the oppression of women has taken many
forms, and the changes in form are related to the history of civilization; this is largely, though not entirely, the history of changing
modes of production. We have seen that for Braun the first form of
the oppression of women was the transformation of the woman into a

slave, into a working animal. To be female meant to be condemned to ignoble, hard, boring work, in unfreedom and total dependency on the lord and master. It meant being an inferior being, a menial, a person unworthy of honor, and unfit for great tasks. By definition, the woman could not be a citizen; she could not participate in public life. It need hardly be added that she was an object also in sexual life, that she did not have control over her own body.

To this general oppression of the woman as a work horse without status or dignity, Christianity, according to Braun, added a new form of oppression—namely, the degradation of sexual functions into something sinful and disgusting. If Greek, Roman, ancient Judaic, and other pre-Christian societies had made woman into a slave, Christianity also alientated her from her sexuality. Love, to which the ancients had erected shining temples, was dethroned and declared a satanic force.

> The heathens erected glistening marble temples to the goddess of love, while the Christians pushed the demure, beautiful one into the filth of the bordellos. Nobody bears greater guilt for the moral depravity of our youth than the church, the sole source of salvation, which branded Nature herself a great sinner.[4]

Braun never tired of writing that the religion of love has blasphemed against creation itself by defaming love.[5] A beautiful and natural human activity thus was stigmatized, and the sexual urge banished into the murky world of our subconscious. Our bodies, in the grace and power of which Nature urges us to glory, were turned into vessels of sin and impurity, to be hidden from view and indeed from thought. Braun was rarely more eloquent than in her insistence that sexuality was healthy, while Christian morality and its continuation in bourgeois form were sick.[6] There is hardly a theme to which she returned as persistently as her angry denunciations of the damage Christianity had done by making us repress our natural sexuality, hardly a myth which she rejected more indignantly than the idea that women have no sexual urge; she called this a web of lies which enslaved women more powerfully than any juridical deprivation of rights could have done.[7] She is rarely more compassionate than when she describes the consequences of this sin against nature: the insidious double standard, the enforced lifelong celibacy of the woman who cannot find a husband, the criminalization of the prostitute, and the hypocrisies of Christian states that license this profession while barring women from other work because practicing medicine or law might "endanger their femininity." Some of her essays show much perceptiveness about the role of sexual repression in generating various kinds of neurotic or deviant behavior.[8] Repression, she argued in a public lecture, damages the female psyche. An artist, she continued, can create great works only if she acts out all her erotic needs, whatever form they might take.[9]

Throughout her life Braun expressed envy and admiration of prostitutes. As in her analysis of famous concubines or whores in Ancient Greece, she believed that prostitution might be a form of self-liberation. In one of her works of fiction, one of her characters says about prostitutes,

> These girls are free; no clippers of considerations or etiquette cut and trim their feelings, . . . no husband makes them their private property similar to his dog, whom he teaches not to take a piece of bread from anyone else even when he is hungry.[10]

In a public lecture on "The Enslavement of Love" given in Berlin on 9 November 1906, she asserted that the flourishing of culture is often tied to the phenomenon of the outstanding courtesan, but never to the institution of marriage. Courtesans appear in periods during which people develop positive attitudes toward life and its joys, and the free use of talents and potential is encouraged in such periods. Love, too, can then go public, and the courtesan becomes an agent of liberation. Having fought for the liberation of eros, she can awaken great impulses for awakening a new culture and a flourishing new intellectual life.[11]

In all this advocacy of "free love" and these bitter denunciations of repressive moral codes, Braun was also crying out her sorrow for having remained a virgin for thirty years, instead of enjoying her body and its pleasures to the hilt. Christianity, with its perverted sexual morality, had robbed her of her youth, and had done the same to hundreds of millions of other unhappy human beings. When they visited the Louvre, her son asked why Venus de Milo has no arms, and Braun told him that this had been her punishment for not holding the men and women who had run away from her temple. In the final analysis, Lily Braun was convinced that erotic love ennobles, if not men, then at least women.[12]

If Christian morality made love into something filthy, capitalism has transformed it into a purchaseable commodity. The way Braun liked to put it: love is perverted as long as the sexual union between women and men takes the form of an economic institution—the family—which, as a unit within the competitive capitalist society, has to participate in the Darwinian struggle for survival. The union of lovers should be a natural sacrament. Instead, as an economic unit it is a business deal, a pragmatic search for partners who can best help each other accumulate wealth. Those two conceptions are incompatible; and the fact that the union is sanctioned by the church only makes the church an accomplice in the violation of the natural sacrament. " 'The road to marriage leads through the church,' Mama used to say; but is there not a golden idol standing at the altar instead of a priest?"[3]

Here I must say more about the role Darwinism played in the Marxist movement around the turn of the century. To accept Darwinist ideas was part of being progressive or avant-gardist; rejecting them smacked of religious fundamentalism. Life as a struggle, and struggle as a process which results in the evolution of ever higher organisms, seemed to many orthodox Marxists a confirmation of the dialectic as a natural law. Marx himself had made remarks to this effect, as had Engels to a much larger extent.

Yet Marxist theorists objected to *social* Darwinism—the application of the Darwinian model to human society. They defined the human being as a cooperative, collectivist creature, a species being, to use a term from the 1844 manuscripts; and they argued that the assumption of an intraspecific war of all against all was nothing more than the projection of capitalism, in all its viciousness, on human relations. A truly human society would be cooperative, not competitive.

From this position, generally taken by Marxists, Braun's own ideas deviated significantly. While she agreed that the competitive war of all against all which capitalism creates is an abomination, she did think the Darwinist model should be applied to the human animal with respect to its natural, biological function, of which the most important, to her, was the choice of a mate. In that area, principles of natural selection were applicable; and it was here that capitalism was doing its greatest damage: for capitalism compels us to violate the rules of natural selection by making us choose our mates on the basis of economic considerations. But in fact, only if men and women were allowed to select each other for strength of character and beauty of body would they produce new generations of healthy, beautiful children. Braun was convinced that, if young people were allowed to follow their natural mating instincts, they would be drawn to the healthiest, strongest, most attractive specimens, those most worthy of procreating; and she thought that in some backwoods areas, not yet spoilt by civilization, such a natural selection was still taking place among the peasant population.[14] But, with selection as it functions within capitalist society, the species can only degenerate.[15] I do believe in the so-called fairy tale, she wrote, which says that children produced in love are especially blessed.

> Place all genuine children of love—not those of alcoholism, irresponsibility, or rape—into favorable physical and intellectual soil, and they would develop into a generation of human beings who will surely put the children of legal marriages of convenience in the shade.[16]

Children born out of wedlock, she said in the same spirit, are potentially the elite of humanity, because they are the product of pure love, hence of pure natural instinct. Yet it is precisely these most valuable members of humanity who are treated so poorly that they perish in capitalist and Christian society.[17]

These ideas of Braun's echoed the New Morality proclaimed around the turn of the century by Scandinavian and German feminists, such as the prominent Ellen Key and Helene Stöcker. I previously mentioned the New Morality in chapter 2. Far from merely being a hedonistic call to shake off the shackles of old-fashioned repressive moral codes, it was primarily a theory of practical evolutionism based on Darwinist and Nietzschean ideas. It substituted eugenics, also called racial hygiene (which later entered the vocabulary of National Socialism), for sexual abstinence, preaching volitional breeding for the purpose, not just to procreate, but to elevate humanity to a higher level. In the selection of mates, it urged all people to trust their instincts, but demanded that such freedom of sexual choice be aided by full knowledge of reproductive functions. In short, the New Morality advocated general sex education, as well as a free rein to erotic urges. "Be true to yourself," was the motto of the New Morality. "Chastity consists in the harmony between the soul and the senses, and no sexual relationship is moral without such a relationship."[18]

By implication, freely following the call of love is moral. But, in denouncing the institution of marriage, Lily Braun insisted that love was a tender growth that thrived only in the utmost privacy—the most intimate personal relationship possible between two human beings. Such relationships, she insisted, must be beyond all conventions and public scrutiny. Hence to regulate them by a contract is a desecration; to depersonalize the woman by making her abandon her former name means certifying that now she is a man's property. "Love should always be a secret about which only the people closest to the lovers know anything. Conventional matrimony cries out to the entire world and cynically tells every little guttersnipe: Look, this woman is that man's property!"[19]

According to Braun, in modern marriage, the woman is indeed the man's property; and an unmarried woman is every man's potential property. This is a sexist society, she recognized, in which all relations between the sexes keep the woman in a dependency relationship, so that even women with strong personalities lose their identity and become empty characters. Most often, wrote Braun, they do not even notice this themselves.

> What tremendous power of domination lies in this compulsion wielded by the husband over the wife as long as he clothes, feeds, and houses her. This lets us understand why the man expends such tremendous amounts of money, effort and persuasion on attempts not to let this power slip out of his hands.[20]

As a result, once love has cooled (if ever it was there) and sex has become routine, the average wife is compelled to go on living with a *stranger*, whose life she cannot share because he does not treat her as an equal.

> Today more than ever, there are lonely women whom the world calls happy, except that they themselves most often do not recognize how degrading it is to live side by side with a stranger; for a stranger is that husband to the wife who sees in her only the female, but not the friend [*den Freund*—Braun here uses the masculine form]; who in his working life, among colleagues, subordinates and superiors is a thinking, striving human being, while with the one who should be closest to him on earth he remains the sensual lover.[21]

Braun added to this passage that the *moral* solution in such cases is for the woman to leave her husband and join a man she really loves. In other contexts, she explained and excused prostitution on similar grounds.[22] In voicing such sentiments, she echoed much contemporary literature, foremost perhaps the writings of Artur Schnitzler. In Schnitzler's plays the only honest people are "loose" women and prostitutes; and among all the many dishonest relationships he depicts in his *Reigen*, the most dishonest one is that between husband and wife: in their scene together, not a single honest word is spoken.

To sexism, according to Braun, capitalism has added yet another mode of oppression. For her, the history of Western civilization in the last few hundred years was the history of a developing society which more and more defined a person's worth by his or her material and intellectual contributions. Creative and productive work, despised as unworthy of a free man among the Greeks, Romans, and feudal lords, had turned into the only activity which gave meaning to life. Consequently, the oppression of women in the early modern period, when this new culture of the dignity of labor was developing, took the form of eliminating women from many lines of work in which they had previously participated. Chapter 3 of *Die Frauenfrage* treats this process in some detail, and the next chapter discusses how women were simultaneously excluded from participation in higher intellectual pursuits. Yet with the coming of the machine age and of modern capitalism, the trend to exclude women from productive work and from intellectual creativity was reversed for a number of reasons. First, within the bourgeoisie, modern means of mass production relieved the housewife of many tasks she previously had to perform, making her more and more useless, a mere object of decoration and pleasure, a doll for her man. Bourgeois feminism, according to Braun, was the self-consciousness of the woman as a mere doll. Hence the first aim of the self-conscious bourgeois woman, bored with her useless life, was to fight for the right to work. Work liberates; Braun shared this conviction with Engels and Marx. It confers dignity and purpose; it is a means toward self-actualization.

> The entire development of women's work, as it meets our eye in the form of dry statistics, must clearly demonstrate to everyone who is not—or does not wish to be—blind, one thing: no other modern phenomenon has such a revolutionizing effect as it. Without it, the

restructuring of economic and social life desired by the working class would remain an illusion. For it strikes the old society at its very roots. It converts the female—this most conservative element in the life of nations—into a striving and thinking human being; it alone is her great emancipator which will lead her from slavery to freedom.[23]

Braun believed that work not only will liberate women; it will also place them into positions of leadership, and will encourage them to make contributions for which they, as females, are particularly fit. Noting that women have not made outstanding contributions to philosophy or art, and that they are not really brilliant as cooks or tailors, she suggested that

the genius of women is fated to manifest itself in a totally different area, an area which only now is opening up for humanity.

We have seen that the professions preferred by women—educator and school inspector, nurse and physician, social worker and factory inspector, commercial employee and office clerk—correspond to the motherliness of her character; and, despite insufficient experience, we might already find that they distinguish themselves particularly in these professions they choose. We also know that almost all welfare endeavors, even the most ambitious ones, owe their existence and development almost exclusively to women, that women everywhere and increasingly participate in everything falling under the rubric of social reform, and that here they perform most excellently both as agitators and as scholars. Whereas ordinarily they used to cling to the traditional, and left the difficult position of avant garde to the men, they now turn to the youngest of the sciences, the social sciences, with astonishing understanding and rare energy, and they fight for the right to practical activity within them. They are facing a tremendous field, whose tillage corresponds to their aptitudes, and in which their personality can express itself most perfectly; for the aim here is to find ways and means to help the miserable and the weak, to comprehend, manage and dominate the economy of the world just like, earlier, the economy of the home. . . .

. . . the power of muscles loses its value, the power of the intellect and the heart gradually steps into its place. To be sure, today, when the first steps on this road are being taken, there are as yet no female geniuses who march ahead as trail blazers, but I have no doubt whatsoever that they will come. In this sense, the enemies (of feminism) are right in foreseeing an age of feminism; but they are wrong in believing that it will be an age of weakness and degeneracy. For only the complementing of male talents by female ones, the collaboration of both sexes who live on earth with equal rights to existence, can produce effects which do not damage the one part by their onesidedness. If the intellectual and emotional aptitudes were equal, then the entry of women into public life would be altogether valueless for humanity and would only imply an even wilder competitive struggle. Only the recognition that the entire character of the female is different from that of the male, and that it will mean a new, re-envigorating principle in the life of the human species, makes the women's movement into what it is—despite the opinion of ill-willed enemies and lukewarm friends: a social revolution.[24]

Work liberates. But, for the men and women at the bottom of society, for the proletariat, work has the opposite effect. These people, who have no property except their mere crude labor power, and who must therefore do hard, demeaning, boring, health-destroying work for starvation wages, without having any control over their products—these people are not liberated by work; their work oppresses and destroys them. It even transforms adult women into children—women into "girls"—as when the married working woman in England is called a "married girl."[25] Work in the factory or in cottage industries, work as a maid, or a waitress, or a lowly farm hand, is alienated work, and a pure burden; very often it is unmitigated hell. A vast proportion of Lily's writings about the world of female work, including the bulk of her major book, consists of bone-chilling descriptions of these many circles of hell.

The slogan "work liberates," therefore, is a lie where the proletarian woman is concerned. She must be liberated *from* work, or at least from the kind of work which now oppresses her. Much of Lily Braun's thought went into ideas about the dealienation of work. She was convinced that in the long run, only the restructuring of society from capitalism to socialism would accomplish this; but in the meantime, unlike Zetkin and other orthodox Marxists, she believed one ought not to abandon the exploited and oppressed working women to their fate; one should press for reforms to ease their lives as much as possible.

Suppose, however, that work has been dealienated—an expression Braun did not use, but which conveys her ideas quite well. Suppose capitalism were reformed so that women had full equality of opportunities, and were free to make their living in any way they saw fit; or even suppose that a socialist society had managed to transform work into a pleasurable activity, and distributed the burdens of toilsome and boring labor evenly among all citizens. For Braun, such freedom and equality in the world of work would still pose one major problem for women; it would interfere with one other essential activity indispensable for women's self-actualization—motherhood. The more a woman is active in the world of production and public affairs, the more her work and her citizenship fulfil and absorb her, the less time and energy will she have for motherhood.

At this point, I want to reformulate what has been said so far to show the relationship between Braun's theories and other contemporary theories of oppression.

Braun's theories of feminism may be restated most simply by taking Marx's *Economic and Philosophic Manuscripts of 1844* as points of departure. In his manuscript on the alienation of labor, Marx argues that the human being achieves self-fulfillment and self-actualization in creativity. From the context of other works by Marx and Engels we know that Marx means productive work, intellectual activity, and artistic creation. In the 1844 Manuscripts, he argues that under capitalism, work becomes a burden—we need not rehearse his supporting arguments here. Labor, when it is applied to the production of commodities, is alienated labor. Similarly, in his *Critique of Hegel's "Philosophy of Right"* and his essay "On the Jewish Question," Marx implies that public life in a class society is a life in which true citizenship cannot be exercised, because instead of being the democratic self-government of a genuine community, politics under capitalism is a conflict between selfish interests and the maintenance of an unsatisfactory, doomed system by force and fraud. The capitalist state is alienated freedom; class politics is alienated citizenship.

Though this terminology was not then in vogue in the Marxist movement (these early manuscripts had not yet been published), throughout her political life, Braun subscribed to sentiments such as these. However, she added two important aspects of alienation to this diagnosis, aspects to which Engels, Marx, and their followers paid little or no attention. First, she implied that human beings actualize themselves not only in creative work, be it the fashioning of art works, useful things, or innovative ideas, but also in sexuality. She insisted that the exercise of our sexuality in sexual acts, most typically with a love partner of the opposite sex, was as necessary to the human organism as eating, sleeping, or creating. Human beings fulfil themselves by love as much as by work. Yet love, she argued, has been alienated; and our sexuality is a curse more than a blessing. Love has been alienated, first, by being branded sinful and disgusting in Christian doctrine; further, by being regulated in the monogamous family which alienates love by linking it to the concerns of an economic unit, so that economic considerations, not sexual needs, determine the choice of partners, the duration of their bond, and the number of children to be produced. Finally, love is alienated because it is regarded as legitimate only when it is practiced within the framework of a church-and-state-certified union—whereas, ideally, sexual communion is an intimate matter which should be of concern only to the two or more individuals involved.

Braun thus complemented Marx's theory of alienated labor with a parallel theory of alienated sexuality. She linked this to Marxism in many ways, arguing that it was not only Christian doctrine but also the capitalist market society which served to alienate it.

To this analysis of alienated sexuality, Braun, as a feminist, added one other theory of alienation which, she argued, was perhaps most important because it had the most disastrous consequences: the alienation of labor enslaves us; the alienation of sexuality makes us into psychological cripples. But the alienation on which she concentrated her attention was the alienation of motherhood; and that alienation, she asserted, threatened the survival of the human species. Capitalism, she says in her memoirs and in her *Frauenfrage*, destroys the health of mothers, and therefore endangers humanity. Capitalism destroys motherhood; if we want to survive, we must destroy capitalism.[26]

Moreover, the alienation of motherhood is dehumanization at its worst. For Braun, motherhood was the most human of all human relations; its alienation, therefore, is the most grievous form of victimizing women; hence mothers, of all human beings, are the most alienated ones.[27] How did she arrive at such a view?

Self-actualization depends on creative work, the exercise of citizenship, and the release of sexual energies with a love partner. But in women, she argued, one other potentiality slumbers which must be actualized if they are to be total, fulfilled human beings, instead of caricatures. That potentiality is motherhood. "A woman who has no child is a second-class woman," she suggested many times.[28]

> Motherhood is the acme of womanhood; and there is no legal emancipation of women which will be able to hide the actual enslavement of the female sex as long as one pregnant woman still pants under heavy loads, as long as one mother who has given birth forces her exhausted body to work, and as long as one abandoned infant cries for its mother.[29]

All of her work is a glorification of motherhood, of the woman as the genitrix of future generations and hence the essential link between successive generations, the one and only guarantee of the survival of the species. In many of her writings it appears to be a means of self-actualization more noble and more satisfying than creative work, sexual activity, or the enjoyment of beauty. So that women, being the only ones capable of motherhood, at times appear as superior beings in her writings: they share all the means of self-actualization possessed by men, but the best one, the highest one, is theirs alone. For "the primeval moral tie between human beings is not the relationship between man and woman, but that between mother and child."[30]

Given this glorification of motherhood as the most fundamental human relationship, we can at last fully understand why Braun included Rousseau among the pioneers of women's liberation. She shared not only his view in this matter; her entire theory of alienation, like that of Marx, can be seen as derived from the Rousseauian notion that human relations in civilized, advanced societies are inversions and perversions of natural ones. Like Engels, she argued that modern capitalist civilization robs women of their femininity and men of their masculinity.[31] And despite exaggerated, condescending ideas about what constituted femininity and masculinity, it was Rousseau who proposed the solution which Braun accepted: become mothers! "As soon as women once again begin to be mothers, the men will once again learn to be husbands and fathers."[32]

"And if I were to speak with human or angels' tongues and did not have love, I would be as sounding brass and a tinkling bell"— this applies especially to women. No equal right, no freedom can be useful to them and make creative human beings out of them, nor can they benefit from freely living out their sexual urges, if they allow themselves to be robbed of the one good that nature has bestowed on them alone: maternal love. It is this emotion which is the source of women's deepest social instincts: compassion and the courage for self-sacrifice.

This emphasis on motherhood as the most essential destiny of woman, as the precondition for women's self-actualization, will offend and possibly enrage many contemporary feminists, as it did feminists in her day, just as Braun herself was offended by the age-old assertion that household work was the "natural" area in which a normal woman fulfilled herself. The insistence that the proper function for women was to give birth, and that their proper place, therefore, was in the obstetrics ward and the nursery, had too often been the basic argument of those who wished to keep women out of public life, the so-called higher professions, and the factory. Maternalism, if we may coin this term for such ideas, has traditionally been a reactionary, anti-feminist argument. In Braun's own day, the argument came to be advanced even by members of the socialist movement, most blatantly by Edmund Fischer, in a series of anti-feminist articles he published in Bernstein's *Sozialistische Monatshefte*. [33]

Yet, maternalism is also an old feminist theme, and around the turn of the century a good deal of feminist agitation and argument concentrated on demands for the protection of motherhood, or the liberation of mothers from all those obstacles preventing them from acting out their maternal destiny and desires. The writings of Ellen Key in Sweden, Adele Schreiber in Germany, and Charlotte Perkins Gilman come to mind as examples of this kind of feminism. [34]

In Braun's writings, it is important to recognize the unbreakable link between her maternalism and her militant demand for the liberation of women from all forms of oppression, inequalities, and restrictions. For her, the way to dealienate motherhood presupposed the socialist transformation of society; the rejection of conventional sexual morality; the destruction of the monogamous family as an economic unit and as a clerical or governmental licence to practice intercourse; and the elimination of all forms of male domination. Her theory, therefore, might be labeled—if it needs a label—Revolutionary Maternalism. It is thus diametrically opposed to the theories of

Shulamith Firestone: not liberation *from* motherhood, but liberation *for* motherhood.

Let me once again stress the affinity of such theories with the Marxist theory of alienation. The Marxist approach to women's oppression, Joan B. Landes has argued, is based on the understanding of women as social beings whose life activity is productive labor. Under capitalism this life activity is alienated not only in the sphere of commodity production, but also in the private sphere, the family.[35] Lily Braun, while fully accepting this diagnosis, adds sexual love, the enjoyment of beauty, and especially procreation and parenthood to these life activities, unconsciously going back to the *Economic and Philosophic Manuscripts of 1844* which identify the relationship between male and female as the paradigmatic human relationship; and to the first pages of Engels's *Origins of the Family*, where he identifies productive work and procreation as the two essential life activities. The Marxist movement, however, has never paid attention to any of these pursuits except productive labor. In its tunnel vision, Marxism shows how much it is the heir of the classical political economists.

Conversely, for Freud and his disciples, the driving force of all human actions appears to be eroticism; one narrow interpretation is substituted for another. In Lily Braun's theories, both of these interpretations of what is essentially human are fused; but the mother-child relationship is posed as a third essential life activity; and ultimately it is considered primary over all others:

> Maternal love is the strongest feeling in the world, stronger than sexual passion, stronger than hunger. Once it has been freed from the chains into which tradition forced it, it will have to become the moving force which will change society from top to bottom.[36]

Dealienated motherhood, in Braun's opinion, would save humanity. Before adding some critical comments to these theories of feminism, let us examine the practical proposals resulting from them.

X

FEMINIST POLITICS

Little or nothing in these ideas was new: Socialist theory had explored the alienation of labor and had called attention to the special problems of female workers; middle-class feminists had long agitated for equal access to education and professions, equality under the law, and the right to participate fully in public affairs; the institution of marriage and the sexual morality of the Victorian age were under attack; and the importance of motherhood as a means of women's self-actualization was a familiar theme. The advocates of these ideas usually fought each other, accusing each other of misreading the root cause of women's oppression. Lily Braun, however, recognized their interdependence, and tried to combine all of these ideas and a whole range of other, less important, feminist ideas into one grand synthesis. This synthesis included political and legal equality, the right to all work, clothing and language reform, liberation from economic exploitation, sexual liberation, the destruction of the family, and the protection of motherhood. These would no longer contend with each other, but would support, and reinforce, and presuppose each other. To the extent that any of these interrelated goals was declared the exclusive or primary task of feminism, Braun rejected them, and criticized their advocates for their narrow-mindedness. Yet she did not hide her agreement with all these demands, just as she continued to support all those women rebels who, each in her own way, were rattling at the prison bars of convention and law.

Still, she insisted that genuine feminism must attempt to solve all the problems faced by women, and that any movement which did not offer a really comprehensive program was inadequate and would end up solving nothing.[1] Every time she stressed this need for a total feminist program, she naturally dwelled on the inadequacies of all other feminist movements.

In the mid-nineties, Lily had been in the forefront of the fight for women's suffrage, and throughout her life she maintained her interest in seeing women participate in politics; but she also argued that this alone would not solve women's problems.[2] She had been sympathetic to the German women's agitation, in the late 1890s, against the new German civil code (Bürgerliches Gesetzbuch, abbreviated as BGB) with its several provisions which discriminated against women. (*Männerrecht* is what German feminists called it, in analogy to Bachofen's *Mutterrecht.*) During the same period the discussion of sweeping anti-obscenity legislation, the famous *Lex Heinze,* provoked wide discussion among feminists about the problem of prostitution. In the sharp conflict that divided the women's movement on this question, Braun sided with those who advocated the decriminalization and decontrol of this trade. During the war of 1914–1918, her son Otto saw prostitution come out into the open right behind the front lines; in fact, he was once quartered next door to a bordello. When in his letters to his mother he expressed his disgust, she warned him repeatedly not to fall into the male-chauvinist habit of condemning prostitutes. Rather, he should see them as victims not only of economic need, sexual deprivation, and the sudden lure of easy money, but also of the exploitative urges of their male customers. Supply in this trade, she argued, is generated by demand. His disgust should be directed at the officers and men who create this trade, not at the suppliers of the merchandise.

In discussing prostitution, she suggested several times that sexual deprivation should be considered a more significant cause than economic need. Such remarks are in line with her recognition that female sexuality is a strong natural urge, the repression of which causes damage. She sympathized with love-starved women, and believed that such women are more frequent among the middle and upper classes than among workers and peasants. Yet she also tended to criticize those who thought they could solve the women's question by advocating free love, and those who believed that the woman fulfils herself primarily in sexual intercourse. Condorcet, a character in one of her novels, argues, do not demand freedom from morality, but moral freedom, i.e., the freedom to act morally.[3] Moreover, she argued that a policy of "free love," if it were not accompanied by other trenchant changes, would only bring women greater oppression.[4] Her good friend Werner Sombart had suggested to her that "the highest flower of culture will not be the working woman, the free, emancipated female, but the *femme amante*"; to which Lily replied that she could not acknowledge the existence of the *femme amante* as long as the truly free woman is not her premise.[5] Within the German women's movement, the most important representative of this view of female sexuality as the heart of the women's problem was Helene Stöcker; and within the League for the Protection of Mothers, a Stöcker faction was opposed by a faction led by Adele Schreiber and Lily Braun. In the final analysis, Lily seems to have had a bit of contempt for women preoccupied with their sex life. About a young cousin who was unhappily in love she wrote:

> She is the type of those unhappy girls cheated out of their lives who became feminists for lack of a man and in addition—this for me is the most disgusting trait of hers—have a certain feverish interest only for sexual matters.[6]

And still, in the final analysis, she insisted that freedom of cohabitation must be granted unconditionally, whatever the motives,[7] even though, by itself, this freedom would solve little. And since freedom of cohabitation was merely one aspect of the woman's right to control her own body and its reproductive functions, Braun linked this demand with the demand for freedom to restrict births, including the freedom to abort.[8]

The same ambivalence marks every other problem she examined. She was aware of the sexist nature of the entire society and believed that at some point all understanding between the two genders would break down. She wrote to a friend:

> I do not want to claim that all men are . . . tyrants, or whatever foolish accusations are made against them by one-sided feminists, but I do assert and am ready to prove that men are *incapable* of understanding large areas of concern in women's lives or of understanding profound problems that result precisely from the fact that women now are stepping out of the narrow confines of the home.[9]

Nonetheless, she scorned those women who saw men as the one and only enemy, or who rejected any contribution made by a male chauvinist simply because he was a chauvinist: Schiller held women in contempt—shall we therefore reject his poetry? That would be like judging the music of Beethoven in accordance with the degree of his sympathy for the proletariat, she wrote, knowing well that many of her antagonists in the Marxist movement were ready to do precisely that.[10] True, men enforce their dominance and are an enemy. But the principal enemy, she insisted, was capitalism—its culture, and its morality, of which contemporary sexism was an important part.[11] At the same time, Braun had hardly any sympathy for those feminists who advocated equality to such a degree as to wipe out the differences between the sexes. She was opposed to the ideal of androgyny, and its notion that the human being of the future ought to be unisexual or bisexual. As she put it: it is ridiculous to conceive women's emancipation as the masculinization of women, and to convert the idea of equal rights and equal validity into the notion of equality in kind.[12]

While she ridiculed those women whose rebellion against male domination made them reject men in one form or another, she also warned that women must, in the final analysis, liberate themselves. For this they cannot and should not rely on men; nor can they afford to tie up their own liberation too much with that of men, the way orthodox Marxist women proposed.

> The man chains us and he opens the chains, he makes us happy and he breaks us to pieces. The man must help if woman wants to become free! That is indisputably correct in many individual cases, but one cannot make it into a strategy for our struggle. In matters of personal freedom and personal development, there is, in the contemporary proletarian marriage, *no* community of interests between man and wife, there only are contradictions. . . . Where her personal freedom is concerned, the worker's wife, too, cannot expect her man to offer either understanding or help in advance, and voluntarily. Her personal rights she must wrest from the husband by force, as long as bourgeois philistine morality is still so engrained in him that he wants to deny them to her, and if she does not have sufficient insight to muster this energy, it should be given to her through proper enlightening.[13]

One might argue that a program for women's liberation as comprehensive as Braun's proposal could not have a well-developed strategy; and Lily would probably have been the first one to agree. What her action program amounted to, therefore, was to fight the problems now contributing to the oppression of women, chief among them the bourgeois-feminist fight for equality of rights and the proletarian-feminist struggle against capitalist exploitation. Success in either or both of these principal struggles, however, would not solve the fundamental conflict between the urge to work and the urge to motherhood. Hence, she concluded, once women had achieved economic, legal, and political equality, once they had succeeded in attaining both full democracy and socialism, the truly revolutionary feminist struggle would only begin.[14]

In the meantime, women must fight on all fronts, against all forms of oppression. But—and here Braun was emphatic—inevitably these various preoccupations, struggles, goals, and strategies contradict and interfere with each other. Because of this, Braun's own strategy was to focus on attempts to mitigate these conflicts, to find common ground, to compromise solutions, or, better yet, to think boldly to transcend these conflicts. A brief survey of her proposed solutions follows; the reader may judge their adequacy.

Let me start with a discussion of the problem of work as a right vs. work as a burden. When she first joined the Marxist movement, she was prone to speak contemptuously of bourgeois feminism, which concentrated its efforts on demanding equal rights for women to dispose over their property, to get access to the university, and to participate fully in public life. These were, for her, demands made by women from the propertied classes, interested in sharing their men's exploitative advantages. Why should a proletarian woman help them do this? Within a few years, however, Braun had convinced herself that both struggles were necessary for women's liberation, and that therefore they ought to be waged simultaneously, each class of women pursuing its own interests. The two struggles need not interfere with each other; and it would be desirable if proletarian and bourgeois women would at least learn to understand and appreciate each other's preoccupations. In promoting such understanding, Braun was more successful among bourgeois feminists than among proletarian feminists, for obvious reasons: it is easier to generate sympathy among the most privileged for the most oppressed, than to make the most exploited muster any understanding for the sufferings imposed on the women of the rich.

Braun adopted a similar two-pronged approach to the question of how to combine the fight against sexism with the necessary collaboration with men. Here, too, she argued that both were necessary and desirable, and that, in general, one need not exclude the other, even though in certain circumstances it might be quite clear that the interests of men and women obviously coincided, or obviously were irreconcilable. Thus, on this question of feminist strategy, she tended to be flexible and pragmatic.

But she found it impossible to be as sanguine about the conflict between the need for work and the need for motherhood. On the contrary, these two needs, which she thought essential for women's self-actualization, were in sharp conflict, and she insisted that this conflict be recognized and acknowledged.[15] In saying this, she did not mean to agree with her friend Ellen Key who had argued that femininity and intellectual creativity exclude each other, and that the genuine woman therefore would renounce intellectual and professional pursuits.[16] Instead, Braun visualized the woman as wanting to participate fully both in production and in reproduction. Yet these two pursuits do interfere with each other; and for Braun this remained one of the central dilemmas to be faced by the women's movement. In one of her last pamphlets, Braun wrote: "The women's question is not a mere bread-and-butter question, nor is it adequately summarized as a demand for general human rights; instead, it revolves around the conflict between the natural function of the woman and the socio-economic position she is forced to assume within modern society."[17] She suggested that this dilemma was a multiply tangled knot that would have to be disentangled slowly and patiently, loop by loop.[18]

For her, the dilemma was linked to a slightly less profound one, namely, the conflict between professional life and housekeeping roles. Here she thought that the communal household would at least approach a solution. She herself hated housework; she found it unchallenging, repetitive, demeaning, and time-consuming, an unmitigated agony which prevented her from doing her real work. Indeed, she argued that for any woman who has outside interests, household work is purgatory.[19] Braun also insisted that the individual household was highly inefficient and wasteful, and that the average wife was by necessity a rank dilettante in food preparation, nutrition, and related activities. Pooling these chores in communal households would, therefore, not only release women for work and/or motherhood, but, by professionalizing and rationalizing these service functions (e.g., the feeding, cleaning, maintenance, and mending), better service would also be provided.

She was emphatic in pointing out that she did not mean this as a demand primarily for day care centers, kindergartens, and other institutions designed to relieve the working mother of some child rearing burdens. Such kinds of bureaucratized child care, she argued, were a mixed blessing, to be condemned since they usually were based on the assumption that the man is the principal breadwinner. That assumption was to be rejected. Men should not be eliminated from child rearing, but, instead, should be enlisted in it. Hence the progressive idea of day care centers must be linked with efforts to restore the parenting functions of the workers themselves. She believed that the communes should take the form of family associations in which communal parenting should be one of the principal tasks.[20]

In connection with this, she warned against one assumption often made by German feminists, which was that it was the infant who was most of all in need of the mother. Wrong, said Braun: the infant's many needs are much more effectively met by a well-trained pediatric nurse.

> It is much rather the awakening intellect which needs the mother's eye, which sees every one of its stirrings, and the mother's care, which is the only one to know which of its many shoots should be pruned, which ones should be supported, which ones are ready to be exposed to sun and bad weather; and millions of women are prevented from doing this! Never has our social order seemed more absurd to me: it forces the government to build jails for criminals and correction institutions for delinquent youths, whom it has robbed of their mothers.[21]

Just as communal housekeeping would not solve the "women's question" but only contribute toward its solution, so Braun's proposal for a system of maternity insurance was meant only as a temporary and partial response to a need. But she thought it would be an important step, for, if it were administered generously and comprehensively, it would make it possible for women to be both members of the work force and mothers. Arduous proletarian work, Braun argued, endangers pregnant women and their fetuses, and hinders lactation. Many proletarian women need to work for wages to survive, but under existing insurance they cannot do so; such schemes either are inadequate or can be circumvented much too easily; also they cover far too few working women.

> Virtually all eras and all peoples have erected altars to motherliness and have praised motherhood as a holy state, declared maternal love to be the most precious good. Should that have become a half-forgotten pious legend for the civilized nations of the present?[22]

Both the socialist movement and the women's movement, she claimed, had neglected this problem. All previous schemes discussed or enacted have been poorly funded; or they have tended to restrict work opportunities, thus driving needy mothers into non-protected lines of work (e.g., the notorious cottage industry or prostitution). In fact, argued Braun, truly effective motherhood insurance is against the interests of capitalism, so that no truly effective measures can be expected from the present ruling classes.

What, then, would be effective measures? Her list begins with the demand that employers should be compelled to insure the safety and health of all their employees. It demands a paid furlough of two months for women about to give birth, suggests the creation of a centralized motherhood welfare administration which should not only administer this insurance scheme, but also administer preventive medicine and pregnancy care, establish maternity hospitals and homes for this purpose, and pay special premiums for nursing mothers. All this should be financed through a progressive income tax.

Eventually, this scheme would not only ease life for the working proletarian mother, but would help solve one very different problem, namely, that of the unmarried woman. Citing the percentage of women between eighteen and forty who were unmarried, Braun complained that a frightening number of nubile, healthy women were excluded from all sexual activity and condemned to celibacy. For a variety of reasons, she thought this percentage was likely to rise. From the point of view both of the nation's interests and the interests of the species she deplored this, for often it was the best potential mothers who were thus excluded—i.e., the most independent ones, the ones who were most freedom-loving. Motherhood insurance, as she proposed it, was designed to make motherhood possible for such women also. It certainly would be healthier than the frighteningly high number of abortions. She ended her pamphlet with the words: "For every child the mother—for every healthy woman, motherhood."

Braun had advocated such a scheme, first in a review article, then in her *Frauenfrage,* and finally in the pamphlet I have just summarized. By the time that pamphlet was published, she could agitate for her proposal within an organization that had been created at the end of 1904, the League for the Protection of Mothers and for Sexual Reform (*Bund für Mutterschutz und Sexualreform*). Founded by Ruth Bré (herself an illegitimate child), Helene Stöcker, Walter Borgius, Maria Lischnewska, and Dr. Julian Marcuse, this organization set itself the aims of assisting unwed mothers, prostitutes, and "girls in trouble," rescuing children born out of wedlock, removing the prevalent prejudice against them, and fighting against the legal discrimination to which unmarried mothers and illegitimate children were subjected. The League created urban and rural homes for single mothers, and in other ways tried to help single mothers establish their economic independence while keeping their children. (One of the maids the Brauns hired around 1910 was a woman whom the League had referred to them.) The League had support among avantgarde men and women including Max Weber, Werner Sombart, August Bebel, Sigmund Freud, and a number of radical feminists outside the socialist movement. However, its aims and activities raised eyebrows among feminists in general, who were loath to see unwed mothers raised to the level of martyrs, who denied the League's contention that all children enrich the nation, and who regarded the encouragement given to single mothers as an attack on morals. After much debate, the League of German Women's Associations declined to accept the Mothers Protection League among its member associations.[23]

Lily Braun herself had been one of the League's founding members, together with Heinrich; and in 1906 she became secretary of the organization, to be succeeded, eventually, by her friend Adele Schreiber. The ideology behind the League's activities was not only compassion for young women and small children who were victims of a repressive morality and an exploitative system, but also that mixture of elements of libertarian, Nietzschean, and Darwinian ideas called the New Morality. A healthy sexuality was to be encouraged for the purpose of fostering a healthy species.[24]

Both the program of the League and its actual practices make it clear that its work was applicable primarily to poor mothers, to women whom economic need compelled to work, and who because of this economic compulsion were forced to neglect their children, born and yet unborn. Similarly, Braun's own proposal for motherhood insurance, which the League adopted as part of its program in 1906, was part of a scheme, not for liberating women for work, but of liberating mothers *from* work, at least temporarily. Incidentally, Braun resigned from the League when a proposal she had made to agitate for the decriminalization of abortion (abolition of the infamous Article 218 of the Reich Penal Code) was voted down. On this point, as on so many others, she obviously was ahead of her time.

Her ideas about marriage and the kind of union between men and women that might replace it were among the most poorly developed of her theories. Perhaps she was much too personally concerned with the dilemmas still to be confronted to sort her many ideas out in systematic fashion. As mentioned, the contemporary institution of marriage was an abomination in her eyes. Moreover, despite the efforts of conservative-minded people to save it, she was convinced that it was beyond saving, and that all efforts to save it would only contribute to its destruction.[25]

In conventional thought, the family was the sphere for intimacy, subjectivity, and personal authenticity. Within the bosom of the family, a person could be truly herself, whereas in the "outside" world of economic competition and public affairs one had to wear masks. Marxist theory around the turn of the century was barely beginning to challenge this separation of private from public spheres by suggesting that the seemingly private world of the family was, in fact, very much a function of political-economic relations, the mating couple being joined on the basis of economic considerations, and their union regulated by church and state. Engels already had suggested that the liberation of women depended on the destruction of the family as an economic institution, and on women's escape from economic dependency—an idea which eighty-five years after his death a contemporary writer expressed much more sharply: "If the ties of sex and survival were taken apart, we might envision a means of overcoming alienated sexuality as well as alienated work. This would indeed be a feminist revolution."[26]

In her own ideas concerning matrimony, Braun went beyond this statement by suggesting that even if capitalism were abolished, even if women were liberated from economic dependency on men, even if marriage could be a union of independent, autonomous individuals, it would still be an oppressive institution. Even in the best of societies, marriage would turn into a jail.

To be a morally acceptable union, Braun argued, marriage should be based on love, and it should be love between equals—equals in status and freedom. What conservative apologists for the contemporary institution of marriage call marital bliss, she argued, is based on the total subjection of women to men, in which women must give up their name and even their own ideas and will. This kind of partnership between unequals, however, destroys marriage by intellectually and spiritually impoverishing both partners.[27] Braun believed that today, such marriages are less and less possible, since women are beginning to step into public life. If marriage in the past was a miniature state, with the husband as ruler over wife and children, today it is a confrontation of two autonomous individuals. One can still force them into the old mold of the monogamous family, but it will break them as individuals; and in so doing will also destroy their love. Love thrives only in total freedom and grows only through the "pathos of distance."[28]

From a dependency relationship, marriage was turning into a partnership, a union of autonomous equals, based not only on love, but also on mutual respect. But this, in Braun's opinion, was leading to a new crisis: Love, respect, friendship, comradeship, partnership—all these various aspects of a marriage relationship were not necessarily compatible with each other. Indeed, in her writings, love, sexual passion, and the total surrender of the self to the other which she associated with it, often appear as incompatible with any kind of relationship, including that of mutual respect between two autonomous, active, creative modern individuals. The very notion of uniting for a lasting union seemed to her to be frightening: any union for life becomes a jail, she seemed to argue; it puts people too close together for comfort, it makes them oppress each other, so that in the end they flee from each other and lie to each other. "How many people who grew up straight have had their spines broken by it!"[29] Love needs a festive mood, she wrote in another place, while matrimony deals with the everyday. Matrimony inevitably generates rough winds which make the tender blossom of love wilt. Love is ecstasy, while matrimony is sober; and even in the best cases, where a marriage leads to genuine partnership and friendship, that very transformation spells the death of love.[30] Even children, usually considered the glue piecing a breaking union together, can become a wedge between the partners. It is precisely the happiest marriages which are most sorely tested by children: "The period in which the children develop into human beings always is the most dangerous; the preceding and following periods are the most harmonious ones."[31]

We see that the liberation and protection of love were of supreme importance to Braun as a feminist and as a human being. Underneath her acceptance of the work ethic and its underlying definition of human beings as conscious, purposeful, and creative creatures capable of remaking the world in their own image (appropriating it, in the Marxian phrase), there was a thoroughly romantic glorification of sexual love. She envisioned sexual love as the one relationship that can bring ecstasy, and therefore, if only for moments, lead to a kind of self-transcendance which ennobles and humanizes more thoroughly than any other activity or relationship. Her entire life's work as a feminist was a song in praise of love.

But even more, we have seen also, was it a song in praise of motherhood; and her deepest dilemmas, her most tragic conflicts, are those in which love and motherhood interfere with each other, situations in which a woman has to choose between keeping her child and keeping her lover not only because here two powerful and positive natural urges were in conflict, but also because she believed that children produced in love are especially blessed. The works of fiction that impressed her most were those like Hermann Sudermann's *Heimat,* in which the heroine confronts a cowardly lover who is willing to marry her, but does not want the child he fathered years ago. The lover has the support of the conventional father, who insists on the marriage to save his daughter's "honor." But the daughter chooses her child, and freedom.[32] This heroine, Magda,

Lily Braun ca. 1905 (International Institute for Social History, Amsterdam)

became something of a role model for Lily; and in some of her fiction similar heroic mothers appear. Ultimately, she believed that the conflict between love and motherhood could be overcome only by instilling in all women the will to motherhood.[33]

With this reference to the heroine of feminist fiction, we have at last come to the one element of liberational strategy which, in Braun's thinking, might resolve all seemingly insoluble dilemmas: her idea of the modern woman, the woman of the future, i.e., her version of the New Woman we encountered in chapter 2. As Braun imagined her, the New Woman would be autonomous, creative, versatile, responsible, all civic-minded, eager to participate in the economy and in politics. She would want and receive as much education as she was capable of absorbing, and all professions would be open to her. In all human affairs she would participate on equal terms with men. Society, in its turn, would be sufficiently solicitous to every single individual that even the people with minimal talents, as well as the homely, the ungainly, the shy—the wallflowers of life—would get a chance to make their modest contributions and receive their share of recognition.[34]

For these rights, women would have to fight. The first requirement of the new woman would therefore be that she would have to be a militant rebel fighting against all the old restrictions keeping women in their place. If dependency was the quintessence of the old woman, a fighting spirit of independence would have to be that of the new one. Never mind the exaggerated forms this might take; in fact, the excesses are necessary to show women the limitations under which they labor and the great distance they will still have to travel; for the genuine freedom which is to grow out of this struggle is, so far, only a dim vision.[35] Better to do too much than too little. Better to perish in heroic struggle than to go on living in dependency. "What I wish you most of all," she once wrote to her closest female friend, "is a woman's destiny, a really rich one. It is the highest, the most desirable thing, even if it destroys you."[36]

The heroic woman of Braun's imagination would liberate herself and create herself. She would not beg, she would not ask, nor would she wait for sympathetic or chivalrous men to give her what she needs. Receiving presents is demeaning; giving them, an act of condescension. The new woman thus must be a heroine, unafraid of being alone and misunderstood. But she must also realize that by herself she will be nothing. Women will liberate themselves only if they achieve solidarity. The self-liberation of the oppressed must be a collective struggle. Yet, Braun argued, women are often oppressed so deeply that they are not even aware of it; and men, too, however compassionate they may be, often do not notice the most abject victims of oppression.[37] It is therefore essential that women be enlightened, mobilized, organized, and taught solidarity. Let us organize the prostitutes, wrote Lily; a hooker's strike of just one week everywhere would prove that even the lowest of all the oppressed are capable of liberating themselves.[38] Let us organize domestic servants. That will be terribly difficult: They are duped by their employers; and they have little solidarity. But nonetheless, if we could get them to strike against the semifeudal relationship under which they work now, that might lead to a fundamental restructuring of the domestic economy.[39] Let us organize the actresses who get jobs only by sleeping with the directors, and who survive on starvation wages only by submitting to rich stage-door cavaliers; perhaps we can awaken their feeling of solidarity so that they can "shake off the yoke of their slavery *through joint efforts.*"[40]

Fighters, independent spirits, enlighteners, and leaders—those were the women whom Braun wished to see. But the women of the future, the activists in the women's movement, should also be lovers, pressing for the right to have sexual relations with partners of their choice, and insisting also for the right to have children. Lily Braun visualized her ideal woman as *feminine.* She seems to have echoed the stereotypical understanding of femininity as compromising all those qualities which men like in a woman: "her grace and modesty, her devotion and willingness to make sacrifices, her warm, loving, maternal heart."[41] Femininity, in her opinion, was properly defined according to male standards, as Quataert points out;[42] her definition thus would offend those who believe in an androgynous ideal, just as other contemporary feminists would be offended by another sentiment she often expressed: her horror of lesbianism and male homosexuality.[43] Obviously, her own views were decidedly heterosexual. She had few female friends and disliked intimate contact with women.[44] Like Plato and Rousseau, she very much believed that the sexes were complementary; she rejoiced in this, and saw it as something worth preserving and cultivating. Her conception of femininity is one jubilant cry of *vive la différence,* an assertion of the worth of being feminine.

It is in the spirit of this belief in the complementarity of the sexes that Lily, when she talked of love, often lapsed into sexist language and ideas. Female love, she insisted, is surrender to a superior person: "Only the de-sexed, the alienated from nature, artificially construe a female love desiring the equal. The woman wants someone who stands above her; for blind trust and a childlike need for protection is the very essence of her being."[45] This is a far cry from the image of the autonomous heroic woman! Again: "Female love is surrender to one standing above, regardless whether the heart which feels this beats under the rough blouse of the servant maid or under the doctoral gown of the woman jurist."[46] We will see below that these strange statements might not be absolutely incompatible with her assertion of the superiority of being feminine.

Further, in the same spirit of *vive la différence* she insisted that women have an inborn *need* to be beautiful (*ein Schönheitsbedürfnis*),[47] as well as the *duty* to be beautiful; and that anything which hides or de-emphasizes their feminine charms is an offense against nature. Every bit of joy we can create in this nasty and ugly world is worth something, and a beautiful woman is a joy to behold.[48] But note that her ideal of female beauty did not necessarily coincide with the norms accepted in her society. She believed, first, that the feminine fashions of her time were contrary to good taste. She thought they were dictated to women by an unrepresentative elite.[49] Further, she argued that modern life was destroying feminine beauty: "The old standard of beauty was defined by the man. It is being destroyed by modernization. The new standard of beauty has not yet been defined; women themselves must develop it out of changed conditions."[50]

If Lily Braun had written *Faust,* the tragic victim, Gretchen, would have turned into a heroine. She would have kept her child instead of murdering it, and she would have emancipated herself through her love relationship with the great Renaissance man. But, in lifting herself beyond her former self through love to a superior man, she would also have lifted Faust beyond himself. For if a woman's love is surrender to a superior being, a man's love, in

Braun's opinion, should be the same. He too, ideally, merges his self with someone whom he respects, whom he admires, and through whom he hopes to transcend himself. Women's liberation, for Braun, is incomplete if it is not profoundly related to men's liberation. The heroic women whom she hoped to inspire, the autonomous females whose duty it would be to be totally themselves and not to let any of their potentials lie fallow, would be successful only if in their struggle they worked with, and for, and through, similarly heroic men. In praising Hermann Sudermann for having created, in his play *Heimat*, a genuine modern woman, a realistic heroine for women who wish to liberate themselves, she asked, "Will he now create a male hero who will one day be the equal of this heroine?"[51]

Earlier I asserted that Braun wanted to humanize Marxism by feminizing it; that statement can now be extended to the assertion that she wanted to feminize all of human society. Women must liberate themselves and their rich potential so that they can *inseminate men* intellectually, emotionally, and culturally. This would be the feminization of human society, the fertilization of masculine civilization with the spirit of motherhood, hence the merger and collaboration of male and female principles which alone generates anything that is genuinely alive.[52]

"Old feminism," Lillian S. Robinson recently pointed out, "concentrated on legal and human rights within essentially unaltered institutions."[53] To this, Braun would have added that her kind of feminism would elevate human beings to a higher level. For ultimately, Lily Braun was convinced that a consistent feminist would have to work for human liberation. Of course, one can raise serious questions about her conception of what that liberation would require. One can easily agree with her diagnosis of all the modes of alienation. Let us further suggest that in her diagnosis of work as both a means of emancipation and a mode of oppression she was right on the mark, and that in identifying women's double or triple burden as wage workers, housewives, and mothers, as the gravest problem for a program of women's emancipation, she anticipated one of the principal concerns discussed by feminists today. Yet many contemporary feminists will find several of her positions objectionable. One of them is her conception of femininity as complementary to masculinity, and the resulting stress laid on the joys of heterosexual love, courtship games, and the beauty of young women's and men's bodies, culminating in her notion that women have both an innate urge and a moral duty to bring out their feminine beauty. Without doubt she was aware how easily the display of feminine beauty lends itself to exploitation, and she also felt deep compassion for women less favorably endowed by Nature—those whose bodies somehow did not come up to masculine conceptions of attractiveness. Yet this compassion was also mixed with contempt. Ultimately, her emphasis on the duty to be beautiful was related to theories of eugenics then part of avant-garde anti-Christian ideology both in Europe and in the United States. That these theories some decades later would become the basis for fascism, racism, and genocide, she really could not have guessed.

Equally controversial, of course, was the stress she laid on motherhood as indispensable for women's self-fulfilment, a position which more often than not is the chief argument of those who wish to reinforce patriarchalism. To be sure, even in contemporary feminism her views have strong echoes, most obviously in the writings of Adrienne Rich. But it seems clear that today's feminists in the United States are likely to be more sympathetic to the idea that the concept of mothering should be replaced by that of parenting, i.e., to a pattern of child rearing in which women and men would participate and contribute equally.[54] To be sure, this idea occurred to Braun as well, as indicated above, but more as an afterthought than as a principal position.

Most of her ideas about female emancipation, finally, are tied together by her conception of the woman of the future as a superwoman, exercising leadership in public life, in the professions, and in the self-government of the community, freely living out her sexual urges, and gently rearing her children to even greater autonomy. Here too we easily recognize the influence of eugenics theory, with its Romantic, Darwinist, and Nietzschean notions about the evolution of a new race of superior individuals and a superior species. It is a beautiful, lofty ideal. But can it be the basis for a practical program?

XI

CHILDREN'S LIBERATION

Braun's socialist feminism was an attempt to make the revolution a *total* revolution, a revolution which would overthrow oppressive institutions and relationships in all human affairs. In her discussion of total revolution, Batya Weinbaum distinguishes between three historic paradigms—the struggle between classes, the struggle between the sexes, and the struggle between generations.[1] Here, obviously, three revolutions are to be waged simultaneously, the workers' abolition of capitalism, women's liberation, and children's rebellion against adult oppression. Weinbaum makes ingenious use of certain Freudian theories to explain why the socialist movement has neglected the fight for women's and children's liberation. Braun was not familiar with these Freudian theories. But in her identification of workers, women, and children as oppressed groups who needed to liberate themselves, Braun clearly anticipated Batya Weinbaum.

That children were oppressed in a variety of ways was argued by a number of reformers around the turn of the century. During the 1890s, shocking instances of child abuse had been discussed in the press; and the misery of children had become the subject of several works of fiction, especially of the Naturalist school, foremost perhaps Gerhart Hauptmann's play, *Hanneles Himmelfahrt*.[2] Both Frank Wedekind's provocative play, *Frühlings Erwachen*, and Braun's own pamphlet calling for a children's revolution[3] took the alarming frequency of children's suicides as their point of departure.

The misery of the children of the poor was a public scandal, as it had been since the beginnings of the industrial age.[4] Throughout Europe, industrialization and urbanization had brought a rapid increase in the number of illegitimate births. Although the illegitimacy rate had begun to decline by the end of the nineteenth century, about 180,000 children were born each year in Germany to single mothers, most of them from among the urban poor. Of all illegitimate children, 32.7 percent died during the first year of life, as against 19.8 percent of all children; and a mere 18 percent of all illegitimate male children (as against 66 percent of legitimate boys) lived to military recruitment age.[5] Of those who survived, most were doomed to stay at the very bottom of society; a very high proportion of fatherless children ended up among the unemployed, in jails, and in insane asylums. A hero in one of Braun's novels, Lucien Gaillard, is the misshapen son of a procuress and a nobleman. Braun has him say, "The children of the future must not have mothers like mine. That is the highest goal of the revolution."[6] Meanwhile, of course, abortionists flourished, plying their illegal trade in unhealthy and demeaning conditions.

Handicapped children often were treated with abuse or neglect. In a health resort, Braun once noticed a Downs Syndrome child being beaten regularly by his nurse. She was indignant, the more so because, like many Downs Syndrome children, the boy was so obviously good-natured. She reported the beatings to the physician in charge of the resort, and learned that he had noticed them also. Yet he had done nothing to stop them. Whereupon Braun angrily told him, "If you physicians are not compassionate enough to free such children from the burden of life on this earth, you should at least protect them against cruelties."[7]

But even healthy children, if their mothers were of the working class, grew up in poverty, squalor, and generally, neglect. In Braun's opinion, many mothers, of whatever class, were unfit for motherhood:

> Being a mother is the highest and the best in the life of a woman, but . . . not every woman who has given birth to a child is, by this token, a mother. . . . It would mean doing the children bitter injustice if one were to leave them all to the care of their mothers.[8]

Proletarian mothers in particular, she thought, were virtually condemned to make their children's life hell. If the mothers worked, the children had to grow up in the street. If she did not, they grew up in material and spiritual poverty. "Hardly one proletarian mother these days can be a real mother, and all proletarian children are stunted not only physically, but also in their psychic life."[9]

Braun denounced wealthy mothers' practice of hiring wet nurses for their infants. The mothers did so in the belief that nursing their babies would enlarge their breasts and thus spoil their figures—a sentiment for which Braun had little sympathy. Braun was convinced, moreover, that the peasant mothers hired as wet nurses would have to neglect their own suckling infants, as well as the other mothers' children; she considered this practice a most cruel exploitation of poverty. In her eyes, nothing could be more reprehensible than depriving a baby of its own mother's milk.[10] Another pattern of child abuse which aroused her indignation was the readiness with which adults, especially upper-class adults, interfered in the squabbles of other people's children, meting out instant retribution; in general, many adults felt authorized to discipline and admonish any child, and Braun was angered by this audacity.[11]

Around the turn of the century, German youth rebelled against this oppression by forming socialist and other radical youth organizations. These organizations were immediately subject to harassment by the public authorities. While some members of the SPD urged the party to incorporate the demands of young people into its platform, the party leadership showed considerable reluctance, arguing that a separate youth organization would disrupt party unity; this question was discussed both at the Bremen party congress of 1904, and, two years later, at Mannheim. Here, too, the innate paternalism of the SPD leaders prevented the party from mobilizing the rebellious spirit of the young for its own purposes.[12]

Not only lower-class children were abused; the children of the rich, powerful, and educated were also being oppressed. There was a "children's question" in addition to a "women's question," and even while Braun was writing her book on the latter, she expressed the hope that she might follow up with a book on the former.[13] Had she not felt in her own life what it meant to live the life your parents planned for you, not the one you wished to live? To be shaped according to the specifications of social convention, rather than being free to take the natural forms your body and soul were seeking? From her memoirs it is clear that her first attempt to write down her ideas—the unpublished manuscript "Wider die Lüge"—was primarily a protest against the upbringing she had received: hypocritical Christian morality, empty knowledge good only for cocktail party chatter, false forms of politeness, imposed "truths," pretense rather than essence.[14] The one thing she would have wanted, the only thing she thought she had a right to expect, she did not receive: the opportunity to create her own personality through self-education. She had written:

> We have to choose between alien truth and our truth. We turn into liars when, lazy and thoughtless, we reach for the ready-made truths of others.
>
> Whoever wants to be true must be free. Free of the chains into which education, training and tradition have locked us, free of the magic spectacles with which the priests darken our sight, free of the lackey's livery into which the powerful of the earth force those who are dependent on them. Whatever you have not acquired yourself, whatever you are not yourself, is lie and slavery.
>
> Education is like an iron mould into which the soft souls of children are pressed. All it ought to be is a stake for supporting the young tree while it is growing. In the life of the child, the question "Why?" signifies the birth of the human being. Education slays it as soon as its limbs begin to stir. The penitentiary/school puts under one and the same yoke the gifted and the ungifted, the imaginative and the sober. It stuffs their brains full with names, numbers and rules; the best student is he who absorbs quickly; the worst, he who in painful thought seeks to appropriate what he has heard. In this process the "Why?" dies, the brain dries up, the heart shrivels, and historic charts, bible quotations, and rigid judgments about the world and about people take the place of independent thinking, of live enthusiasm for the good, the true and the beautiful.
>
> Woe to whoever contradicts the teacher: Thinking leads to wrong roads, doubt creates heretics and rebels.
>
> Go and swallow that soft, sweet pap they are placing before you ready to eat, you spoon-fed baby; and you will surely forget how to use your own teeth![15]

This outburst suggests that her indictment of adults included several counts, and in subsequent writings, she specified these counts. Most fundamentally, the aim of all education and child rearing ought to be to create autonomous personalities; to give people freedom and pride and confidence, the morality of masters, not of slaves. But, in fact, conventional education aims to break the will of the children, to make them dependent and weak. It destroys character rather than building it.[16] It does this for the purpose of making them obedient subjects and disciplined wage slaves. It also channels them into those careers or adult lives which the parents think proper or profitable, and this alone is enough of a false direction to skew the children's character systematically. Daughters, particularly, are the victims of an upbringing designed to prepare them for their specific service roles. Child rearing, furthermore, is shaped, not to accommodate the child, but the parent's convenience. Parents emerge out of Braun's writings as basically unfit to rear children. They have all the wrong attitudes: they consider children their property, their servants and subjects; they shape or rather misshape them according to parental specifications; and oftentimes they shunt them.

Perhaps an even more evil force confronting the child was the school system of the time, thought Braun and many other critics in Wilhelmine Germany. At the age of six, all children entered primary school, where during the first four years they learned the three Rs and other grade school subjects, in addition to receiving religious instruction. After these first years, the system divided; those who showed academic promise (as measured by their grades) could, if their parents had the money for tuition, transfer to a secondary school. The poor, and those with lower grades, continued in the primary school for another four years; at age fourteen their formal education ended, and they entered the world of wage work.

In all public secondary schools the sexes were strictly segregated; that is, schools were either entirely for boys or entirely for girls. But this statement alone is misleading because secondary schools for girls were barely beginning to be created, and the proportion of female children who received an education that might prepare them for higher studies was infinitesimally small. Hence, whatever will now be said about secondary education applies almost exclusively to boys. The standard secondary school was the classical Latin school (*Gymnasium*); the basic form of this institution was created in the sixteenth century. In this nine-year school the boys learned Latin, Greek, and French (Hebrew also, if they aspired to become pastors), as well as a great deal of ancient history. They were introduced also to more recent history, to geography, mathematics, literature, and a tiny bit of natural science and philosophy. Only graduates of these *Gymnasia* were admitted to German universities. Hence whether or not a young man would be able to enter any elite profession demanding a university degree was dependent on his successful passage through the *Gymnasium*. His success in this school also decided the nature and length of his military service. All young men were obliged to serve. The normal term of service was two years. But for those who had successfully completed six years of the *Gymnasium* or another kind of secondary school (*Realschule*), the term was reduced to one year. A number of privileges were attached to the status of the "one-year volunteer." Even for those sons of upper- or middle-class parents who did not wish to enter a university, the pressure to get through at least those first six years was great.

There was a time when the *Gymnasium* was an important source of enlightenment for the rising bourgeoisie; its teachers were courageous humanists who, by reference to the classics of Greece and Rome, sought to instill the ideals of active citizenship in the young generation. When Hegel served as teacher, and later director, in a *Gymnasium*, one could imagine that his lessons might have made a tremendous positive impression on the boys in his classes. By the end of the nineteenth century, however, the best of these humanists had converted their preoccupation with the classics into a cozy ivory tower which kept them safely away from the grubby bourgeois world. While they were still fairly young, they might inspire a few students with their humanist spark. As they got older, they became funny Mr. Chips figures, like the group of teachers described in Theodor Fontane's *Frau Jenny Treibel*. The best of these *Gymnasium* professors are depicted as lovable, even though a bit irrelevant. The worst of them were intellectual drill sergeants who were staunch supporters of the established system, sharing all its prejudices and wielding their considerable authority and power to instill those prejudices in their students.

Anyone reading the works of fiction written after 1890 that deal with the *Gymnasium* (and a great deal of fiction dealt with it) will come away with the impression that at best it was irrelevant, and at worst it was nine years of torture. Teachers taught bone-dry subjects that prepared the students for nothing they would ever want to do. Some devoted scholars became role models for future academics. But even they must have had a hard time imparting enthusiasm for Aeschylus or Tacitus to most of their charges. Many therefore succumbed to the temptation to force the material onto their students. Teachers had parental authority, which they could wield in school as well as in public. They had considerable disciplinary powers, including the power to inflict corporal punishment, and, in serious cases, banish the student to the school jail.

The atmosphere of these schools, as German literature from the period conveys it, was a mixture of boredom, terror, and very unhealthy rivalry, which brought out nasty traits in the boys' personalities. One is reminded of similar accounts of public schools in Victorian England: the same tendency toward sadistic pranks, directed either against good-natured teachers or against outsiders within the class; the same public stereotypes about the teachers as figures of ridicule, but also as potential tyrants. Read the dreary depictions of *Gymnasium* classes in Thomas Mann's *Buddenbrooks*, Heinrich Mann's *Professor Unrath*, or the portrait of the *Gymnasium* professor in Ludwig Thoma's *Moral*; or go through the pages of the satirical journal *Der Simplicissimus* for devastating cartoon portrayals of these teachers.

The system, as reform-minded people saw it, spoiled the children's characters by teaching unnecessary subjects with faulty methods. It killed whatever intellectual sparks they had. By being accessible only to a small minority of male children, it promoted class antagonism—arrogance among the lucky few who managed to graduate, envy among the many who had never even entered. By excluding girls, it obviously oppressed females. Meanwhile, it helped thoughtless parents use their sons as pawns in furthering their own parental ambitions.[17]

Braun's accusations, in effect, add the *alienation of youth* to the list of alienations which concerned her. In modern society, she argued, labor, citizenship, sexuality, motherhood, and aesthetic enjoyment are alienated; and, in addition, parental abuse and systematic miseducation rob children of their childhood. The period of youth is turned into a painful process of socialization for an alienated world, a socialization which reproduces the class structure, the authoritarian state, and the patriarchal family by terrorizing children into submissive subjects.

No wonder, therefore, that young people rebelled, and in their rebellious mood went in many unhealthy directions—delinquency, crazy fads, and deplorable excesses. Such excesses, Braun observed, are inevitable when youth begins to stir against obsolete moral authorities. That is the price we pay for liberation. The rebellion of youth demonstrates that humanity is preparing for great battles; and inevitably some weaklings will fall by the wayside.[18] Note that her sentiments are similar to an opinion Engels held, that the self-liberation of the proletariat begins with an increase in working-class criminality.[19]

One way in which youth sought to escape its alienation was through flight into romantic love, which often led to disastrous conflicts and a rash of suicides by frustrated lovers. Lily Braun thought that these *Romeo and Juliet* stories were also an accusation hurled against the miseducation and oppression of youth. She wrote:

> Barely grown up, our young people are forced into an arid, narrow professional life. There they go under and die of thirst and end up by regarding every glass of stale water as nectar.[20] Give them time and space so that their intellects and hearts can fill with ideals worthy to live and fight for, and they will cease making superficial love affairs the contents of their lives and regarding them as tragic events.[21]

Alienation, according to Marx, leads to rebellion. At the least, whoever diagnoses alienation can be expected to issue a call for emancipation or liberation. And, on the basis of her diagnosis of the alienation of youth, Lily called for the emancipation of children. Her theory of children's liberation is based on a determined reversal of the fifth commandment, which orders children to honor their parents—presumably by obeying them. In her journal, Braun printed a quotation from the German writer Multatuli:

> It is not true that a child owes its parents submissiveness and love. This miserable prescription has been invented for the convenience of parents who felt themselves lacking in intellectual weight and were too lazy, and too arid of heart, to merit love.[22]

Children, wrote Braun, owe their parents nothing. They have rights against them and against all their elders; and parents have duties toward their children. Parental love, to be meaningful, must be unselfish. Children are not their parents' property, but have been entrusted to them. Nor are the children's claims for autonomy selfish; on the contrary, they are made for the good of the development of the species. The present system of child rearing and education reproduces all the ills of a repressive and exploitative society. By claiming their right to the free development of their individual personalities, a right to lead their own individual lives, children will make a free and equitable society possible. She asserted:

> Every human being who is prevented from exercising the powers inherent in him or her must become unhappy. . . . Hence it is the parents' duty to awaken these powers, to carefully examine every talent, every pronounced intellectual inclination, for its value and to further its development.
>
> It is the mother's duty to educate her daughters for life, not to conjure up fantasy images of this life.
>
> Are daughters being educated for life? Most of the time it is only the lower classes whom the bitter struggle for existence compels to educate their daughters for this struggle.
>
> The times are past when one thought he ought to rear his daughters in the hothouse; wherever that is still done, a great injustice is done to the daughters, because such a tender plant will wither as soon as the rough air outside hits it. And it must be reared not only with regard to the possible external life situation, which might compel the girl to work for her own support, but also with regard to her personal happiness in life which, after all, should not be weighed lightly by loving parents.[23]

In response to the question of whether parents should force an adolescent to go through the rite of confirmation even though the child was doubting the religious teachings, she urged parents to recognize that even at age fourteen their children had judgment.[24] Always take your child seriously, she warned parents in her memoirs: intellectually mature children are embittered by the fact that adults belittle them, finding them cute and childish.[25] The duty of parents, she wrote, was to transform themselves as early as possible from feared, awe-inspiring authorities into friends, to elevate the child to their own adult level, as it were. As friends, they would be able to know the child's potentials, aptitudes, and inclinations; and in testing or probing for these slumbering capabilities, they should have the child's satisfaction in mind, not their own.[26] All child rearing and education should bring out individual traits as much as possible; nothing is more harmful than standardization or leveling through education.[27] She warned parents against trivializing important decisions of this kind, or treating them as empty conventionalities, as her own parents had done. And she urged those parents who felt societal pressure to conform to band together with like-minded people.[28]

To be sure, at other times Braun warned against instilling a destructive spirit of criticism into children, and she warned against the excesses of some avant-garde educational experiments.

> I consider it a grave injustice toward youth to educate them for criticism rather than reverence while they are still immature. To be sure, they should learn to think for themselves, but one should not place everything great and high onto one and the same level with them, as it were, so that they get the idea they might be entitled to judge it as if it were like them. One should also recognize the holy right of sentiment. Fine sentiment often makes much more correct decisions than cool reasoning.[29]

Further, she warned that children's upbringing is much more effective if it consists of examples rather than preaching.[30] And, finally, she warned parents against hovering over their children too much. Mothers who never leave their offspring out of sight and out of control make them into dependent, weak, bored children who do not know what to do by or with themselves. It is good for children to be without their mother for several hours every day. If she sacrifices too much of her energies on them when they are very little, she will not be able to function as friend and helper to her sons or daughters once they have become adolescents and adults.[31]

In short, enlightened parents should work for the emancipation of their children. Similarly, enlightened teachers ought to help liberate children from the school as presently constituted. Learning should not merely prepare youth for various practical pursuits; it should, at the same time, "enrich the child's current life, should warm the heart, and expand the intellect."[32]

In "Wider die Lüge," she wrote:

> A well-formed [*gebildet*] human being is the aim of education. Marvelous! If it were true. Forming well means to develop the given material to its highest perfection—not to make marble columns out of plaster, iron constructions out of wood, diamonds out of glass. But the characteristic trait of our *Bildung* is to replace being with deception. Whoever talks about anything and everything, always having a judgment ready at his fingertips, and rarely admires anything, is considered *gebildet*. The ability to judge, indeed, is the criterion of *Bildung*, but only if the judgment is the person's own. Yet the road to this *Bildung* is long and steep, and the ever-ready judgment should make us suspicious.

The aim of education is not an encyclopedia but a free human being. Knowledge is not an aim in itself but a means to the end of enriching life and strengthening the human being. Do not ever kill a "Why" but lure it out from wherever it hides, the way the gardener, through careful cultivation, lures the tender shoots out of the ground. Guide, but do not impose yourself. Be aware that your truth is not that of the child, that you are teaching the child to lie whenever you force your truth onto him. Belief in fairy tales is the truth of children. Leave it to them. Therefore tell your child the myths of nations as if they were fairy tales: from Isis and Osiris to Odin and Baldur, from Jehova to Jupiter and the heavenly father of the Christians. Show him how under a thousand names and forms people knelt in adoration before the holy mystery of creative life. Teach him to see and admire it in every fragrant flower, in every cloud, every star, every law of nature.

And then introduce him or her to the history of the human race. Do not create angels and devils in the fullness of your own unlimited powers—but do not disturb the children if they create heroes of their own. Modestly step back with your own egos behind the slowly forming ego of the other. Whatever the child himself cannot judge, do not teach him to judge. The wish to spare children experiences of their own through ours is false sentimentality; for experience of one's own is the only sure stepladder of self-development. If this leads the child away from you, do not lament, for he is not your property but his own and that of humanity. Do not press rules for life into him; instead, show him the way to find his own rules for his own life.

And for his heart, a religion of his own.[33]

Childhood, Braun insisted, was not to be regarded as a mere preparation for adulthood. Instead, "every period of a person's life has its own validity, like every season of the year."[34] Hence, her statement that a child's truth is different from that of an adult, and that children need fairy tales as much as adults need to study objective reality. Yet she also emphasized the need adults have for play, suggesting that they should learn to retain some of their childish character. The complete human being would have not only a healthy, strong body and a well-honed intellect, but also a rich fantasy life; so that fairy tales were also part of the training for adulthood.[35]

One area where she objected vehemently to fairy tales was the area of sex education, which she considered an important parental responsibility. Reticence here, as well as lies or pretty fables, could only lead to disaster, distrust, and ultimate alienation between parents and children.[36] She demanded coeducation through all school grades and wanted boys and girls to learn each other's bodies by playing together naked. Moreoever, she insisted that the upbringing of children should be such as to liberate them from sexism, from the convention that stereotypes behavior as either male or female. Why should not boys be allowed to play with dolls? Why should not girls be permitted to roughhouse or play with soldiers? Once all children have the same opportunities for all and any kind of play, they will turn out to have talents, aptitudes, interests, and ideas which will not be stereotypical.[37]

For some of these ideas, Braun found support in Charlotte Perkins (Stetson) Gilman's booklet, *Concerning Children*.[38] But in fact she had formulated her ideas long before she read Gilman, and most of her thoughts on children's education and children's liberation are easily identified as Goethean and Nietzschean. In fact, some of her earliest monographs on the women around Goethe show that in these notions of a humanist education she took Weimar as her model.[39] Yet neither Nietzsche nor Goethe went as far as she in writing a veritable manifesto calling for a children's revolution. Written in 1911, this 28-page pamphlet begins with a heart-wrenching evocation of the ghosts of all the children and adolescents who have killed themselves because of parental abuse, oppressive schools, puritan morals, or demeaning and shaming treatment by adults. Rejecting all the many remedies others have proposed against this scandal, she argues that children, like slaves, proletarians, and women, must liberate themselves. "Never in the course of human historic development has one social class liberated another, or one generation another."[40]

Become rebellious, she urges the youth of her country, make yourselves known and heard. Parents, she tells them, usually do not know their children well, because children have been taught to keep silent and out of sight.

> Have the courage to make your parents acquainted with you! Speak up about your wishes, your views, your hopes and fears, even when at first you meet only astonishment, admonitions, prohibitions, and commands. Obedience is no virtue if it is not a joyful agreement with the command.
> Listen to one of our greatest modern poets, Richard Dehmel, who sang to his own son,

"And when one day of filial duties,
My son, your aging father talks to you,
Obey him not, obey him not—"

Speak freely about all that the school takes from you and keeps from you. Your parents' class prejudices have not yet so deeply eaten into your hearts that they could suppress your inclinations. Demand the right to choose your profession according to your aptitudes. Protest against the fact that Mathematics or Greek or Latin poison the most beautiful years of your youth while the artist or the engineer in you demands entirely different intellectual nourishment.[41]

On the road toward the self-determination of youth she identified a few way stations. Among them were school communes run democratically through general assemblies of the entire community, where students determine their own curriculum. What was important in these communes was not so much what was studied, but how it was studied; and even more important: both teachers and administrators respected the children as autonomous human beings. Another institutions that would educate children for self-determination were boys' towns and similar experiments in the rehabilitation of abandoned or delinquent children. Here, too, what she liked was the principle of autonomous self-administration, and to her, these institutions gave proof that only freedom can make us responsible. Only by being free can we learn to be free.[42]

In the end, she expected oppressed children to transcend themselves just as she expected other oppressed groups to throw off the chains of their own alienation. "In the final analysis," she called to them, "you have only one enemy—yourselves. Your careerism, your hypocrisy, your cowardice. Overcome these, and the road is free."[43] The pamphlet ends with a call to revolution:

History tells us about a children's crusade. Today more is at stake than the liberation of Christ's grave from the hands of the infidels.
    The century of the child, which so far has been no more than a pious wish, should be the work of the children![44]

In closing this chapter I cannot refrain from commenting on some relevant facts from Braun's personal life. First, it is obvious that when Braun calls on children to liberate themselves, when she demands reforms in child rearing patterns, she is lamenting her own wasted youth, her many years of frivolity, and the formal education that was denied her.

Now children often protest and rebel against their parents and against societal conventions. But all too often, having themselves become parents, they behave toward their own children just as their parents behaved toward them. Did this happen also in the case of Lily Braun? There are some analogous inconsistencies one could adduce to show that she did not always practice what she preached. For instance, twice in her life she was attracted to men who were remarkably similar to the father she was repudiating, and one of these men became her husband. Was she similarly inconsistent in her ideas about child rearing once she had a son of her own?

This question must be answered with an unequivocal "no." While I will refrain from describing her relationship with her son, Otto, in detail, let me simply assert that quite self-consciously she raised him in such a fashion that he would grow beyond her and away from her. It is the duty and the pleasure of parents, she wrote to him, to serve as stepping stones for their children; and she expressed satisfaction that she had done this. Blessed, however, are those parents who after enabling their children to their full potential are in turn lifted beyond their own level by their children; and she felt that Otto was beginning to do this with her.[45]

Self-transcendence through your progeny! All her life Lily Braun was in search of superior people to whom she could look up, from whom she could learn, with whose help she might herself rise to her full potential. She had found quite a number of them: her father, her grandmother, some writers of the past and the present, her two husbands; and now there was Otto. "My son," she wrote to a friend, "has gradually turned into my friend—a friend to whom indeed I surrender often and gladly, whenever I am permitted the delightful feeling that he is superior to me."[46] Otto was but fourteen years old when his proud mother wrote these words. In the light of her theories of children's liberation, one must conclude, Braun's relation to her son was a model of revolutionary praxis.

XII

GROWING ISOLATION

As we will see presently, the birth of her son, Otto, in 1897 became the occasion, or the pretext, for Lily's reconciliation with her father. Otto himself became the focus of her life, always in her thoughts, and most of the time in her presence. From earliest childhood until he went off to fight in World War I at the age of 17, he accompanied her on most of her frequent travels, and certainly on every one of the many long working vacations away from her husband. She seems to have spent altogether more time with her son than with Heinrich.

Heinrich himself, though obviously proud of his son, seems to have had little interest in parenting. After marrying Lily he obtained custody of his two sons from his first marriage, but after a few months of having them at home sent them off to a boarding school and from then on saw them only rarely. Eventually the younger one ran away and disappeared without trace, while the older one was able to develop a tolerable relationship with Heinrich, and a cordial one with Lily. The baby boy born to Heinrich by his second wife was given away for adoption. And, again, anyone reading the correspondence between Heinrich and Lily gets the impression that Otto was much more her child than his. At the same time it is remarkable that this correspondence, so replete with mutual recrimination, as we will see, contains hardly any arguments about child rearing. Perhaps in this they found themselves in general agreement; or else Heinrich was too disinterested to interfere.

Later on in this chapter I will say more about this strange marriage which quite early turned into an intense love-hate relationship that often was on the verge of disintegrating. One of the things that kept it together was the fact that, for better or for worse, Lily and Heinrich

Braun were a beleaguered minority of two within the organizational juggernaut of the SPD. Their antagonists in the party lumped them together; the real or imagined offenses of either one were always adduced to accuse the other. Hence, to secure their own political and financial survival they were condemned to stick together.

Two developments coincided to bring the relationship of Heinrich and Lily Braun with the party to a crisis point. One was the publication by Eduard Bernstein of his reformist views and his critique of party orthodoxy, which set off a heated debate for and against Revisionism. In this debate, the Brauns, though having their own serious disagreements with Bernstein, were generally regarded as belonging to the Revisionist camp. Hardly had this ideological crisis developed when in the Reichstag elections of 1903 the SPD made spectacular gains,[1] with the result that a substantial number of new Social Democratic deputies entered that parliamentary body, some of whom, including Heinrich Braun, were inclined to voice their own well-developed views about socialist politics and were therefore prone to defy the party leadership. At this point, August Bebel, who had up to then shown little interest in the ideological disputes, apparently sensed that control of the party might be slipping out of his hands and decided to reassert his authority. He did this by using the 1903 Congress of the party, which took place in Dresden, to crack down on Revisionism, decry the new influx of what he called fellow travelers into the Reichstag caucus of the party, and denounce all dissent within it as heresy. At the Dresden Congress, the Brauns were among a half dozen party leaders whom Bebel singled out for the most scathing condemnation and indeed for accusations of moral unfitness. In the end, the Congress passed a resolution condemning Revisionism.[2]

The effect of this for the Brauns was that in the party they now stood branded as troublemakers and heretics. Bebel made no move to expel them, he would probably have failed in such an attempt. But henceforth the Brauns were shunned. They were no longer asked to give lectures, except by local organizations that sympathized with Revisionism, and their written contributions were no longer accepted in regular party journals. Thus they were prevented from earning a living as party journalists or agitators; and publishing in non-party periodicals was now branded as a betrayal of party loyalty.

Before discussing their desperate attempts to survive in such a situation, we must for a moment return to Lily Braun's relations with her family. In the summer of 1897 her son, Otto, was born, and from that moment on his care and upbringing demanded a great portion of her time. Nonetheless, during the first few years of his life she managed to remain active within the party and do the research for her major work, *Die Frauenfrage*.

The birth of Otto led to a reconciliation between Lily and her father. Since his forcible retirement, the general's health and will to live had declined rapidly. A feeling of uselessness and particularly nagging financial worries caused him to age very quickly. He owed his brother-in-law a fortune. If he were to die without paying his debt, his honor and the good name of his family would be forfeited, for aristocratic gentlemen do not default on their debts. We are entitled to assume that one reason why he was willing to receive Lily back into the fold of the family was the fact that he had mortgaged her prospective inheritance from his sister Clothilde to secure his debt. Nobody knew about this, not even Lily's mother or her aunt, but there was an urgent need to inform his daughter.

The old man confessing his financial recklessness to Lily and begging her to assume his debt, pledging her, moreover, to reveal his dishonorable secret to no one ever, must have cut a pitiful figure; and it is clear that Lily at that moment regarded him as weak and contemptible.[3] Yet she was sufficiently imbued with aristocratic notions of honor that she made him the solemn promise to cover his indebtedness and to keep the entire sordid business secret from all including her mother and Heinrich. Eventually she did manage to pay the entire amount back. It took her nearly fourteen years to do so, and the financial sacrifice required for this effect destroyed her.

How she envied people like Kautsky, Luxemburg, and Mehring, who had regular jobs as editors of party journals! She herself could not expect any lucrative assignments from the party. To be sure, her husband doled out household money rather carelessly, so that she could begin to pay off her father's debt in tiny installments. Until 1903 she managed to place occasional articles in journals, both those approved by the party and others. After 1903 this was no longer possible. For her book, *Die Frauenfrage*, she must have collected some royalties, but she made much more money with two books that she published after her mother's death in 1903. Both books were exercises in ancestor worship. One of them, *Im Schatten der Titanen*, was written to honor the memory of her grandmother and to introduce the reader to the history of her family. It paid particular attention to her blood ties to the Bonapartes and to her grandmother's relations with the Goethe household. The other book was written to honor the memory of her father. It was an edited collection of the letters he had written to his wife in the wars of 1866 and 1870/71. The book showed Hans von Kretschman from his best side as a humane officer who genuinely cared for his troops. They also presented realistic images of war as a sordid business, and contained some unkind remarks about some German units that had participated in actions against the French. The general's letters debunked and demystified war and thus went counter to the cult of war then fostered in Imperial Germany. That made the book controversial. Consequently, her cousin Fritz von Kretschman[4] was able to convince Aunt Clothilde that in this book Lily had in fact dishonored her father's memory, and the old lady allowed herself to be persuaded to cut Lily out of her will. The rich inheritance that her father had mortgaged was thus denied her. From this blow Lily Braun never quite recovered.

Political considerations complicated her situation. Having been criticized and insulted as Revisionists, she and her husband wanted to fight back; indeed, they felt it their duty as socialists to do so. They desperately needed to find means to make their views known to the party and to the world. What was at stake for them was nothing less than the future of the socialist movement which they saw imperiled by Bebel's authoritarian leadership, by orthodox dogma, and by the cultural backwardness of the party's rank-and-file.

They therefore decided to create a journal of their own. This, of course, required considerable capital, and so they sought to obtain support from like-minded people inside and outside the Marxist movement. When such support did not come forth, they decided to sell Heinrich's highly successful social science journal, the *Archiv*, to a group of scholars headed by Max Weber; and the large sum of money they received for it they invested in their new journal, *Neue Gesellschaft*. Within two or three years, however, that journal had to be abandoned. It was in an impossible political position, neither within the party nor outside it. Its financing was poorly conceived, with generous honoraria for contributors but a very low subscription rate. Nor did it have a clearly defined clientele, for while its themes were to be high-brow, its tone and format were to be popular; and in any event the clientele would have to be built from zero. This, however, turned out to be impossible, not only because of the journal's inherent flaws, but also because the party leadership denounced, ridiculed, and boycotted it. The substantial capital the Brauns had invested in the paper had now been spent. Heinrich and Lily Braun were ruined.

And once again she fought back. This time she did it by writing her memoirs, in fictionalized form, to be sure, but with the various persons in it so thinly disguised that most were easily identified. Its two large volumes were meant to be a self-vindication and a severe reckoning with all the people with whom she had once been associated. It was the skillful self-portrait of a self-styled heroine whom all those around her had misunderstood, wronged, abandoned, and betrayed. Naturally, the book angered many of the people who appeared in it. In the party it was denounced as an inexcusable indiscretion, because it aired disputes and tensions that the party leadership would have liked to remain hidden. Precisely for that reason, of course, it appealed to a broad reading public both inside and outside the movement. It became a best-seller and netted Lily a great deal of money.

In writing this autobiography she had discovered her talents for writing fiction; and in fairly rapid succession she then managed to produce genuine works of fiction—two novels, one of them another tremendous financial success; a play which saw only a few performances; and an opera libretto, for which she tried in vain to encourage Puccini to write the music. It was turned into an opera more than a decade after her death by another composer.

Her works of fiction deal with the themes that preoccupied her all her life: revolutionary defiance of alienating conventions; sexual liberation as a precondition for general emancipation; conflict between conjugal and maternal love; the oppressive effect of organized religion; and the evils of patriarchy.

To the extent that her labile health permitted, Braun also continued to go on lecture tours throughout Germany and Austria, speaking on feminist and socialist themes to socialist groups and women's organizations. She often pushed herself beyond her physical or emotional limits. Her letters often expressed despair; they sighed for unattainable little luxuries, bemoaned her terrible loneliness, or cried out in sorrow over her failing health and her lost youthful charms. But in the end she always came up with words of heroic resolve to go on fighting.

It may be appropriate at this point to quote a lengthy passage in which she expresses this heroic resolve. This is the Introduction to volume I of her memoirs:

TO MY SON
The roses are in bloom and the lime trees spread their fragrance. High above dark forests and lush green meadows the mountains of my home country reach up toward a sky in which the stars glitter and shine, not clouded by the smoke of the cities or the fog of the plain. The grey rocky giants shimmer like silver in the light of the moon, and snow still glistens in their thousand fissures and folds.

This is the most beautiful night of the year, the night when forest and field are a-whisper and a-murmur with old fairy tales, the night, my son, which presented you to me: a midsummer-night's child, a Sunday child. Eleven years ago it is today. And yet to me it is as if it were only yesterday that you lay at my breast, that you babbled the first words, put your little feet one before the other for the first time. And now you are a big boy! Your childhood is preparing to bid you farewell.

It was almost on the same day, and it is more than three decades ago, that I too celebrated my eleventh birthday at the foot of these mountains. The table at that time was bending under the mass of presents—on your table, my son, only a few books were lying today next to our old Maria's fragrant cake!—, and parents, relatives and friends surrounded me, celebrating the birthday child with bubbling champagne and flattering speeches, —while we today were alone and had only Tirolean country wine in our glasses. The birthday child then was a pale, gangly girl with a grown-up arrogant-sarcastic expression around the mouth, whose smile of gratitude was no more than the result of proper upbringing; you, however, are a beautifully thriving lad, who in joyful exuberance whirled first his mother and then old Maria around the meadow in a mad dance. Only two things have remained the same—then and today: on your table as well as on mine lay the first, long-desired diary, whose white pages are as alluring to the heart of an eleven-year-old as the entrance gate to the magic kingdom of life itself; and before you as before me the same

mountain giants were towering, and the same forest rustled around
our childhood dreams.

My diary has accompanied me all my life, and I have always remained faithful to the habit of accounting for the day's debits and
credits in it every night. At the end of every year I have used it to
contemplate the past segment of my life and to draw up a balance
sheet about it. Its laconic remarks—mere dry factual material—constituted the firm framework which memory then filled with the colorful
images of life; and from this my own self looks at me undistorted by
those worst portraitists in the world—hatred and admiration.

When this time I fled into our quiet mountain retreat out of the
treadmill and the factory atmosphere of my Berlin working life, I
took the thirty-two year books of my diary with me. It is time for a
general reckoning.

On steep mountain trails I have climbed to where I am now,
trusting in my experienced eye and my energies, far removed from
the spheres of life which tradition and custom have amply stocked
with road signs so that even the thoughtless might not err from the
path. But now I must stop to catch my breath, for the great loneliness around me makes me shudder. Whither now? Down into the
valley, to the road signs? Or further up on a trail I will pick myself?

The people are angry at me, and all those who at one time or
another have accompanied me part of the way on my life's travel call
me a deserter; but in my eyes it is they who are the disloyal ones.
Who among us is right: they or I? In order to find the answer, I want
to trace the very last roots and the outermost twigs of my being; and
of you, my son, I will be thinking when I do that, so that, when you
have matured into a man, you might understand your mother.

I am summoning the spirits of the past in the mid-summer night
which gave you to me, in the mid-summer night when all around me
on the heights the bonfires are glowing, in the mid-summer night in
which whatever was worthy of eternal life rises again from the dead.

—Obergrainau, 24 June 1908

With the passing of the years, her loneliness increased markedly.
For one thing, her marriage with Heinrich came under ever-increasing
strain; we will discuss the reasons for that before long. Meanwhile, the
financial troubles resulting from the promise she had made to her
father eventually led to estrangement from the last one of her relatives
who had remained loyal to her, her sister.

Mascha seems to have been no less a rebel against upper-class
conventions than Lily. But she may have been handled more tact-
fully by her parents, and, at the same time, warned by her sister's

fate, she was more cautious in voicing her nonconformist views. In her teens, when their father had forbidden her all contact with Lily, she had secretly continued to see her occasionally and later acted as Lily's ally against the family. In 1898, when she was twenty-one years old, she married Otto Eckmann, a highly regarded and very successful artist and interior decorator who was one of the pioneers of art nouveau, which in Germany was called Jugendstil.[5] The Eckmanns were respected members of the artistic avant-garde. The few articles Mascha contributed to Neue Gesellschaft, written in fresh, imaginative, and forceful style, reveal her to have been a radical feminist, socialist, and anarchist.[6]

Otto Eckmann died early after a long and painful illness. His widow herself suffered some serious ailments, had to undergo surgery several times, and was given so much morphine to kill the pain that she became an addict. She had a number of lovers and married at least two of them. Although she had inherited a considerable fortune from Aunt Clothilde and also had title to some of the family land holdings in East Prussia, her morphine needs and other expensive tastes eventually drained her financial resources. During the war she volunteered for work as a German agent, first in South America and then in the United States, where she conducted anti-British propaganda in alliance with a group of Irish revolutionaries. In 1918 she was caught, spent a year or so in federal detention awaiting trial as a spy, testified in court against her Irish coconspirators, and was at last released on parole. She had meanwhile joined the Catholic church, and she was therefore released into the custody of a convent in Manhattan. There she died in August 1920.

When their aunt Clothilde died in 1904, leaving her wealth to Mascha and five Kretschman cousins, Mascha generously gave a seventh of her portion of the estate to Lily but did not manage to persuade the cousins to do likewise. When later the financial edifice of the Brauns collapsed, she again helped out with a substantial loan. In the end, the amount owed her by the Brauns was the fantastic sum of 45,000 marks.[7] Meanwhile, she herself was in financial need, but when she asked for her money back, she received nothing. She then sold all or part of her claim to a friend, who went to court to try to collect. His litigation started a chain reaction of counter-litigations between him and Heinrich Braun, in which accusations of blackmail, libel, and fraud were exchanged. It turned into an unbelievably ugly affair that dragged on for years after Lily's death and cost the Brauns a fortune and unspeakable aggravation. In the course of it, the love Mascha had had for her sister turned into hatred, and this was yet another cup of bitterness Lily had to drain.

Under all this load of troubles, the Braun's marriage eventually became badly strained. One must ask why they had married so hastily in the first place; indeed, Lily Braun herself asked this at the time of their sixth anniversary. Her answer was that psychologically she had been ready to fall in love and that she had taken him to her heart without knowing him: "What were you to me then? A man whom I loved most ardently without really knowing him. Perhaps I would have fallen in love with someone else instead of you—I just had to love someone."[8] What she was saying here is that after Georg's death she had been lonely, and that her sexuality had re-awakened. She was thirty years old, still a virgin, and was once again mourning her wasted youth. In her letters to Tilly she expressed her envy at the sight of lovers and mothers. Men seemed to sense that she was making herself available: a very rich man proposed to her in September of 1895—but she had already met Heinrich.

Heinrich's immediate infatuation for her, so shortly after his marriage to Frieda, must be seen as a sign of his irresponsibility and immaturity. But it also says much about the tremendous appeal Lily must have exerted. Even though she was in mourning, he seems to have been struck by the radiance of her appearance, her beauty, her enthusiasm, her obvious intelligence, her readiness to be loved. The glamor of an aristocratic name appealed to his imagination; for him she was something like a princess, a figure from a romantic fairy tale, while her body suggested to him that she was Venus de Medici come to life.

Of course, Heinrich Braun not only satisfied her sexual and financial needs. He was obviously an interesting and admirable man. She was impressed by his erudition and by his contacts with radical intellectuals throughout Europe, was in general sympathy with his views on politics and shared his deep compassion for the underdog. In marrying him she looked forward to a lifelong genuine partnership in fighting for their ideals. But this kind of partnership never developed. Even though he in his turn admired and adored her, he rarely treated her as his intellectual equal, often irritated her with critical comments that showed he had not fully understood her writings, treated her like a child in money matters even though she seems to have been more responsible in this regard than he, and in general condescended, calling her his stupid little pussycat. In personal relations, too, he showed himself unwilling to share. During his frequent and prolonged bouts of melancholy or anxiety, he would not open up to her about his worries. Whether sick or depressed, he absolutely refused to be helped or comforted by her. Her own complaints, worries, anxieties, and bouts of depression he angrily dismissed. Moreover, the two were simply incompatible in many ways. The puritan austerity of his life style grated on her just as much as the useless luxuries he heaped on her. His harsh judgment of others, his brusqueness, and his open detestation of all social life alienated her friends and deepened her isolation. In many respects he seems to have been a replica of her father: charming when he wished to be, lavish in giving presents but financially inept; irascible, petty, and authoritarian; thin-skinned and imbued with an exaggerated sense of honor; and in many respects quite patriarchal.

Heinrich and Lily spent an inordinate amount of time apart from each other because when he was present she could not get any work done. Before any meeting with him after a lengthy separation, she was apprehensive: would he be in a good or rotten mood? Whenever they were apart, they exchanged letters almost daily and until the very end continued to declare their love to each other in passionate terms. Both had invested much in this marriage and could not even think of letting it be dissolved. Nonetheless, in the spring of 1913, a few weeks after she had finally paid off the last installment of her father's debt, it nearly did dissolve. What happened was that Heinrich discovered her secret—subconsciously she must have wanted him to do so, though consciously she felt she had betrayed her father's trust and therefore threatened to commit suicide. When her husband learned the financial sacrifice Lily had made for fourteen years, he exploded with rage, and an all-night dialogue ensued, a most melodramatic scene in which they shouted and wept at each other. In this night of mutual recrimination they dug deeply into all the unforgiven old hurts they had administered to each other. The night ended with a resolve to go on living together and even loving

each other. But their marriage had become little more than two
strangers living under the same roof. Joining them under this roof,
after some months, was a young art historian whom Heinrich had
introduced to Lily, Julie Vogelstein. After Lily's death, Heinrich
married her. There is evidence suggesting that even before Lily's
death, Julie had become his lover.

Lily Braun herself had been yearning for a lover for some time. In
the summer of 1911 she and her son went on a pleasure cruise to
Tenerifa, and on board ship she struck up a friendship with a fellow
passenger. Later she expressed regret that residual feelings of propriety had prevented her from sleeping with him. One year later she
spent a summer vacation in Trouville on the coast of Brittany, and
in her letters to her husband frankly envied the younger people on
the beach their amorous dalliances. In the spring of 1913, shortly
after the crisis in their marriage, while on vacation in Florence she
allowed herself to be picked up by a stranger, of whom the only thing
I know is his first name, Tancredo. Tancredo and she at once became lovers, and between March 1913 and August 1914 the two met
each other in Florence or in Southern Germany several times. Each
encounter was felt by Lily Braun to be an interlude of great happiness. The coming of the First World War, however, destroyed this
relationship. It also challenged many of her ideological positions and
caused her to abandon many of her feminist views, her pacifism, and
her membership in the Social Democratic party.

XIII

WORLD WAR I

The First World War broke out as a result of tensions that had been building up inside and between the several European nations for many years; and large numbers of people who had felt these tensions as oppressive greeted the war as a cleansing fire, or the breath of fresh air during a violent storm that chases away all stuffiness. This feeling of relief explains the jubilation with which everywhere masses of people hailed the war—a jubilation so noisy that it drowned out the laments of those who had tried to prevent the disaster and the worries of those who foresaw some of its dire consequences. Even among those who were wise enough not to rejoice in the coming of the slaughter, most were grimly determined to fight until victory. Almost everywhere, in Germany and France, in England and Russia, the vast majority of the people, as well as their political and intellectual leaders, convinced themselves that this war had been forced upon their nation by reckless leaders in other countries, and that it was therefore a just war. In Germany, many conservatives welcomed the war as a chance to assert the virtues of Prussian authoritarianism and discipline, or the superiority of German culture, against the alleged weaknesses, vices, or degeneracy of British and French societies. At the same time, many socialists honestly believed, just as Marx, Engels, and Lenin believed, that a defeat of tsarist Russia would remove the most powerful bastion of reaction from European politics, so that a victory over Russia would pave the way for the proletarian revolution. In various ways, most political leaders, right and left, managed to persuade themselves that their own ideology sanctified the war.

Lily Braun, together with the vast majority of the socialist leadership in Germany, adopted this line. She, like the majority of Germans, demanded that a victorious Germany should secure her borders by annexing various territories in the East and West. She wrote to Otto:

> As much as I am opposed to the rape of nations, it does seem impossible to me simply to go back to our old frontiers. It would be an admission of weakness. In any event, the separation of Poland from Russia is a necessity, but also our access to the Channel, i.e., the line Liege-Louvain-Antwerp would have to be secured for us somehow.[1]

In a later letter, she went so far as to voice the purest militarism:

> A peace without strong safeties would be our economic ruin; a peace with strong safeties will necessarily lead to continued strong armaments, and, in the final analysis, wars again and yet again. I do believe, incidentally, even though I am a feminist . . . and a socialist, that wars are part of the conditions of life and development of the world.[2]

Despite the professed internationalism of the socialist movement, it is useful to remember that Marx and Engels, in 1848 and also later, voiced similar sentiments about the healthiness of an occasional war, and the need of the German nation to secure its frontiers at the expense of less developed or less civilized peoples. Braun's positive attitude toward the nation state, her support of Italy, and her distrust in the viability of the Austro-Hungarian empire could have come straight from Marx's *Neue Rheinische Zeitung*. Braun wrote to Otto:

> On account of its historical development, Austria is a moribund body, or, better, a body in the process of dissolution; for what your Pa [Heinrich] praises as Austria's great achievement in the last few decades, namely, that all the different nationalities under its rule have developed so well, e.g., the Czechs, appears to me precisely as a sign of its weakness and dissolution. Compared to Austria, Italy, for instance, appears to me entirely as the young lad striving forward. Its inner unity conditioned by race and language, predestines it for development; and here I find its hatred of Austria entirely understandable from a historic point of view. In short, I believe that Austria can become the chain on our foot, if there is not going to be a clean separation of its non-Germanic nationalities and a firm union of the Germans with us.[3]

Statements of this kind are representative of what German politicians and intellectuals, with few exceptions, took for granted in the first two years of the war. In the popular press, and in popular opinion, this expansionist ideology was usually mixed with fervent hatred of the French, the Russians, and the English; but here Braun's upbringing and background forbade her to agree. To hate the French was impossible; she herself had far too many French relatives, to say nothing of her intense pride in being a descendant of the Bona-partes. To hate the Italians, as most Germans did, was impossible for her for very personal reasons. In Florence was her lover, Tancredo, with whom she hoped to be united. She was therefore filled with deep longing for Italy and for Florence. Connections of this kind made her sensitive to the suffering that the war caused, not only among Germans, but also among people of other nations. In her letters during the war, she often expressed sympathy with the soldiers and their wives and mothers on both sides of the trenches.

Yet in the final analysis the war convinced Braun of the need to engage in power politics. In her letters she began to extol the ideal of the strong state and of tight political leadership, and she voiced contempt for critical intellectuals who she thought were undermin-ing authority.[4] Like many other Germans of that time, she also began to romanticize war in general. In a letter to Otto she wrote: "Rest assured, my child. *Nothing,* but *nothing at all,* not even hunger, if it really should become a threat to us here at home, can deter me from unconditionally saying Yes to the war. . . . How else could I travel from town to town preaching constructive life in the midst of war?"[5] Despite all the miseries it was bringing, the fear and suffering and horror, she was willing to assert: "We need the war. And, despite all my great heartache, I must add: We are not yet permitted to wish for peace. We must win *total* victory, if the victory is to be more than a perilous armistice."[6]

Braun welcomed the war because she hoped it would secure Ger-many wider and safer boundaries, subdue her rivals, and do away with obsolete empires. She also believed, as some of the most radical socialists did, that it was speeding the transformation from capitalism to socialism. Wartime solidarity and austerity, to her, were foretastes of socialism; the emphasis on duties, rather than rights, was cleans-ing society of many degenerate trends of the past; similarly, rationing and the imposition of a command economy were steps toward social-ism; both she and her husband Heinrich lamented that the government did not take such measures with greater energy.[7] While in their assessment of the consequences of wartime austerity measures they were in agreement with Lenin, Lily Braun sharply disagreed with Lenin on one important point. While she believed that the war was an important step in the development of socialism, she thought that one principle of Marxism had been overthrown: its internationalism. In her opinion, the war had abolished the cosmopolitan, and replaced him with the patriot and citizen, even in the working class. The international brotherhood of all men and women, she wrote, is a beautiful goal, but for the time being it is utopian; we are not yet ready for it. Instead, we must go through the stage of national citizenship if we want to realize the dream of universal brotherhood.[8]

With dismay, she observed tremendous abuses which the war was uncovering—inefficiency, corruption, and profiteering—high living, in the midst of general misery, by people from the Crown Prince on down. And she believed that this naked display of moral and political degeneracy would speed the coming of the revolution. Braun wrote: "Never before has the shameless character of capitalism revealed itself so totally. For money everything is to be had. I hope that some day it will not be peace which will be purchaseable also!"[9]

The war, to her, seemed like an iron broom, ruthlessly sweeping away all softness and flabbiness, all weakness of character and indulgences, including intellectualism and aestheticism, to replace them with natural instincts—virile fighting and leading instincts in men, serving and self-sacrificing instincts in women, instincts of solidarity in all.[10] This broom would sweep away the entire generation of leaders who had allowed the war to break out; and, out of the resulting chaos, a new order would be forged by a Rousseauian legislator, a hero, a leader forged in this same hot fire, emerging from this terrible schooling steeled in body, mind, and soul.[11] Lily's husband Heinrich wrote to their son Otto:

> If socialism is the goal, then it depends on the historically given conditions of the period whether a great statesman, destined by providence to be the architect of this socialist state, makes use of one kind or another of political methods. If he reaches the *goal*—of course, this must be understood in all its depth and multiple facets—then he will have fulfilled his task, and the aim sanctifies the means. But where is this statesman? I do not see him. Perhaps he is only

growing up now, and the war will turn out to have created this steeled hero who will shape a new world from the ruined elements of the old one.[12]

Heinrich Braun's socialism, by now, had become a strange mixture of Marxist, populist, elitist, and nationalist ideas, in which the proto-fascist thoughts of Lagarde had begun to play a strong role.[13] Together with other nonconformists, he had helped found a new association, *Deutsche Gesellschaft 1914*, formed in analogy to the Deutsche Gesellschaft of 1814 led by Ernst Moritz Arndt. Both associations combined a strong commitment to national defense with an equally urgent striving for radical domestic reforms.

While Heinrich hoped for a Siegfried-like leader to emerge after the war to lead Germany toward a better society, Lily placed her faith in their son Otto's entire generation, hoping against hope that enough of them would come back from the war to do the job. She wrote: "There will not be any improvement in our domestic politics until the old, dusty, rusty generation has been swept away. The crazy thing is only that one cannot send these people who are intellectually dead into the trenches."[14] She, too, hoped for a revolution, but was less optimistic than Heinrich about what it would bring; it might turn out to be no more than a change in ruling classes, with those now oppressed becoming the oppressors. While that would be preferable to the present state of affairs, it would not be enough, and the price to be paid for such a change would be high. She wrote to Otto:

> I, too, consider a revolution possible, perhaps even probable, but I cannot attach such great hopes to it, because the mass of those who will carry it out does not, in the final analysis, want anything else than to eliminate the present bourgeoisie and to lie in their warm beds. Measured against the ghastly misery now prevailing, that alone would be immense progress, to be sure. But the danger is great that at the same time culture will be destroyed, rather than there being a higher culture created, as we wish it. For that reason, I consider it so tremendously important that the truly educated youth march together with the socialist workers, so that, at the given moment, they might be able to repress crudity and barbarism.[15]

The war, with all the sacrifices and deprivations it brought, obviously emphasized the idealist in her, i.e., that side of her revolutionary ideology which sought to overcome our dependence on material possessions and selfish advantages. In stressing individual and collective heroism, sacrifice, discipline, government authority, and the need to safeguard cultural values, she felt herself more and more the disciple of Nietzsche, whom she quoted as a philosopher of heroism.[16] And this revolutionary idealism increasingly crowded out the Social Democrat's preoccupation with economic problems. In her mind, such a preoccupation was the quintessence of the bourgeois way of life. During the war, she always referred to this capitalist culture as Americanism; for her it was represented in Germany by the war profiteers' shameless hunt for profit even while the young generation died in the trenches. But she also came to believe that the German SPD, with its narrow emphasis on economic problems, represented this spirit as well: "That the innermost essence of *contemporary* social democracy is nothing else than part of this capitalist spirit is something we have at last come to recognize," she wrote to Otto.[17]

If in this dismissal of the SPD as essentially bourgeois she sounded surprisingly like Lenin, she was even more surprisingly Leninist in her appreciation of the one major contribution the SPD had made— that of having organized and disciplined the working class in exemplary fashion.

> It is beyond all doubt that the brilliant organization and the efficiency of our armies is due in part to the success of the social democratic movement in disciplining the people. Yet the judgment of our enemies about us as being "barbarians" equally is caused by the reputation which our party has gained abroad. I, too, must confess that I bear my share of the blame here.[18]

Like Lenin, she declared the SPD to be bankrupt, even while calling for a socialist revolution: "Social Democracy is dead—long live socialism!" she cried; and, like Lenin, she related this repudiation of the SPD with growing doubts about the importance of liberal democracy. Looking at the Western allies, she suggested, one might become skeptical about its value.[19] In December 1915, a few weeks before the party split in two, she sent a letter of resignation to the local organization of the SPD to which she belonged. Her membership in the party had at last come to an end.

Her doubts about democracy and her repudiation of the SPD as infected by capitalism signified the deep ideological crisis into which the war had thrown her and her entire generation of people whose faith had been in inevitable progress and the infinite perfectibility of the human species. The war cast doubt on all these optimistic axioms; and behind her anger at pacifists, war profiteers, and slackers, behind her contempt for all political and intellectual leaders of the past, from the Emperor on down, was the disturbing realization that the old world had collapsed without a new one emerging. Bewilderment, anxiety, helplessness, and ignorance were all that remained: "Ignorance is the characteristic feature of our time. Strange that there was another in which we seemed nearly all-knowing to ourselves."[20]

Like other people crying from the depths, she expressed a yearning for religious certainty, but in the next breath dismissed this as a confession of weakness:

> The more monstrously the chaos of our time becomes apparent to us, the more strongly I feel how we lack religion; we are seekers of God, much more than seekers of life. [Her last novel was entitled *Lebenssucher*—The seeker of life.] One more and more feels like a ship which has lost, not its rudder, but the compass, and now no longer knows in what direction to set the rudder. Incidentally, I am not altogether clear whether the religious need might not be nothing more than a product of anxiety, just as the child, when it gets dark, clings to the mother's apron; mature adults should not be afraid in the dark at all, but should wait for the light of dawn.
>
> I was preparing my lecture and approached it with the idea that I had to say a lot, and important things; and suddenly I really know nothing! I am standing face to face with the monstrous, the mysterious of the present and the future, and I am ashamed to have to chatter about it, because I no longer know how to interpret it.
>
> For the first time I *fully* understand Goethe; for in the depth of my heart I had never before understood how precisely in the period of Napoleon he could stand so far apart from the world events. Now I know: The greater and deeper he is who experiences a tragedy of world proportions, the quieter he must be, the more awestruck an onlooker. . . . In any event, . . . my next novel is to be located far from the present time.[21]

Still, she hoped that someone, a Nietzschean hero, would come along who might bring a new, positive, humanist faith. To be sure, the world tragedy was awe-inspiring; but—Goethe notwithstanding—the feeling of awe was not identical with religion:

> If a new savior were to come who found the right word to give form to all our longing, in order to proclaim—right now, in the face of

death—a religion of life (I do not mean this in the usual trivial
sense of a religion for daily life, but one of creative, eternal life
forever—giving new birth to itself), it would be the axe which
would cut Christianity out at its root.[22]

Meanwhile, the future seemed dark and foreboding. The war was
causing social transformations which in themselves constituted something close to a revolution, but these were undesirable changes. To
Braun, these transformations spelled the americanization or the barbarization of Germany. The middle classes, especially professionals,
artists, and higher-salaried officials, were being proletarianized, some
of them made destitute, while at the same time the proletariat and
the riffraff of war profiteers were rising—people without higher cultural needs and aspirations. What kind of spiritual and intellectual
life would such a new elite produce after the war? she asked herself.
She saw the entire population being split between the young ones at
the front, who were being steeled by their experience of deprivation,
discipline, and comradeship, and the weak and the selfish who
stayed at home—vampires who in the midst of the war were displaying their new wealth garishly and shamelessly.[23] The entire population, she thought, was dividing into patriots and internationalists;
and the latter, whom she loathed, included not only the ultra-left
wing of social democracy, but those aristocrats who before the war
had become anglicized or americanized, and also that part of the
liberal bourgeoisie which tends toward pacifism and humanitarian
ideals.[24]

How to cope with the growing chaos? What should a revolutionary
socialist-feminist *do* at a time when all previous ideologies were revealed as outdated? Braun expressed contempt for people who lapsed
into Spenglerian pessimism, predicting the decline of Europe.[25] She
responded to the long-range puzzles posed by the war by returning to
vigorous public activity. Her first thought, after the war broke out,
was to seek an assignment in Italy, presumably to stir up or keep
alive pro-German feelings, and, of course, to be close to her lover,
Tancredo. But her negotiations with the Foreign Office and the
Prussian War Ministry came to nothing. When an acquaintance
suggested she travel to the United States to do propaganda work
among German-Americans, she declined, arguing that she thought

Lily Braun in 1916 (Ullstein, Berlin)

political work inside Germany to be far more important for the time being.[26] And, in fact, she plunged into intensive work as a domestic propagandist, going on one extensive lecture after another.

The themes she discussed were elaborations of her new views. In lectures entitled "The War as Educator" she urged her (primarily female) audiences to be brave, tough, and heroic. Reaffirming her feminist convictions, she suggested that the war would be an opportunity for women to show how well they could work and manage their households and the entire nation. Yet the war had already shown that many women still had a lot to learn. Women, she suggested, are by nature individualists, hence reluctant to practice discipline, self-sacrifice, and other patriotic virtues; they are gentle, yet must learn to be tough; they are soft, sentimental, and domestic, too much interested in preserving culture and comfort, yet they must become heroic. The Germany which will emerge from this war, she wrote in a lengthy pamphlet, will be a virile Germany, sloughing off everything effeminate, while accommodating and promoting everything feminine.[27]

In other lectures she tried to mobilize women for work on the home front, arguing that this would not only support the war effort, but also keep idle women, whose jobs the war had eliminated, and sex-starved women, whose husbands or lovers were at the front, off the streets. Prostitution practiced by soldiers' wives seems to have been a fairly frequent phenomenon. Braun regarded it as a matter of grave concern. To counteract it, to make sure that women would contribute to the war effort, and to assert the equal worth of the contributions women could make, Lily proposed that a law be drafted which would institute universal service for all women. During two years of such service they would be trained to be soldiers of peace, i.e., to carry out a wide variety of public functions. Once they had served their two years, they would return annually for exercises to refresh their skills, just like soldiers in the reserve.[28]

While this emphasis on equality of duties, as well as rights, was well within the radical feminist tradition, Braun's heated denunciation of pacifism and internationalism as appeasement offended large numbers of women in the women's movement. But feminists were even more offended by the theme that came to predominate in her wartime lectures: the duty of women to become mothers.

Motherhood had become a patriotic duty, she argued, now that the nation's youth was bleeding to death in the trenches. A peaceful, productive, civilized postwar world could only be built if a new generation were born, and raised in the new socialist spirit. War, she argued, liberates primeval instincts, which in women are maternal instincts; and she urged her listeners to go back to nature by cultivating the strong will to motherhood, despite the hardships this would imply in time of war. Only if women heed this call, she wrote, would they be able to face the front-line heroes without having to be ashamed. And once the war is over, she added, we women will not, remembering our weakness, sigh: "That was a time of great suffering"; rather, proudly, remembering our strength, we will say, "That was a great time of suffering."[29] Braun was well aware that her call to motherhood was in conflict with her demand for service or for wage work outside the home. She therefore believed that it would be the duty of public authorities to make a continual renewal of the population possible. By hygienic, economic, and legislative measures, the government should promote pregnancies on the part of healthy young women. Meanwhile, the women's movement should set aside all other interests and issues, and strive to attain only one goal, that of making sure that every healthy young woman become a mother.[30]

With pronouncements of this sort, Braun placed herself in opposition to those radical feminists who, out of pacifist motivation, had responded to the outbreak of the war with a call for a pregnancy strike.[31] She polemicized angrily against these feminist pacificists:

> Let me put it straight to those women who today render faithful service to their country in all areas and to those who are mourning at the graves of our heroes: Your deeds will one day be forgotten, your tears will be valued no higher than crocodile's tears, if the will to motherhood will not come to live in you again. All the blood now fertilizing Europe's soil everywhere will have been spilled in vain if the women fail in their task; they will be the ones bearing the monstrous burden of guilt for the possibly far more frightful wars of the future, for the victory of Asia over the civilized nations of the West, if the pregnancy strike now being preached by fanatic pacifist women will become reality in even greater measure than today.[32]

What are we to make of Lily Braun's behavior and ideas during the war? Can they be reconciled with the directions in which she had gone in the preceding twenty-five years? For many readers of this book, the image I have presented of her as a radical feminist, socialist, and general liberator will be seriously flawed by the turn which her ideas took after August 1914. We have seen that she became a nationalist, and supported German annexationist aims. She turned toward an authoritarian cult of the state, and a belief in the need for an inspired young leader. In some of her letters, which posit the contrast between the heroes at the front and the slackers, profiteers, and degenerate intellectual at home, she seems to be leaning toward the notorious stab-in-the-back theory by which the German Right after the war sought to explain the defeat. In exhorting women to bear children for the fatherland, she began to sound suspiciously like later National Socialist sermons about the need to propagate the Aryan race. Altogether, the themes which she struck during the war included some of the principal building blocks of subsequent fascist and National Socialist ideology. It would therefore be improper to end this chapter without exploring the relationship of her wartime views to the ideology of German fascism.

Like Marxism, fascist and National Socialist ideas originated as reactions to alienation, i.e., to the diverse human costs of material and industrial development. But, while Marxism seeks to explain oppression, exploitation, and alienation by a rational analysis of the principles underlying the capitalist order, fascists and National Socialists preferred to advance conspiratorial theories singling out various villains—Jews, foreign agents, intellectuals, Freemasons, Marxists, Liberals, bankers, and others. Further, while Marxists defined the socialist goal as a democratic community of equals who enjoy material plenty by using society's resources in rational planning, the fascist or National Socialist collective utopia is a hierarchical order based on charisma, instinct, and coercion. Both visions assume that the society of the future will provide material affluence through maximal use of modern technology. Lily Braun anticipated some of the rhetoric on which Hitler and his storm troopers rode into power in 1933: in projecting a powerful Germany, and lording it over conquered Slavs; in hoping that heroic youths would rebel against discredited oldsters and that an inspired leader would take command over the herd of the all-too-many; in demanding a true community held together by discipline and emotional feelings of unity; in extolling emotions, feelings, and instinct over cold, objective intellect; and, finally, in stressing the political importance of charisma and public festivals.

One cannot, I believe, stress sufficiently the shock effect of the war, and the degree of bewilderment, despair, helplessness, and self-searching it caused. If war, in general, signifies a breakdown of an old order and of the norms by which this order has survived, the intellectual results of this breakdown approach what one might call collective madness. For Braun, the war threatened all the beliefs by which she had lived, especially her previously unshakable faith in progress through reason and human perfectibility. August 1914 served to discredit both liberalism and Marxism by revealing the monstrous strength of irrational motives.

Of course, August 1914 did not appear out of nowhere, and neither were her doubts altogether novel in the European intellectual world. For some decades prior to 1914, the age of imperialism, colonialism, and finance capitalism had shown that for one thing, the revolutionary scenario of Marxism had little predictive value; and many other certainties of the nineteenth century had long been shattered or challenged by philosophy and science. Einstein's theories of relativity, Bergson's stress on unfathomable life energies, and the Freudian awareness of the unconscious are outstanding examples of such challenges. Gumplowicz, Mosca, and others had added to them the idea that social life was a war between the strong and the weak, and that progress and justice were illusions. Expressionist painting and the dissolution of tonality in music may be seen as artistic expressions of these trends at thoroughly and soberly redefining reality.

Like everyone else, Marxists found themselves compelled to make intellectual adjustments, if they did not retreat into self-assuring dogmatism. Sorel explored the importance of myth and advocated the general strike as a theatrical, dramatic event with which to usher in the revolution. Lenin ingeniously merged Russian Narodnik notions of a peasant-supported revolutionary conspiracy with the organizational fetishism of the SPD. Bogdanov, Lunacharsky, and other Russian revisionists sought to give Marxism a religious note to appeal to the religious urges in human beings. Lily Braun, as we have seen, incorporated Romantic humanism and radical feminism into her economic theories of oppression through capitalism. In most of these cases, August 1914 merely accelerated and intensified the process of diversification.

Both the war and its outcome also intensified a trend that had been apparent before, namely, that some former Marxists or former radical socialists found themselves moving toward the extreme right, a move that usually was triggered by some profound crisis, such as the Dreyfus scandal and the failure of the 1905 revolution in Russia, to name but two. Among those people that come to mind are several who once were close friends of Braun's: Werner Sombart, Peter Struve, and Henri de Man. Had she lived into the 1920s or longer, would she have drifted to the far right with them?

The question is speculative, but must be asked. What hints do we have about how she would have behaved? One feeble hint is the observation that her husband Heinrich did not make the move to the right. He remained in the party, still very much on the sidelines, but loyal to the spirit of socialism and general liberation. Like him, many other German intellectuals, after flirting with protofascist ideas, returned to their previous liberal or socialist convictions; a prominent and well-known example was Thomas Mann.

In contrast, Lily Braun's sister Mascha found her answers in the mysteries of the Catholic church, and, after the war, she expressed deep loathing for the liberal democrats and moderate socialists who had taken power in Germany. Had she been younger, and male (and had she survived), she would have been prime recruiting material for one of the paramilitary groups formed around 1920, that helped to pave the way for Hitler's NSDAP.

As for Braun herself, one can only suggest that, in the final analysis, all her moral and aesthetic sensibilties would have made her recoil in disgust from the know-nothing rhetoric, the sheer rowdyism, and the bloody political practice of National Socialism. What her wartime writings (and those of many of her contemporaries inside and outside Germany) do show vividly is how brittle humanitarian, liberal, and socialist ideas can be in periods of political, social, and cultural disintegration. In its turn, her ideological transformation between 1914 and 1916 illustrates the decisive break with the past that occurred in August 1914; the war had dealt a death blow to most assumptions on which her ideas were based. When she died, she had hardly begun the painful job of restructing her image of reality. But, had she lived, she would not have written *Mein Kampf,* or supported the Hitler movement; she would have fought German fascism.

XIV

CONCLUSION

What unites Lily Braun's wartime ideas with the thoughts of the preceding period is the stress she laid on the need for heroic defiance and the attempt she made to live up to that command. Throughout her life Braun self-consciously strove to become one of those New Women whom German feminists had idealized in novels and on the stage—a woman of superhuman energy, intellect, persuasiveness, compassion, and capability for enjoyment. In thus defining herself or, rather, her ideal self, she freely borrowed from Nietzschean and Wagnerian ideas, from the aristocratic tradition of *noblesse oblige,* from her understanding of practical Christianity, and from her feeling that revolutionaries must reshape not only social institutions but, first of all, themselves. The life she sought to lead was one of heroic struggle not only against external enemies but also against internal weaknesses. From her upbringing as a refined young lady who moved in the highest aristocratic circles she had retained a taste and a hunger for fine things—elegant clothes and precious jewelry, luxury foods, a stimulating social life, leisure and money enough to enjoy theater, good books, beautiful resorts, and travel in exotic places. In the life she actually led she enjoyed very few of these pleasures, but often ached for them and then had to remind herself that these longings were unworthy of a heroic fighter. She fought also, though not perhaps quite vigorously enough, against her ambitious eagerness to be recognized as a leader, against her pride and arrogance, and against her oversensitivity to criticism.

Most of her life Lily Braun lived on the brink of financial disaster, and the continual struggle for economic survival must have been one of the chief causes of her early death. She fought with equal tenacity and desperation for the survival of her stormy marriage with Heinrich Braun. Most of her life, finally, she was desperately lonely, having burnt her bridges to former friends, relatives, and associates; and, defiantly, she wallowed in the bitterness of her isolation.

Her health was never very good. Childhood diseases had left her with damaged kidneys and a weak heart. During the last two decades of her life she fought losing battles against painful and debilitating disorders and often had to recover slowly from heroic measures attempted by her physicians. Early in life she began to bemoan the loss of her youth, her energy, her health, and her slim figure. Once the war had begun and her son had enlisted in the army, daily worrying about her child and the unfulfilled longing to be with her Italian lover further aggravated her. In August 1916, on her way to meet the mailman who she hoped was bringing a letter from Otto, she simply collapsed, of a heart attack or a stroke; neighbors carried her home, and within a day or two she was dead.

In death she received more recognition than she had been given in life. In between a vast number of routine one-paragraph obituaries that appeared in the German and foreign press, there were many elaborate tributes by people who obviously knew her well, appreciated her contributions and her sacrifices, and loved her.[1] Even people in the SPD and the women's movement, who had fought her bitterly, now wrote words of deep sensitivity about her. To be sure, the obituary in Vorwärts was cool and condescending, but many other party papers transcended pettiness and wrote with warmth, acknowledging the party's mistake in not accepting her fully, or not valuing the many painful sacrifices she had made for the cause.

Some of the more perceptive obituaries, in trying to explain why she had never been accepted fully by her party comrades, stressed the fact that even as a fighter for the proletarian cause she had always remained a lady. An anonymous obituary contained the following:

> Twenty years ago, we young people tended toward some sort of student anarchism, which petered out in a good deal of explosive verbiage. At that time, in Zürich, a young German writer, John Henry Mackay, made an extraordinary impression on us because, a consistent individualist, he attended revolutionary workers' meetings always clad in his elegant black salon garb, preferably with a top hat or a black bowler. Compromising types would on such occasions put on a floppy felt hat; groveling conformists would go so far as to take

off their stiff shirt collar and to wear a necktie with a good deal of red in it over their sportshirt. After all, democracy too has its laws of etiquette and is no less strict than other societal powers in punishing those who offend against them. Mackay's top hat was of conscious political significance: it was a towering protest against the sloppy hats' state of the future. Poor Lily Braun, who died in Berlin a few weeks ago, was another member of this tribe of rebellious top hat wearers. When I think of her, I see a tall woman striding with her head raised high, in a rustling black silk robe, a lush red rose on her breast. . . . It is thus that I saw her in workers' meetings about fifteen years ago, or at least that is the way my memory—which, of course, depends on my intellectual conception of what she was like—places her before my eyes. Mackay's top hat was a provocation of the democratic petit-bourgeois. But Lily Braun had no intention whatever of evoking bad feelings among her comrades. But she was, as it were, born with a black silk robe on; it would have rustled around her even if it had been made of cheap cotton.

To be sure, one cannot . . . imagine this leader of German women in a shabby cotton dress. Without wanting to do so, she . . . towered over the goodnatured, hard-working party members and all her life had an illicit tendency toward the Dionysian which is offensive to the bourgeois. Of her efficient and honest comrades in her work she demanded that they wear "grape leaves in their hair" and was amazed that her audiences began to boo and to applaud as soon as she crossed the threshold. . . .[2]

Clara Zetkin wrote a truly spiteful obituary. It began, to be sure, with words of appreciation for her heroic qualities; but it went on to dwell on her inadequacies. First, it argued, at the time Braun joined the party she was insufficiently cognizant of proper theory; the essence of the Marxist movement had escaped her, and she never made up for this deficiency. Second, Zetkin denounced her memoirs as trash, because of the perverse shamelessness with which Braun bared herself in it, and because it presented a distorted image of the party and its leaders. The book, she concluded, was an exercise in sensationalism without historic or artistic value, interesting only as a document of the perverse psychology of aristocrats.

Zetkin condescendingly described *Die Frauenfrage* as an honorable failure, honorable because Braun had worked so hard, a failure because of the author's insufficient mastery of historical materialism. Altogether, she argued, Braun was not a creative thinker, had neither depth nor originality. Her works are flashy but shallow, and

they are much too smoothly polished. Braun, she wrote, was a second-rate writer unable to express her immediate experience. Her
talent was not up to her intentions. Hence, she disappointed herself
and was a disappointment to others. In the end, she showed that it is
impossible to transcend one's inherited class position.[3]

Even before Braun's death, Julie Vogelstein had begun to write her
biography; and within a few years it was published as the introduc-
tory essay to a five-volume selection of Braun's works. Vogelstein
had by this time become Heinrich Braun's fourth wife. The biography is brief. It is based on inadequate knowledge or use of source
materials, and in its appraisal of Braun's personality and contributions is, at best, ambivalent. Vogelstein was convinced that Lily
Braun had ruined her poor husband's life. She, too, believed her to
have been a shallow dilettante intellectually and, by character, a
spoiled aristocrat. A few years after Heinrich Braun's death she also
published a biography of him, in which Lily Braun's life is treated in
much greater detail, and even more negatively.[4]

Lily Braun's books continued to sell well for several more years and
gave her widower a steady income until his death in 1927. But by
then the memory of her had already begun to dim; today she is
virtually forgotten. The reason is easy to see: she was never quite in
tune with her times; in some senses she still lived in the age of
Goethe and Napoleon; and in many another sense she was far ahead
of her time. Hence in all the many causes in which she participated
she was seen as a misfit, particularly in the socialist party and in the
women's movement. In their histories, these two major political
currents tended to give her the silent treatment. Political movements
write their first histories in self-congratulatory fashion: the successful
leaders become the heroes; their rivals are dismissed as troublemakers, loudmouths, or revisionists, if they are mentioned at all.

If her identification with the great intellectual liberators of the late
eighteenth and early nineteenth century—with Rousseau, Condorcet, and Goethe—made her ideas obsolete in the high capitalism of
the Wilhelmine period, her faith in progress and human perfectibility through socialism and women's liberation would have made her
even less at home in Germany after the war. And one wonders how
she would, in the end, have coped with all the disasters that occurred after her death—the defeat and the Versailles settlement, the

failed German revolution and the rise of bolshevism in Russia, the inflation of 1923, and the great depression of 1929.

Lily Braun did not fit in very well with any of the many classes and cultures then forming part of German society. She was in touch with many, but at home in none. The culture of Potsdam and that of Weimar—Prussian militarism and Goethean humanism, patriotic authoritarianism and liberal cosmopolitanism—had left strong impressions on her since early youth. Protestant and Catholic Germany, places in the north, south, west, and east had been important parts of her experience. Aristocracy, bourgeoisie, proletariat, and peasantry, as well as academic intelligentsia, artistic avant-garde, and political figures from the furthest right to the most radical left— she had lived and formed friendships among all of them, while keeping them all at arm's length. Few people managed to experience the rich and confusing mix of their own culture in such breadth and with such intensity; and among those who have this chance, few possess Lily Braun's gift of transforming every concrete experience into provocative questions or ideas by fitting it into the larger condition of their class, their sex, their society, or their world view. Since Braun was able to do this, we improve our understanding of Wilhelmine culture in general by studying her life and her ideas. For this reason, it does not matter that by upbringing and convictions she may have been behind her times. On the contrary, her ideas and her very life were interesting precisely because she was not altogether in harmony with her society and its many subcultures.

For this very reason she seems, at least in the short run, to have been more influential abroad than in her own country. Some of her works were translated into Russian, Czech, Polish, and Serbian; some of her views were accepted, some of her proposals tried out. Watching her polemics against Zetkin, influential women within the Marxist movement often sided with Braun, among them Aleksandra Kollontai and Adelheid Popp. Yet, overall, Lily Braun was forgotten very quickly. Indeed, what she herself had feared before she joined the party had come true; by becoming a member of the SPD, she ended her effectiveness both as a feminist and as a socialist. This was true not only because of incompatibilities due to her background and personality, but also because of many of her progressive ideas. As a feminist, as a Marxist revisionist, as an advocate of children's liberation, she asked questions and raised issues which were too uncomfortable for her contemporaries. But for this very reason she is of interest to us several generations later. The questions have not gone away, nor the problems they addressed; however, the suggested answers she offered are still worthy of examination. Meanwhile, her personal dedication to a life of revolutionary praxis, with its meticulous emphasis on constructive reforms rather than destruction, on the preservation of cultural values, including good manners, rather than barbarization, transcends the problem and ideologies of the movement, and should make her a heroine of freedom-loving people throughout the ages.

In short, her political style remains attractive; and her issues are still current. In their totality, they amount to a pioneer attempt at providing a synthesis of socialist with feminist concerns, which would transcend the narrow sectionalism of both movements, enriching them both. In analogy with contemporary Neo-Marxist schools, one might label her ideas feminist humanism, because both as a socialist and as a feminist, she thought of herself as a humanist, concerned with the liberation of all, women, men, and children, from oppression. Hence she was also a pioneer of Marxist humanism, a precursor of Reich, Marcuse, Bloch, Fromm, and Habermas.

When I have shown drafts of this book to friends and colleagues, I have received some sharply negative reactions to Lily Braun: that she was confused and that she sowed the seeds of confusion; that her personality was immature; her style too florid; and her optimism naive and exaggerated, hence easy to turn to despair. Foremost, many of my friends have suggested that she was less radical than she pretended to be: Her feminism was suspect because of her emphasis on femininity, motherhood, and heterosexuality, and because she stayed with her husband Heinrich even though the marriage made them unhappy. Her socialism was suspect because she sided with Revisionism, or because she was too much a feminist, an aesthete, or a believer in aristocratic values. Finally, her very radicalism was suspect because it was too individualistic, because it was mixed in with her personal ambition to become a leader, or because she would not submit to organizational discipline. To these objections I can only reply that I, for one, wish there were more radicals who refused to conform to the dogma of any one Movement, opting instead to bridge ideological barriers in an attempt to create a holistic revolutionary perspective.

Does this mean that I consider her attempt to provide her grand synthesis of liberational philosophies to have been a success? Certainly not. Like any other such attempt, however impressive, Braun's theories are full of contradictions, inconsistencies, omissions, and prejudices. She leaves important questions unanswered, and fails to ask many more. But about what philosophy can this not be said? We cannot but admire her for her courage in making the attempt in the first place, and for the fearlessness with which she confronted difficult problems. Moreover, Lily Braun's life and her ideas, inspiring and puzzling, ambitiously conceived and faultily executed, offer important insights for our own times.

NOTES

Abbreviations

NOTE: Unless indicated otherwise, all letters cited in the end notes are contained in the Lily Braun archives at the Leo Baeck Institute, New York.

JOURNALS:
Archiv   Archiv für Sozialgesetzgebung und Statistik
AZ   Arbeiter-Zeitung, Wien
EK   Ethische Kultur
FB   Die Frauenbewegung
GL   Die Gleichheit
NG   Neue Gesellschaft
NZ   Neue Zeit
SM   Sozialistische Monatshefte
Zu   Die Zukunft

BOOKS BY LILY BRAUN:
Frauenfrage   Die Frauenfrage, ihre geschichtliche Entwicklung und ihre wirt-
               schaftliche Seite. Leipzig: Hirzel, 1901.
Liebesbriefe   Die Liebesbriefe der Marquise. München: Albert Langen, 1912.
Im Schatten   Im Schatten der Titanen: Erinnerungen an Baronin Jenny von
               Gustedt. Stuttgart: Deutsche Verlagsanstalt, 1903.
Memoirs   Memoiren einer Sozialistin; vol. I, Lehrjahre; vol. II, Kampfjahre.
               München: Albert Langen, 1908, 1911.

Preface

1. Alfred G. Meyer, "Marxism and the Women's Question," in Dorothy Atkinson, Alexander Dallin, and Gail W. Lapidus, eds., Women in Russia (Stanford, Calif.: Stanford University Press, 1977), pp. 85–112.

Introduction

1. Die Bürgerpflicht der Frau, p. 22. Berlin, G. Bernstein, 1895.

I. Early Life

1. Her actual baptismal name was Amalie. I have seen only one legal document—a petition to the Prussian Ministry of Education—in which she used it. Reference: SG Darmst, ZK 1896(s) Lily Braun, Staatsbibliothek Preussischer Kulturbesitz, Berlin.

2. I know about the book from her letters, but have never seen a copy and therefore will not cite it. It was published under a male pseudonym, Ludolf Waldner, the last name being the maiden name of her favorite great-grandmother, Countess Diana Waldner von Freundstein.

3. Lily Braun to Heinrich Braun, 8 June 1898.

4. *Kriegsbriefe*, pp. 199, 208, 224–225.

5. *Memoirs*, vol. I, pp. 14–15, 245–246. Lily to Tilly [Mathilde] von Colomb, 14 June 1890, 25 October and 15 November 1896.

6. Ibid., I, p. 27.

7. Ibid., II, p. 441.

8. Hans von Kretschman, "Ethische Kultur—Deutsches Heer." *EK* I/2–3.

9. Lily Braun to Theodor Gomperz, 7 December 1909. Gomperz Collection, Honnold Library, Claremont, Calif.

10. Jenny von Kretschman to Lily von Kretschman, 16 September 1891(?).

11. Lily Braun to Heinrich Braun, 13/14 August 1904.

12. Pastor Hans served on the local arrangements committee for the 14th Congress of the General German Women's League (ADFrV), which met in Augsburg 24–26 September 1887.

13. The manuscript is apparently not in her *Nachlass*. We have to rely on the portions of this fragment which is in *Memoirs*, vol. I, pp. 328–329.

14. Letter to Tilly von Colomb, summer 1982.

15. *Memoirs*, vol. I, pp. 41–43. Since the barbaric practice of tight lacing was customarily begun at this age in a girl's life, it is plausible to assume that these instructions were part of a sort of initiation into female sexuality that took place on this occasion.

16. See Katharine Anthony, *Feminism in Germany and Scandinavia* (New York: Henry Holt & Co., 1915), pp. 70–71.

17. Letter to Tilly von Colomb, 26 September 1886.

18. This is a persistent theme not only in her letters to her cousin but also in published essays and novels written during the last twenty years of her life, especially *Die Liebesbriefe der Marquise*, and the opera libretto, *Madeleine Guimard*. Braun also lectured on the theme of the courtesan; thus in the fall of 1907 she presented a cycle of five lectures on the *grandes amoureuses*, according to the following outline: (1) the courtesan in antiquity and today; (2) Female Maecenases in the Renaissance; (3) The *grande amoureuse* as ruler and inspirer; (4) The *grande amoureuse* as artist; and (5) Death and resurrection of the *grande amoureuse*. Reference: Pr. Br. Rep. 30 Bln C Pol. Präs. Nr. 16082 Bl.55. Deutsches Zentralarchiv, Potsdam. I

would like to express my appreciation to the archival services of the German Democratic Republic for making these and other police files on Lily Braun available to me.

19. Letter to Tilly von Colomb, 11 September 1886.
20. Ibid.
21. Letter to Tilly von Colomb, 31 January 1889. Emphasis added.
22. Letter to Tilly von Colomb, 13 January 1889.
23. Letter to Tilly von Colomb, 26 July 1883.
24. Letter to Tilly von Colomb, 29 August 1886. See also letter of 21 September 1888.
25. Letters to Tilly von Colomb, 16 April 1889, 24 April 1889.
26. Letter to Tilly von Colomb, 12 May 1889.
27. *Memoirs*, vol. I, pp. 433ff.
28. Letters to Tilly von Colomb, 11 May 1890, 14 June 1890, 26 December 1890, and 27 January 1891, provide the sketchy outlines of this romance. In her memoirs it has been fictionalized beyond recognition; and in her sister's unpublished autobiographical sketch, the fictionalized version is reported as if it were fact. Maria von Kretschman's autobiographical sketch was written in 1918/19 while she was in federal detention on Ellis Island as a German spy. It is in the possession of the Leo Baeck Institute.
29. Letters to Tilly von Colomb, 24 May 1891, 18 October 1891, 25 May 1892.
30. *Aus Goethes Freundeskreise; Erinnerungen der Baronin Jenny von Gustedt* (Braunschweig: George Westermann, 1892). "Erinnerungen von und an Jenny von Pappenheim (Freifrau von Gustedt)" in Ludwig Geiger, ed., *Goethe-Jahrbuch, vol. XII* (Frankfurt a/M, 1891). "Ottilie von Goethe und ihre Söhne: Aus den Erinnerungen einer Zeitgenossin," in *Westermann's Monatshefte*, vol. 70, 1891, pp. 97–109. "Weimars Gesellschaft und das 'Chaos'," ibid., vol. 71, 1892, pp. 235–264. "Briefwechsel zwischen Goethe und Minister von Gersdorff," in *Goethe-Jahrbuch* 1892, vol. 13, pp. 98ff. "Die literarischen Abende der Grossherzogin Maria Paulowna," in *Deutsche Rundschau*, vol. LXXV (April–June 1893), pp. 422–448; and vol. LXXVI (July–September 1893), pp. 58–89. Also Lily von Giżycki, *Deutsche Fürstinnen* (Berlin: Gebr. Paetel, 1893).
31. Letters to Tilly von Colomb, 20 September 1891, 22 December 1894.
32. These include a series of twelve articles under the title "Streifzüge durch die moderne Literatur" published in 1895 and 1896 in different issues of *Ethische Kultur*; several theater reviews, some brief, some of article length, in the same journal; "Die neue Frau in der Dichtung" in *NZ*, vol. XIV, Tome II, No. 36, 1895/6, pp. 293–303; and three articles published in Maximilian Harden's *Die Zukunft*: "Die Frauenfrage auf der deutschen Bühne," *Zukunft*, 1897, No. 21, pp. 26–33; "Ein Frauendrama," ibid., 1898, No. 24, pp. 511–517; and "Die Lieder der neuen Frau," ibid., 1902, pp. 494–505. I could have included essays on Wagner and articles about

contemporary painting; but the above citations sufficiently show the volume and range of her work. I have translated these and many other works by Braun into English and hope to publish a selection of them.

33. Heinrich Braun to Lily Braun, 9 June 1896.

34. See Zetkin's article welcoming Braun to the party, in GL VI/1 (8 January 1896), p. 7.

35. From Friedrich Dernburg's review of Braun's memoirs, "Lily Brauns Abschied von der Partei," *Berliner Tageblatt,* 1911, No. 257 (12 May 1911). I am grateful to the Staatsarchiv der DDR, Potsdam, for calling my attention to this review.

36. See Jean H. Quataert, *Reluctant Feminists in German Social Democracy 1885–1917* (Princeton, N.J.: Princeton University Press, 1979), pp. 126–127. For Zetkin's livid reaction to the book see Rosa Luxemburg's letter to Jogiches of 28 January 1902, in *Comrade and Lover: Rosa Luxemburg's Letters to Leo Jogiches,* ed. and transl. by Elżbieta Ettinger (Cambridge, Mass.: MIT Press, 1979). Zetkin eventually reviewed the book in GL XII/15/115–118 and XII/16/122–124.

37. See Róża Luksemburg, *Listy do Leona Jogichesa-Tyszki,* vol. I, pp. 372, 551 (Warszawa: Książka i Wiedza, 1968).

38. The first journal he founded, and later sold, was *Sozialpolitisches Zentralblatt.* He later created the *Archiv für soziale Gesetzgebung und Statistik.*

39. This credit is given him by Georges Haupt, "Marx and Marxism," pp. 279–280, in Eric J. Hobsbawm, ed., *The History of Marxism,* vol. I (Bloomington: Indiana University Press, 1982).

40. See Karl Kautsky, "Heinrich Braun: Ein Beitrag zur Geschichte der deutschen Sozialdemokratie," p. 157, in *Die Gesellschaft: Internationale Revue für Sozialismus and Politik,* I (1933), No. 1–3. Also Maximilian Harden, "Bebel und Genossen, II," in *Zu,* 3 Oct 1903, p. 16. Also letter No. 309 in the Georg von Vollmar file, Institute for Social History, Amsterdam, and Leo Arons (1860–1919) to Victor Adler, 28 November 1894, in Victor Adler archive, Verein für Geschichte der Arbeiterbewegung, Wien.

41. Undated letter of Mrs. Heimann to Julie Braun-Vogelstein.

42. For some of the facts about the divorce proceedings, see Heinrich Braun to Victor (and Emma) Adler, 14 November 1891, 20 November 1891, 9 February 1892, 5 January 1895, and 19 April 1898, Victor Adler archive, Verein für Geschichte der Arbeiterbewegung, Wien. Also Josefine Braun to Benno Karpeles, 19 November 1897, ibid.

43. Victor Adler to Heinrich Braun, 21 March 1895, ibid.

44. Lily Braun to Heinrich Braun, 31 August 1895.

II. German Feminism before 1895

1. J. G. Zimmermann, *Über die Einsamkeit,* vol. III (Frankfurt and Leipzig, 1785) pp. 339–340. Quoted in Timothy F. Sellner, Introduction to

Theodor Gottlieb von Hippel, *On Improving the Status of Women* (Detroit, Mich.: Wayne State University Press, 1979), p. 39.

2. See Elizabeth Cady Stanton, Susan B. Anthony, and Matilda Joslyn Gage, eds., *History of Woman Suffrage*, vol. I (Rochester, N. Y., 1887), p. 41.

3. For a relevant description of this process, see Lily von Giżycki, "Volksküche," in *EK* II/1/77. For the situation in Victorian England, which in many ways was similar, see Constance Rover, *Love, Morals, and the Feminists* (London: Routledge & Kegan Paul, 1970), pp. 78–81.

4. Louise Otto-Peters, *Das erste Vierteljahrhundert des Allgemeinen Deutschen Frauenvereins, gegründet am 18. Oktober 1865 in Leipzig* (Leipzig: Moritz Schafer, 1890), p. 7.

5. Ibid., p. 23.

6. Lily von Giżycki, "Deutsche Arbeiterinnen-Interessen," in *FB* I/1/6.

7. For a summary of these trends, see Katharine Anthony, *Feminism in Germany and Scandinavia* (New York: Henry Holt & Co., 1915), pp. 84–87.

8. Quoted in a review of the book by Helene Stöcker in *FB* I/24/194.

9. For a review of some of this poetry, see Lily Braun, "Die Lieder der Neuen Frau," in *Zu*, 1902, pp. 494–505. For some of her reviews of plays and novels dealing with the New Woman, see "Die Frauenfrage auf der deutschen Bühne," ibid., 1897, No. 21, pp. 26–33; "Ein Frauendrama," ibid., 1898, No. 24, pp. 511–517; "Die neue Frau in der Dichtung," in *NZ*, vol. XIV, Tome II, No. 36, pp. 293–303; and a series of about twelve entitled, "Streifzüge durch die moderne Literatur," in *EK*, volumes I and II. See also *Frauenfrage*, p. 201.

10. Editorial in *FB*, vol. I, No. 1, pp. 3–4.

11. See Helene Lange, *Die Frauenbewegung in ihren modernen Problemen* (Münster: Tende Verlag, 1980 reprint), pp. 45–47.

12. Marianne Weber, *Ehefrau und Mutter in der Rechtsentwicklung* (Tübingen: J.C.B. Mohr, 1907).

13. Lange, op. cit., pp. 83–84.

14. Quoted from an article by M. Mellien in *Neue Banen*, 1895, No. 4, by Lily von Giżycki, "Nach Links und Rechts," in *FB* I/7/50.

15. Henriette Goldschmidt, "Erklärung gegen das Frauenstimmrecht," in *FB* I/3/19.

16. *FB* I/22/178.

III. The SPD in the Early 1890s

1. For a discussion of this double personality, see Peter Groh, *Negative Integration und revolutionärer Attentismus: Die deutsche Sozialdemokratie am Vorabend des Ersten Weltkrieges* (Frankfurt a/M, 1973).

2. On Kautsky and his views see Gary P. Steenson, *Karl Kautsky, 1854–1938: Marxism in the Classical Years* (Pittsburgh, Penn.: University of Pitts-

burgh Press, 1978); Massimo Salvadori, *Karl Kautsky and the Socialist Revolution, 1880–1938* (London: N.L.B., 1979); Walter Holzheuer, *Karl Kautskys Werk als Weltanschauung* (München: C. H. Beck, 1972); Hans-Joseph Steinder, *Sozialismus und deutsche Sozialdemokratie* (Hannover: Verlag für Literatur und Zeitgeschehen, 1967).

3. Karl Kautsky, letter to Heinrich Braun, 17 January 1894. Kautsky archive C, pp. 316ff. See also Clara Zetkin, letter to Karl Kautsky, 14 March 1897, in Kautsky archive DXXIII/314 (2–3), Institute for Social History, Amsterdam.

4. Heinrich Braun to Lily Braun, 7 October 1895. He is commenting about the Breslau party congress.

5. F. Stampfer, "Richtung und Party," *NZ* XXIV/1/292–295; Karl Kautsky, "Eine Nachlese zum Vorwärtskonflikt," ibid., pp. 313–326. This, incidentally, contains a polemic against the journal then owned and edited by the Brauns and a bitter personal attack on their friend Kurt Eisner.

6. Barbara Lovett Cline, *The Questioners: Physicists and the Quantum Theory* (New York: Thomas Crowell, 1965), p. 34.

7. For an example of the querulous tone of these disputes, see the public arguments between Bernstein and Kautsky over who had the right to edit the unpublished works of Engels and Marx. *NZ* XXIV, part 3, pp. 167–168, 303–304, 374–376, 470–472.

8. Ignaz Auer to Heinrich Braun, 4 September 1903.

9. The quotation and the observation are from Mark Falcoff's review of *Comrade and Lover: Rosa Luxemburg's Letters to Leo Jogiches,* in *Commentary,* April 1980, p. 90. For a general study of the embourgeoisement of the SPD in Wilhelmine Germany, see Guenther Roth, *The Social Democrats in Imperial Germany* (Totowa, N.J.: 1963), pp. 85ff., 212ff., also Peter Lösche, *Arbeiterbewegung und Wilhelminismus: Sozialdemokratie zwischen Anpassung und Spaltung. Geschichte in Wissenschaft und Unterricht,* No. 20 (1969), pp. 519–533.

IV. The Women's Organization of the SPD

1. Lily Braun to Heinrich Braun, 24 August 1895. Also *Memoirs* I/549–551.

2. Werner Thönnessen, *The Emancipation of Women: The Rise and Decline of the Women's Movement in German Social Democracy, 1863–1953* (London: 1973). Also Hilde Lion, *Zur Soziologie der Frauenbewegung;* Schriftenreihe der Akademie für soziale und pädagogische Frauenarbeit in Berlin (Berlin: F. A. Herbig, 1926). For another complaint that women were treated as second-class party members, see Clara Zetkin, *Zur Geschichte der proletarischen Frauenbewegung Deutschlands* (Berlin: Dietz Verlag, 1958), p. 8.

3. See Margarete Lichey, *Sozialismus und Frauenarbeit: Ein Beitrag zur Entwicklung des deutschen Sozialismus von 1869 bis 1921* (Dissertation, Breslau: Universitätsverlag, 1926[?]).

4. For a telling account of the workers' patriarchal views, see Elżbieta Ettinger, ed., *Comrade and Lover: Rosa Luxemburg's Letters to Leo Jogiches* (Cambridge, Mass.: MIT Press), p. 124.

5. *Memoirs* II/358.

6. Batya Weinbaum, *The Curious Courtship of Women's Liberation and Socialism* (Boston: South End Press, 1978), especially chapter 4.

7. Richard J. Evans, *Sozialdemokratie und Frauenemanzipation im Deutschen Kaiserreich* (Berlin-Bonn: J.H.W. Dietz Nachf., 1979), p. 85.

8. Lily von Giżycki, "Die Frauenfrage auf dem sozialdemokratischen Parteitag," *FB* I/21/166.

9. *Correspondenzblatt der Generalkommission der Gewerkschaften Deutschlands*, VII/34/202. Hamburg, 23 August 1897. For a summary of strike activities, see ibid., No. 14, p. 75.

10. For some relevant figures, see the report about Braun's speech in Vienna of 12 December 1895, in *AZ Wien*, 13 December 1895; also Lily Braun, "Der internationale Frauenkongress in London," *GL* XI/16/123.

11. Reinhold Jaeckel, *Die Stellung des Sozialismus zur Frauenfrage* (Dissertation, Tübingen: 1904), p. 152. Similarly, Hilde Lion, *Zur Soziologie der Frauenbewegung*, argues that Bismarck's anti-socialist laws gave the SPD no alternative: in order to survive they had to enlist the aid of their women.

12. For an excellent treatment of this group, its leading personalities, and the issues with which it dealt, see Jean H. Quataert, *Reluctant Feminists in German Social Democracy, 1885–1917* (Princeton, N.J.: Princeton University Press, 1979).

13. For the ludicrous lengths to which not only the police but also various political parties went to enforce this legislation, see Agnes von Zahn-Harnack, *Die Frauenbewegung: Geschichte, Probleme, Ziele* (Berlin: Deutsche Buch-Gemeinschaft, 1928), pp. 278–289.

14. Clara Zetkin, "Frauenrechtleriche Harmonieduselei" (Women's libbers' pipedreams about harmony), *GL* 1895, No. 1.

15. For typical expressions of Zetkin's essentially anti-feminist stand, see her editorial, "An die Leserinnen und Leser," *GL* VIII/1, or her article, "Frauenrechtlerische Unklarheit," ibid., VI/13/19–20. For a general treatment of her views, see Hilde Lion, *Zur Soziologie der Frauenbewegung*, pp. 24ff; Karen Honeycutt, "Clara Zetkin: A Left-Wing Socialist and Feminist in Wilhelmine Germany" (Dissertation, Columbia University, 1975); idem, "Socialism and Feminism in Imperial Germany," in *SIGNS*, 1979, V/1/30–41; also Jean Quataert, op. cit., Chapters III–V.

16. See her obituary for Lily Braun, *GL* XI/16; also Karen Honeycutt, "Socialism and Feminism in Imperial Germany," pp. 30–40.

17. See Evans, op. cit., p. 186.

18. Klara Blum, "Sozialismus und Persönlichkeit: Zum fünfzehnten Todestag Lily Brauns am 8. August" in *AZ*, Wien, 10 August 1931.

V. There Is No Direction but Forward

1. For the minutes of this meeting, see *EK* I/50/400–401.
2. Lily von Giżycki to Tilly von Colomb, 10 October 1893.
3. Lily von Kretschman to Tilly von Colomb, 27 December 1891.
4. Lily von Kretschman to Tilly von Colomb, 12 May 1889. On the history of the Ruhr miners see Stephen Hickey, "The Shaping of the German Labour Movement: Miners in the Ruhr," in Richard J. Evans, ed., *Society and Politics in Wilhelmine Germany* (New York: Barnes & Noble, 1978), pp. 215–240.
5. Lily von Kretschman to Tilly von Colomb, 28 February 1892.
6. Lily von Giżycki, "Nach Links und Rechts," in *FB* I/7/50. For similar criticism of timidity in the bourgeois women's movement, see her "Stimmungsbilder aus der General-Versammlung des Bundes Deutscher Frauenvereine in München," ibid., I/9/69–70.
7. "Die Stellung der sozialdemokratischen Frauen gegenüber dem Entwurf eines bürgerlichen Gesetzbuches," in *FB* I/16/126.
8. Cited in Lily von Giżycki, "Die Frauenfrage auf dem sozialdemokratischen Parteitag," ibid., I/21/166.
9. "An die Leser," in *EK* II/42. Also "Herrn Förster zur Erwiderung," in *GL*, 25 October 1899.
10. Lily von Giżycki to Karl Kautsky, 16 May 1895. Kautsky archive DVI, No. 584. Institute for Social History, Amsterdam.
11. Clara Zetkin, "Reinliche Scheidung," in *GL* IV/8/63, IV/13/102–103, 15/115–117. See also articles in *Vorwärts*, 9 January 1895 and 24 January 1895.
12. Constance Rover, *Love, Morals, and the Feminists* (London: Routledge & Kegan Paul, 1970), pp. 89–93; also David Pivar, *Purity Crusade, Sexual Morality and Social Control, 1868–1900* (Westport and London: Greenwood Press, 1973), pp. 133–135.
13. Lily von Giżycki to Tilly von Colomb, 30 June 1895.
14. Lily von Giżycki, "Zur Beurteilung der Frauenbewegung in England und Deutschland," *Archiv* VI/I/575–597. The article was reprinted as a pamphlet (Berlin: Carl Heymanns Verlag, 1895). See also Lily von Giżycki, "Englischer Sozialismus," in *Die Zeit* (Wien), IV/45 (10 August 1895).
15. For a report of the meeting, see *AZ*, No. 342, 13 December 1895. I am grateful to the Staatsarchiv der DDR, Potsdam, for giving me access to this report.

VI. An Orthodox Marxist with a Few Ideas of Her Own

1. Clara Zetkin to Karl Kautsky, 25 September 1896. Kautsky archive DXXIII/313. Institute for Social History, Amsterdam.

2. GL VI/1/7.

3. Lily Braun-Giżycki, *Frauenfrage und Sozialdemokratie* (Berlin: Verlag Vorwärts, 1896), pp. 2–3.

4. Ibid., p. 20.

5. For similar denunciations of the bourgeois women's movement, see the following: "Das Frauenstimmrecht in England," GL VII/13/102–103; "Warum kann die Frauenbewegung nicht unabhängig bleiben?" ibid., VII/ 10/76–78; "Bürgerliche und proletarische Frauenbewegung," ibid., VI/ 23/178–180; and "Der internationale Frauenkongress in London," in *Schweizerische Blatter für Wirtschafts- und Sozialpolitik*, 1899, pp. 1–16.

6. Even though she probably would have refused to attend, she resented not having been invited to the International Women's Congress in London, 1899.

7. See her gloss in NG II/9/98.

8. *Memoirs* II/294, 311. Also "Zur Dienstbotenfrage," in NG III/3/34.

9. GL VII/5.

10. Ibid., Nos. 6–12, 14 and 15.

11. Ottilie Baader, *Ein steiniger Weg: Lebenserinnerungen* (Berlin: Buchhandlung Vorwärts, 1921), pp. 63–64.

12. Jean H. Quataert, *Reluctant Feminists in German Social Democracy 1885–1917* (Princeton, N.J.: Princeton University Press, 1979), pp. 114–116.

13. See "Eine Konferenz zur Förderung der Arbeiterinnen-Interessen," in NG III/22/258–259; also "Die bürgerliche Frauenbewegung und die Sozialreform," ibid., III/24/280–283.

14. See Clara Sahlber, "Informationen für die Frau," Bonn, September 1953, quoted in Emmy Beckmann and Elizabeth Kardel, eds., *Quellen zur Geschichte der Frauenbewegung* (Frankfurt a/M: Moritz Diesterweg, 1955), p. 71.

15. Julian Marcuse, "Mütterheime," in *März—eine Wochenschrift*, VI/ 4/405. Herausgegeben von Ludwig Thoma and Herman Hesse.

16. *Die Frauenfrage*, p. 547. For an earlier discussion of this scheme, see her review of Louis Frank, Dr. Keiffer, and Louis Maingie, *L'Assurance maternelle*, Brussels-Paris, 1897, in *Archiv* XI/543–548. See also *Bericht über die 2. Frauenkonferenz 1902, München* (Berlin, 1902). For later summaries, see Alice Salomon, *Mutterschutz und Mutterschaftsversicherung* (1909); Henriette Fürth, *Die Mutterschaftsversicherung* (Jena: Gustav Fischer, 1911); Adele Schreiber, ed., *Mutterschaft* (München: Albert Langen, 1912); and Katharine Anthony, *Feminism in Germany and Scandinavia* (New York: Henry Holt, 1915), pp. 118–119.

17. *Bericht über die 2. Frauenkonferenz,* pp. 296–297. For an earlier rejoinder by Braun, see her "Arbeiterinnenschutz und Frauenfreiheit," in *GL* VII/18/–137–141.

18. For the text of the law, see Emmy Beckmann & Elisabeth Kardel, eds., *Quellen zur Geschichte der Frauenbewegung* (Frankfurt a/M: Moritz Diesterweg), pp. 71ff.

19. See Lily Braun, "Die Frau in der Sozialdemokratie," in *Illustriertes Konversations-Lexikon der Frau,* vol. II, pp. 475ff.

20. On barring women from health-endangering work, see Dr. med. Agnes Bluhm, *Der Einfluss der gewerblichen Gifte auf den Organismus der Frau,* p. 24. Schriften des ständigen Ausschusses zur Förderung der Arbeiterinnen-Interessen. (Jena: Gustav Fischer, 1910). Dr. Bluhm, incidentally, was Braun's physician.

21. *Die Frauenfrage,* p. 49. See also "Die gesetzliche Regelung der Heimarbeit," in *NG* I/8/91–93.

22. *Frauenarbeit und Hauswirtschaft,* originally a lecture given in Berlin, 1901 (Berlin: Verlag Vorwärts, 1901). Also *Was wir wollen; Flugschrift des Vereins fur Hauswirtschafts-Genossenschaften* (Berlin, 1902). Similar ideas were expressed not long afterwards by Charlotte Perkins (Stetson) Gilman. See her *The Home, Its Work and Influence* (New York: McClure, Phillips & Company, 1903), *Women and Economics* (New York: Harper Torchbooks, 1966), and "The Waste of Private Housekeeping," in *Annals of the American Academy of Political Science,* July 1913.

23. "Die Reform der Hauswirtschaft," in *Zu* XXXIV/408–415, 540–543. See also reader's response to these articles, ibid., XXV/171–172.

24. Helene Lange, *Die Frauenbewegung,* pp. 112–113.

25. Heinrich Herkner, "Eine deutsche Beatrice Webb?" in *Zu* XXXVIII/ 314–315.

26. *GL* XI/13/97–99, 14/105–106; 15/113–115; and 16/121–122. For Braun's reply, see ibid., 18/140–144; Zetkin's rebuttal is in 20/155–156.

27. Friedrich Engels, "Grundsätze des Kommunismus," in *MEW* 4/373– 374.

28. Friedrich Engels, *Der Ursprung der Familie, MEW* 21, pp. 75–76, 158. Karl Marx and Friedrich Engels, *Die deutsche Ideologie, MEW* 3, p. 29.

29. Franz Oppenheimer, *Die Siedlungsgenossenschaft* (Leipzig: Duncker & Humblot, 1896).

30. See *Frauenfrage,* pp. 199, 461–462. Also "Eine ungehaltene Rede," *NG* IV/13/391–393.

31. *Frauenfrage,* p. 456. See also "Die Frauen und des Organisationsstatut," *NG* I/25/293–294; "Frauenstimmrecht und Sozialdemokratie," ibid., V/7/205–210; "Die Frauenfrage auf dem internationalen Kongress," ibid., V/9/257–263; "Eine ungehaltene Rede," ibid., VI/13/391–393.

32. "Frauenstimmrecht und Sozialdemokratie," *NG* IV/7/207–209. See also Clara Zetkin, *Zur Frage des Frauenwahlrechts* (Berlin: Buchhandlung Vorwärts, 1907).

33. This outline, in her handwriting, is contained in Bundesarchiv, Nachlass Harden: Lily and Heinrich Braun to Harden, Bestand 20, Heft 2, pp. 5–6.

34. "Die Frauenfrage im Altertum," *Archiv* XIII/155–178; and "Die Anfänge der Frauenbewegung," ibid., pp. 314–381. The former also appeared in *GL* IX, Nos. 1–2, 4, 6, 9, and 12.

35. "Die Frauenfrage im Altertum," in *Archiv* XIII/155–178.

36. "Die Anfänge der Frauenbewegung," ibid., pp. 314–381.

37. *Frauenfrage*, pp. 380–381.

38. Ibid., p. 431; 316. For a similar passage, see *Memoirs* II/468.

39. *Frauenfrage*, p. 556.

40. Ibid, pp. 456–458.

41. Ibid., pp. 456–462; 556.

VII. Revisionism as the Liberalization of Marxism

1. For a discussion of this, see Vernon Lidtke, *The Outlawed Party: Social Democracy in Germany, 1870–1890* (Princeton, N.J.: Princeton University Press, 1966), passim.

2. For a standard critique of orthodox dogma, see Erich Matthias, "Kautsky und der Kautskyanismus," *Marxismusstudien*, No. 2, 1957.

3. Carl E. Schorske, *German Social Democracy, 1905–1917* (Princeton, N.J.: Princeton University Press, 1955), p. 41.

4. Hilde Lion, *Zur Soziologie der Frauenbewegung* (Berlin: F. H. Herbig, 1926), pp. 92–94.

5. *Memoirs* II/622–624. For a discussion of the organizational fetishism in the SPD, see Thomas Nipperdey, *Die Organisation der deutschen Parteien vor 1918*, chapter 7, especially pp. 325–327 (Düsseldorf, 1961). Also David W. Morgan, *The Socialist Left and the German Revolution* (Ithaca, N.Y: Cornell University Press, 1975), p. 21.

6. *Comrade and Lover: Rosa Luxemburg's Letters to Leo Jogiches*, ed. and trans. Elżbieta Ettinger (Cambridge, Mass: MIT Press, 1979), p. 111.

7. Schorske, op. cit., p. 124.

8. Lily Braun to Heinrich Braun, 31 August 1895.

9. "Gräber," *NG* III/26–308–309.

10. Lily Braun to Heinrich Braun, 30 September 1903. For an eloquent denial of the possibility ever to know absolute truth, see *Memoirs* I/413.

11. Lily Braun to Heinrich Braun, 8 July 1905.

12. For expressions of this sentiment, see Lily von Kretschman to Tilly von Colomb, 12 April 1892, 9 February 1896.

13. "Ein Traum von William Morris," *NG* II/34/405–408.

14. "Die Mannheimer Frauenkonferenz," *NG* III/1/5.

15. Lily Braun to Heinrich Braun, 12 August 1903.

16. See Lily von Giżycki, "Politik und Ethische Bewegung," *EK* III/21/164–165.

17. A lengthy article is devoted to this argument: "Die bürgerliche Frauenbewegung und Sozialreform," *NG* II/24/280–283.
18. "Mitläufer," *NG* II/27/313–315.
19. Lily von Kretschman to Tilly von Colomb, 5 June 1892.
20. *Memoirs* II/627–628. Of course, by trying to appeal to "the best" of the bourgeoisie, Braun was indulging in a form of elitism of her own.
21. "Meiner 'Meerfahrt' Tagebuch," *NG* II/28/330.
22. "Londoner Tagebuch," *NG* II/29/341.
23. For one of the many expressions of these ideas, see *Memoirs* II/357.

VIII. Revisionism as the Radicalization of Marxism

1. *Memoirs* II/458.
2. Lily Braun to Heinrich Braun, 18 January 1901.
3. *Memoirs* II/290. See also ibid., I/114.
4. Ibid., p. 483.
5. Ibid., II/624.
6. "Juristischer Kindermord," *NG* II/20/231.
7. "Londoner Tagebuch," *NG* II/29/342.
8. "Meiner 'Meerfahrt' Tagebuch," *NG* II/28/332; also her account of the international women's conference, London, 26 June to 4 July 1899, in *Schweizerische Blätter für Wirtschafts- und Sozialpolitik* (1899), p. 2.
9. For an elaboration of this point see the obituary for Braun in *Neue Freie Presse*, Wien, 30 August 1916.
10. *Memoirs* II/589.
11. Ibid., pp. 208–209, 247, 290–291.
12. Franz Laufkoetter, "Die Taktik des Starken und die Taktik des Schwachen," *NG* II/27/319–321. See also similar remarks by Braun in "Londoner Tagebuch," *NG* II/29/341.
13. *Memoirs* I/548.
14. Obituary for Braun, *Volkswacht*, Breslau, 8 October 1916.
15. *Memoirs* II/287, 410–416.
16. "Leid und Leid," *NG* II/33/394.
17. "Die Anfänge der Frauenbewegung," *Archiv* XIII/346.
18. *Liebesbriefe*, p. 177.
19. "Nichtraucher," *NG* II/27/323.
20. *Memoirs* I/523–524.
21. Isaiah Berlin, *Four Essays on Liberty*, p. 176.
22. Lily Braun to Theodor Gomperz, 21 June 1911. Gomperz Collection, Honnold Library.
23. *Memoirs* II/635–636.
24. Cited in Georg Plechanov, "Henrik Ibsen," Ergänzungsheft zur *NZ*, No. 3, 10 July 1908, p. 31.

25. " 'Bürgerliches' und 'proletarisches' Erziehungsprinzip," *NG* III/8/93–94.

26. "Abseits vom Wege," *NG* IV/4/126. She was convinced that this would always be difficult, even once socialism had become reality. See Lily Braun to Heinrich Braun, 3–4 July 1904.

27. *Memoirs* II/585. For another passage in which Nietzsche's ideas are given revolutionary implications, see ibid., I/412.

28. Ibid., II/480.

29. In pain we can show greatness, can be heroes, / But blissful happiness makes us divine.

30. "Ein Gang durch die Berliner Kunstausstellungen," *EK* I/34/269–270; 35/376–378. Also her review of Hermann Sudermann's *Heimat*, *EK* I/41/328; also "Allerhand Nachdenkliches," *NG* II/34/408; and "Londoner Tagebuch," ibid., II/29/342.

31. *Memoirs* II/547–548.

32. *NG* II/10/117. See also "Gräber," in ibid., III/26/308–309.

33. See especially "Streifzüge durch die moderne Literatur," *EK* I/27/216; 31/244–245.

34. "Maifestnummern," *NG* II/18/208.

35. "Abseits vom Wege," *NG* V/4/121–126; *Liebesbriefe*, passim. For her comments on *art nouveau*, see *Memoirs* II/211, 473. She had a personal relationship to that style because her sister was married to one of the pioneers of German *art nouveau* (*Jugendstil*).

36. See for instance her review of Fritz Mauthner, *Lügenohr*, *EK* I/12/95–96.

37. "Die Pflicht, schön zu sein," *EK* II/8/62. Also many articles dealing with nature, with festivals, with the dignity of dying, and so on.

38. Clara Zetkin to Karl Kautsky, 4 March 1900. Kautsky archive DXXIII, pp. 322, 329. Institute for Social History, Amsterdam.

39. "Wie wir Ungläubigen Weihnachten feiern," *NG* III/12/136.

40. From a police report about her lecture. Reference: Pr. Br. Rep. 30 Bln. C Pol. Präs. Nr. 16082, Blatt 59. Staatsarchiv der DDR, Potsdam.

41. "Karneval," *GL* VII/4/26–28. "Die Predigt von der Freude," ibid., VII/21/161–162. "Ein Gang durch die Berliner Kunstausstellungen," *EK* I/34/269–270.

42. *Memoirs* I/425; also 358, 363–367, II/67. Also "Das ist der Mai," *NG* I/5/51.

43. Lily Braun to Heinrich Braun, 11 July 1903.

44. "Karneval," *GL* VII/4/26–28.

45. "Negerkultur," *NG* II/22/264; also "Auch eine Osterpredigt," ibid., II/15/169.

46. See "Hebel oder Hemmschuh?" *NG* I/10/111.

47. *Memoirs* II/651–654.

48. Obituary for Braun, *Volkswacht*, Breslau, 10 August 1916.

49. Stefan Grossmann in *Vossische Zeitung,* Berlin, 9 August 1916.

50. Carl E. Schorske, *German Social Democracy, 1905–1917* (Princeton, N.J.: Princeton University Press, 1955), pp. 21–22.

IX. The Alienation of Femininity

1. The German title, "Volgelfrei," is a term from medieval German law. Anyone declared to be "vogelfrei"—literally: free as a bird—was thereby branded an outlaw and could be killed with impunity by anyone.

2. "Vogelfrei," NG II/24/286. How contemporary this is can be seen by comparing it with Susan Jacoby, "Unfair Game," in *The Possible She* (New York: Farrar, Straus & Giroux, 1979), pp. 36–43.

3. *Frauenfrage,* p. 13. Also "Die Frauenfrage im Altertum," *Archiv* XIII, p. 166.

4. From a gloss in NG I/3.

5. "Die Entthronung der Liebe," NG I/20/237–239. See also "Das geistige Leben des Weibes," pp. 232–234. Chapter 5 in Robby A. Kossmann, ed., *Mann und Weib, ihre Beziehungen zueinander und zum Kulturleben der Gegenwart,* vol. I, second edition (Stuttgart: Union Verlag, ND).

6. "Wider Moral- und Kirchenpfaffen," NG II/16/183.

7. From a review of Clara Müller-Jahnke, *Ich bekenne: Die Geschichte einer Frau,* NG I/13/155.

8. See for instance "Die Lieder der Neuen Frau," *Zu* 1902, pp. 494–505.

9. Summarized in a police report on a lecture given November 1906. Pr. Br. Rep. 30 Bln. C Pol. Präs. Nr. 16082. Blatt 37. Staatsarchiv der DDR, Potsdam.

10. *Liebesbriefe,* p. 63.

11. From a report in *Die Zeit am Montag,* Beilage zu No. 46, 12 November 1906. Deposited in the police dossier cited in note 9 above, Blatt 38. Braun later expanded this lecture into a cycle of five lectures on the "Grandes Amoureuses," Berlin, fall 1907, ibid., pp. 36, 38, 55. See also "Das geistige Leben des Weibes" (note 5 above, pp. 232; 238–239; 246–247; 267–268.

12. Lily Braun to Heinrich Braun, 17 July 1912.

13. *Memoirs* I/293.

14. Lily Braun to Otto Braun, 8 February 1915.

15. "Die Ehe auf der Anklagebank," NG IV/2/52.

16. Ibid.

17. From a lecture on the right to motherhood given in November 1906. From the police dossier cited in note 9 above, Blatt 42.

18. Ellen Key, *The Renaissance of Motherhood* (New York: 1914), p. 89.

19. *Memoirs* II/432.

20. *Männerkultus,"* NG II/37/442.

21. "Ein neues Drama" (review of Georg von Ompteda, *Nach dem Manöver*), EK III/4/29.

22. Lily Braun to Otto Braun, 20 June 1915.

23. *Frauenfrage,* p. 287.

24. Ibid., pp. 206–207.

25. "Zur Beurteilung der Frauenbewegung in England und Deutschland."

26. *Memoirs* II/345. *Frauenfrage,* p. 557.

27. See her maternalist manifesto, "Ein Aufruf an Deutschlands Frauen," NG IV/7/189–193.

28. "Ellen Key und die Frauenfrage," *Zu* 1899, 28/318–328. Also in her speeches during the war, especially her lecture, "Die Frau von Übermorgen."

29. *Die Mutterschaftsversicherung,* pp. 11–12.

30. *Frauenfrage,* p. 3. "Die Frauenfrage im Altertum," *Archiv* XIII/157.

31. *Frauenfrage,* pp. 199–207.

32. Ibid., p. 205. Also "Die Anfänge der Frauenbewegung," *Archiv* XIII/355. Her interpretation of Rousseau's *Émile* as a contribution to feminism is stated most clearly in "Das geistige Leben des Weibes," pp. 249–251. (See note 5.)

33. "Die Frauenfrage," in SM XI/3/258–266, and subsequent numbers. For replies (other than those by Braun) see Clara Zetkin, "Aus Krähwinkel," GL 22 March 1905; and Emma Ihrer, "Die proletarische Frau und die Berufstätigkeit," SM XI, 1 May 1905.

34. Adrienne Rich, *Of Woman Born: Motherhood as Experience and Institution* (New York: W. W. Norton & Co., 1976) is a recent feminist analysis of the institution of motherhood.

35. Joan B. Landes, "Women, Labor, and Family Life: A Theoretical Perspective," in *Science and Society* XLI/4/393.

36. *Memoirs* II/421. The phrase Braun used here was that attributed to Archimedes, who supposedly claimed that, given a firm point on which to stand, he would be able to move the Earth.

X. Feminist Politics

1. "Ellen Key und die Frauenfrage," *Zu* 1899, 28/319.

2. "Das Frauenstimmrecht in England," *Archiv* X/417–454. *Frauenfrage,* chapter 3. See also her obituary for Susan B. Anthony, NG II/12/134.

3. *Liebesbriefe,* pp. 182–183.

4. *Die Mutterschaftsversicherung* (Berlin: Vorwärts-Verlag, 1906), p. 24.

5. *Memoirs* II/231–232.

6. Lily Braun to Heinrich Braun, 26 July 1905.

7. "Ausnahmegesetze?" NG II/36/340.

8. For a convincing argument that these freedoms naturally reinforce each other, see Katharine Anthony, *Feminism in Germany and Scandinavia*, pp. 98–99.

9. Lily Braun to Theodor Gomperz, 19 February 1911. Theodor Gomperz Collection, Honnold Library, Claremont, California.

10. "Schiller und die Frauen," NG I/6/61.

11. NG I/10/110–111.

12. "Zeitschriftenschau," NG I/13/155–156.

13. "Die 'unterdrückte' Frau," NG II/29/348.

14. "Introduction" to Adele Schreiber, ed., *Mutterschaft: Ein Sammelwerk für die Probleme des Weibes als Mutter* (München: Albert Langen, 1912), pp. 1–4.

15. See her review of Friedrich Naumann, *Neudeutsche Wirtschaftspolitik.* NG II/24/283–285.

16. "Ellen Key und die Frauenfrage," *Zu* 1899, No. 28, pp. 318–328. This was in response to Ellen Key, *Missbrauchte Frauenkraft* (Paris-Leipzig-München: Albert Langen, 1898).

17. *Die Frauen und der Krieg* (Leipzig: S. Hirzel, 1915), p. 6.

18. *Die Mutterschaftsversicherung*, p. 4.

19. Lily Braun to Heinrich Braun, 8 May 1893; 3 April 1900; 4 April 1900; 17 July 1901—to list but a few of these passionate denunciations of housework.

20. "Erziehungsfragen," NG II/39/466–467.

21. *Memoirs* II/420.

22. *Die Mutterschaftsversicherung*, p. 9.

23. Agnes von Zahn-Harnack, *Die Frauenbewegung: Geschichte, Probleme, Ziele* (Berlin: Deutsche Buch-Gemeinschaft, 1928), pp. 33–35. Also Ruth Bré, "Preface," in Ernst Rudolphi, *Mutterschutz in Theorie und Praxis* (Berlin: 1912), p. 4.

24. The original program of the organization specified that only healthy mothers were to be protected, but Braun objected, arguing that the term was subject to arbitrary interpretation, so the word was removed. See Richard J. Evans, *The Feminist Movement in Germany 1894–1933* (London-Beverly Hills: Sage Publications, 1976), p. 160. See also Henriette Fürth, "Entwicklung des Mutterschutzes in Deutschland," in Schreiber, ed., *Mutterschaft*, p. 284.

25. "Das Problem der Ehe," NG I/10/114–116; "Die Befreiung der Liebe," NG I/22/260–263; "Die Ehe auf der Anklagebank," NG V/2/50–57.

26. Batya Weinbaum, *The Curious Courtship of Women's Liberation and Socialism* (Boston: South End Press, 1978), p. 161.

27. "Das Frauenstimmrecht in England," *Archiv* 10 (1897) pp. 452–453. See also *Memoirs* II/539–540.

28. *Memoirs* II/642.

29. *Ibid.*, p. 341.

30. *Ibid.*, pp. 232, 642.

31. *Im Schatten*, p. 293.
32. Reviewed in *EK* I/3/22–25.
33. Lily Braun to Otto Braun, 4 March 1916.
34. For the woman of the future, see "Die neue Frau in der Dichtung," *NZ* XIV/2/36/293–303; also the series of articles in *EK* called "Streifzüge durch die neue Literatur." For the last point, which insists on giving even the physically and mentally most limited people a meaningful function, see "Der Trampel," *NG* II/23/274–275.
35. "Weiblichkeit?" *Zu* 1902, pp. 418–419.
36. Lily Braun to Julie Vogelstein, 25 January 1915. The German word "Frauenschicksal" (woman's destiny) probably is an allusion to Iphigenie's lament in Act I, Scene 2, of Goethe's *Iphigenie auf Tauris:* "To live a useless life is early death; / That women's fate is mine above all others."
37. See, for instance, "Der Fall Kirchhoff," *EK* I/45/355–356.
38. "Dirnen-Streik," *NG* III/4/30.
39. "Sklavenmarkt," *NG* II/35/419.
40. "Hinter den Kulissen," *EK* II/46/361.
41. "Das Frauenstimmrecht in England," *Archiv* 10 (1897), p. 451.
42. Jean H. Quataert, *Reluctant Feminists in German Social Democracy, 1885–1917* (Princeton, N.J.: Princeton University Press, 1979), p. 91.
43. *Memoirs* I/384. Lily Braun to Otto Braun, 3 May 1908.
44. Lily Braun to Otto Braun, 14 May 1914.
45. *Memoirs* I/384.
46. Ibid., p. 362.
47. *Frauenfrage*, p. 200.
48. "Die Pflicht, schön zu sein," *EK* II/8/62.
49. *Die Frauen und der Krieg* (Leipzig: S. Hirzel, 1915), p. 28.
50. Quoted from a lecture on feminism held in Berlin, fall 1906, in *Die Zeit am Montag*. Collected in the archive of the Prussian police. Pr. Br. Rep. 30 Bln. C Pol. Präs. Nr. 16082, Blatt 34. Staatsarchiv der DDR, Potsdam.
51. "Hermann Sudermann und die Frauenfrage," *EK* I/2/25.
52. This paragraph is a condensation of the sentences with which she ends "Das geistige Leben des Weibes," p. 287 (cited in note 5, chapter 9.)
53. Lillian S. Robinson, *Sex, Class and Culture* (Bloomington: Indiana University Press, 1978), p. 20.
54. See the contributions in Joyce Treblicot, ed., *Mothering: Essays in Feminist Theory* (Totowa, N.J.: Rowman & Allanheld, 1983).

XI. Children's Liberation

1. Batya Weinbaum, *The Curious Courtship of Women's Liberation and Socialism* (Boston: South End Press, 1978), chapter 7.

2. For a general discussion of the condition of German children around the turn of the century, see Johannes Schult, *Aufbruch einer Jugend* (Bonn, 1956), which reports several notorious cases of child abuse.

3. Lily Braun, *Die Emanzipation der Kinder: Eine Rede an die Schuljugend* (München: Albert Langen, 1911).

4. For a discussion of the poor health of working-class children in Berlin, see Wilhelm Schröder, "Berliner Kinderelend," NG III/24/283–284.

5. Julian Marcuse, "Mütterheime," *März; eine Wochenschrift*, ed. Ludwig Thoma and Hermann Hesse, VI/4/485.

6. *Liebesbriefe*, p. 413.

7. Lily Braun to Heinrich Braun, 28 July 1911.

8. From a review of an article by the anti-feminist Edmund Fischer, NG I/13/136.

9. "Proletarische Mütter," NG II/22/264. See also the translation of a poem by Elizabeth Barrett Browning, "Arbeiterkinder," EK I/30/241.

10. For one of several such outbursts, see her review of Th. Landmann, *Die Erziehung kleiner Kinder im vorschulpflichtigen Alter*, EK II/50/399. This idea that wet-nursing deprived the wet nurses' own infants of their mother's milk was widely shared by radical feminists at the time. When Adelheid Popp, the leading woman in the Austrian socialist party, had her second baby, she was urged by her physician to engage a wet nurse, but refused for what she called political reasons. In later years she changed her mind: If people can sell their own blood, she wrote, why not their own milk, as long as that does not mean their own babies will be deprived. Adelheid Popp, "Blätter der Erinnerung," p. 41. Archiv des Vereins für Geschichte der Arbeiterbewegung, Wien.

11. For an incidence of this kind which angered Braun, see her letter to Heinrich Braun, 30 July 1901.

12. Alex Hall, "Youth in Rebellion," in Richard J. Evans, ed., *Society and Politics in Wilhelmine Germany*, p. 261.

13. Lily Braun to Heinrich Braun, 13 January 1901.

14. *Memoirs* I/413/ff.

15. Ibid., pp. 413–414.

16. Orbilius, "Kinderrechte und Elternpflichten," and L. Berkheim (pseudonym for Lily von Giżycki), "Nochmals Kinderrechte und Elternpflichten," EK I/2/14–16, 10/75–77. Also "Der Hauptmann von Köpenick als Erzieher," NG III/4/39.

17. NG I/5/49, I/7/75. *Frauenfrage*, p. 202. "Preussens Schule im Lichte amerikanischer Kultur," NG II/22/257–258.

18. "Sich ausleben!" NG II/13/146.

19. Friedrich Engels, *The Condition of the Working Class in England.*

20. Here she seems to be referring to the glass of water theory (or slogan, as Richard Stites prefers) of free love, made famous by Aleksandra Kollontai—an admirer of Braun—and vehemently denounced by Lenin. See Richard Stites, *The Women's Liberation Movement in Russia: Feminism, Nihil-*

ism and Bolshevism, 1860–1930 (Princeton, N.J.: Princeton University Press, 1978), pp. 377–378.

21. "Liebesgrössenwahn," *NG* II/11/122.

22. *NG* II/26/308.

23. "Nochmals Kinderrechte und Elternpflichten," *EK* I/10/75–77.

24. "Eine Gewissensfrage," *EK* III/14/107.

25. *Memoirs* I/44.

26. "Eine Gewissensfrage," *EK* III/14/107–108.

27. *Die Emanzipation der Kinder,* p. 13.

28. "Eine Gewissensfrage," *EK* III/14/107–108.

29. Lily Braun to Geheeb, 13 September 1908.

30. "Kindermund," *NG* II/27/323.

31. "Ellen Key und die Frauenfrage," *Zu* 1899, No. 28, p. 321. See also "Proletarische Mütter," *NG* II/22/263–264.

32. *Die Emanzipation der Kinder,* p. 16.

33. *Memoirs* I/414–416.

34. *Die Emanzipation der Kinder,* p. 15.

35. Review of Th. Landmann, *Die Erziehung kleiner Kinder, EK* II/50/399. Also "Wie wir Ungläubigen Weihnachten feiern," *NG* III/12/136.

36. "Mutter und Sohn," *NG* II/36/430. Also "Ein Aufruf an Deutschlands Frauen," *NG* IV/7/189–193.

37. *Frauenfrage,* pp. 201–202.

38. Charlotte Perkins (Stetson) Gelman, *Concerning Children* (Boston: Sorrell, Maynard & Co., 1900). German translation: *Kinder-Kultur* (Berlin: 1906).

39. See especially "Die literarischen Abende der Grossherzogin Maria Paulowna," in *Deutsche Rundschau* LXXV/424.

40. *Die Emanzipation der Kinder, p. 16.*

41. Ibid., p. 21.

42. Ibid., pp. 24–25.

43. Ibid., p. 24.

44. Ibid., p. 28.

45. Lily Braun to Otto Braun, 5 March 1915. See also *Die Frauen und der Krieg,* p. 49. Otto Braun was indeed an extraordinary person; he was chivalrous, tender, decent, and an intellectual prodigy with fantastic leadership potential. He was killed in action in 1918, two years after Lily Braun's death. A few years later, the publication of some of his poems and essays made him famous in Germany. See Otto Braun, *Aus nachgelassenen Schriften eines Frühvollendeten* (Berlin: Bruno Cassirer, 1920).

46. Lily Braun to Frau Natorp, 14 August 1911.

XII. Growing Isolation

1. The SPD increased its number of Reichstag deputies from 56 to 81.

2. The pretext for the entire debate was an exchange of articles con-

cerning the rude and destructive tone of arguments in the party, which the leadership cleverly turned into a debate over the propriety of writing for non-party journals. Georg Berhard, "Parteimoral" in *Zu* February 1903; Kautsky's attack on Berhard in *NZ* XXI/1 (17 January 1903); Henrich Braun's arguments in *Vorwärts*, 29 March 1903; and articles by Friedrich Stampfer in *NZ* XXI/1, No. 26, and Karl Kautsky, ibid., XXI/2, No. 47 (22 August 1903). Lily Braun's comments appear in *Memoirs* II.

3. Lily von Kretschman to Georg von Gižycki, 24 November 1891. Lily Braun to Heinrich Braun, 6 April 1904.

4. In 1891 Lily's first honoraria for her Goethe articles had gone to support cousin Fritz, who was then a teenage cadet living beyond his means. Lily von Kretschman to Tilly von Colomb, 18 October 1891.

5. Eckmann's memory was honored by an entire issue of *Deutsche Kunst und Dekoration*, March/April 1900. For his ideas of creating art for the people, see Otto Eckmann, *Neue Formen: Dekorative Entwürfe für die Praxis* (Berlin: Spielmeyer Verlag, 1897).

6. Mascha Siémon, "Traum," *NG* III/2; "Kunstgewerbe fürs Volk," *NG* II/9; "Wohnungskünste," *NG* I/21. Also book reviews in *NG* II/17, III/16, V/10.

7. Lily Braun to Heinrich Braun, 5 June 1907.

8. Lily Braun to Heinrich Braun, 6 September 1895, 10 August 1902. Heinrich Braun to Lily Braun, 12 May 1898.

XIII. World War I

1. Lily Braun to Otto Braun, 14 August 1915.
2. Lily Braun to Julie Vogelstein, 8 December 1915.
3. Lily Braun to Otto Braun, 28 January 1915.
4. Lily Braun to Otto Braun, 11 May 1916.
5. Lily Braun to Otto Braun, 19 March 1916.
6. Lily Braun to Otto Braun, 27 December 1914.
7. *Die Frauen und der Krieg*, pp. 10–12, 44. Also Lily Braun to Otto Braun, 13 February 1915; Heinrich Braun to Otto Braun, 8 May 1916.
8. *Die Frauen und der Krieg*, p. 44.
9. Lily Braun to Otto Braun, 22 January 1915.
10. *Die Frauen und der Krieg*, pp. 10–12.
11. Lily Braun to Otto Braun, 18 February 1916.
12. Heinrich Braun to Otto Braun, 5 April 1916.
13. Heinrich Braun to Col. Gen. von Moltke, 16 December 1915.
14. Lily Braun to Otto Braun, 16 March 1915.
15. Lily Braun to Otto Braun, 4 August 1915.
16. "For people who interest me I wish suffering—I feel no pity for them, because I am wishing them the only thing which today can demonstrate whether a person does or does not have worth—that he stand firm." Quoted in *Die Frauen und der Krieg*, p. 10.

17. Lily Braun to Otto Braun, 6 March 1915; 16 March 1915.

18. Lily Braun to Otto Braun, 23 October 1915.

19. Lily Braun to Otto Braun, 22 March 1916.

20. Lily Braun to Julie Vogelstein, 12 December 1914.

21. Lily Braun to Otto Braun, 21 January 1916.

22. Lily Braun to Otto Braun, 17 January 1916.

23. Lily Braun to Otto Braun, 16 July 1915.

24. Lily Braun to Otto Braun, 20 April 1916.

25. Ibid.

26. Lily Braun to Otto Braun, 5 July 1915.

27. *Die Frauen und der Krieg*, pp. 37ff, 43.

28. Ibid., pp. 46–48. See also Lily Braun to Otto Braun, 24 September 1915; 21 September 1915. This idea of a universal national service for women found an echo among radical feminists in Russia who proposed similar legislation. See Richard Stites, *The Women's Liberation Movement in Russia* (Princeton, N.J.: Princeton University Press, 1978), p. 298.

29. *Die Frauen und der Krieg*, p. 54.

30. Lily Braun to Otto Braun, 12 February 1916.

31. For a mild reaction of this kind, see a review of her pamphlet, *Die Frauen und der Krieg*, by Wally Zepler in SM 1915, No. 7, pp. 366–368.

32. Quoted from her lecture, "Die Frau von Übermorgen," in an obituary by M.W. in *Die Frau der Gegenwart*, Breslau, 1 September 1916. See also the obituary in *Die Morgenpost*, Berlin, 10 August 1916.

XIV. Conclusion

1. A very fine example of such an appreciative obituary is that by Wally Zepler in SM 1916, No. 16, pp. 869–870.

2. Obituary for Lily Braun, *Neue Freie Presse*, Wien, 30 August 1916.

3. GL XXVI/25, Beilage für unsere Mütter und Hausfrauen, pp. 97–98.

4. Julie Vogelstein, *Lily Braun; ein Lebensbild* (Berlin: Hermann Klemm, ND). Julie Braun-Vogelstein, *Ein Menschenleben: Heinrich Braun und sein Schicksal* (Tübingen: Rainer Wunderlich, 1932). Also Julie Braun, *Was niemals stirbt: Gestalten und Erinnerungen* (Stuttgart: Deutsche Verlagsanstalt, 1966).

BIBLIOGRAPHY

Works by Lily Braun

Gesammelte Werke, 5 volumes (containing a brief biography by Julie Braun, *Im Schatten, Memoirs, Lebenssucher, Mutter Maria, Liebesbriefe,* and *Madeleine Guimard*), Berlin: H. Klemm, 1923.

Books

Aus Goethes Freundeskreise; Erinnerungen der Baronin Jenny von Gustedt. Braunschweig: George Westermann, 1892.
Deutsche Fürstinnen. Berlin: Gebr. Paetel, 1893.
Giżycki, Lily v. & Georg v. Giżycki (eds.) *Kinder- und Hausmärchen, gesammelt durch die Brüder Grimm. Nach ethischen Gesichtspunkten ausgewählt und bearbeitet.* Berlin: Ferd. Dümmler, 1895.
Giżycki, Lily v. (ed.), Georg von Giżycki, *Vorlesungen über Soziale Ethik.* Berlin: Ferd. Dümmler, 1895.
Die Frauenfrage, ihre geschichtliche Entwicklung und ihre wirtschaftliche Seite. Leipzig: Hirzel, 1901.
Im Schatten der Titanen. Erinnerungen an Baronin Jenny von Gustedt. Stuttgart: Deutsche Verlagsanstalt, 1903.
Braun, Lily (ed.), Hans von Kretschman, *Kriegsbriefe aus den Jahren 1870–71.* Berlin: Meyer & Jessen, 1903. Second edition, 1911.
Memoiren einer Sozialistin. Vol. I, *Lehrjahre.* München: Alb. Langen, 1908. Vol. II, *Kampfjahre.* München: Alb. Langen, 1911.
Die Liebesbriefe der Marquise. Roman. München: Alb. Langen, 1912.
Madeleine Guimard (opera libretto), in *Gesammelte Werke.*
Mutter Maria eine Tragödie. München: Alb. Langen, 1913.
Lebenssucher. Roman. München: Alb. Langen, 1915.

Pamphlets

Die Stellung des Frau in der Gegenwart. Berlin: Ferd. Dümmler, 1895.
Die Bürgerpflicht der Frau. Berlin: Ferd. Dümmler, 1895.
Zur Beurteilung der Frauenbewegung in England und Deutschland. Berlin: Carl Heymanns Verlag, 1895 (also published as an article in *Archiv,* vol. VIII).
Frauenfrage und Socialdemokratie. Berlin: Verlag Vorwärts, 1896.
Die neue Frau in der Dichtung. Berlin: Vorwärts Verlag, 1896 (first published in *NZ*).

Frauenarbeit und Hauswirtschaft. Berlin: Verlag Vorwärts, 1901.
Was wir wollen: Flugschrift des Vereins fur Hauswirtschafts-Genossenschaften.
    Berlin, 1902.
Die Frauen und die Politik. Berlin: Vorwärts Verlag, 1903.
Die Mutterschaftsversicherung. Berlin: Vorwärts Verlag, 1906.
Die Emanzipation der Kinder: eine Rede an die Schuljugend. München: Albert
    Langen, 1911.
Die Frauen und der Krieg. Leipzig: S. Hirzel, 1915.

Articles

1891
"Erinnerungen von und an Jenny von Pappenheim (Freifrau von Gustedt)."
    In Ludwig Geiger (ed.), *Goethe-Jahrbuch,* vol. XII. Frankfurt a/M,
    1891.
"Ottilie von Goethe und ihre Söhne: Aus den Erinnerungen einer Zeitge-
    nossin." In *Westermanns Monatshefte,* vol. LXX, 1891.

1892
"Weimars Gesellschaft und das 'Chaos.' " In *Westermanns Monatshefte,* vol.
    XIII, 1892.
"Briefwechsel zwischen Goethe und Minister von Gersdorff." In *Goethe-
    Jahrbuch,* vol. XIII, 1892.

1893
"Kinderrechte und Elternpflichten." In *EK* I/2, 10. Published under the
    pseudonym L. Berkheim.
"Hermann Sudermann und die Frauenfrage." *EK* I/2.
"Die literarischen Abende der Grossherzogin Maria Paulowna." In *Deutsche
    Rundschau,* LXXV and LXXVI.
"M.v. Egidy." *EK* I/19.
"Streifzüge durch die moderne Literatur." A series of articles in different
    issues of *EK,* beginning with I/27 and up to II/42.
(untitled) Address to the Eisenach meeting for furthering and spreading the
    Ethical Movement. In *EK* I/32. Reply and rejoinder, *EK* I/46.
"Ein Gang durch die Berliner Kunstausstellungen." *EK* I/34, 35.
"Der Fall Kirchhoff." *EK* I/45.
"Ein Interview mit einem Modell." *EK* I/51.

1894
"Aschermittwoch." *EK* II/5.
"Die Pflicht, schön zu sein." *EK* II/8.
"Volksküchen." *EK* II/10.
"Die Frauenfrage." *EK* II/20.
"Zwei Feste." *EK* II/26.
"Der ethische Gehalt des Parsifal." *EK* II/28.

"Eine Pilgerfahrt." *EK* II/32.
"Ein Rückblick auf die diesjährige Berliner Kunstaustellung." *EK* II/35.
"Hinter den Kulissen." *EK* II/46, III/15.
(untitled) Christmas editorial, 1894. *EK* II/51.

1895
"Die Künstler und die Gesindeordnung." *EK* III/3.
"Kunst?" *EK* III/9.
"Eine Gang durch die Volksküchen." *EK* III/10.
"Eine Gewissensfrage." *EK* III/14.
"Nach links und rechts." *FB* I/5,7.
"Politik und Ethische Bewegung." *EK* III/21.
"Die Stellung der Frau in der Gegenwart." *EK* III/23, 24, 25.
"Brief aus London." *EK* III/27.
"Londoner Studien." *EK* III/29.
"Die Litteratur zur Frauenfrage." *EK* III/32.
"Stimmungsbilder aus der General-Versammlung des Bundes deutscher Frauenvereine in München." *FB* I/9.
"An die Leser." *EK* III/42.
"Zur Beurteilung der Frauenbewegung in England und Deutschland." *Archiv* VIII.
"Das Abgeordnetenhaus und die Frauenfrage." *FB* I/10.
Christmas editorial, 1895. *GL* III/26.
"Englischer Socialismus." *Die Zeit* (Wien), 10 August 1895.

1896
"Die neue Frau in der Dichtung." *NZ* XIV/II/36.
Christmas editorial, 1896. *GL* IV/26

1897
"Die Frauenfrage auf der deutschen Buhne." *Zu* XXI, 1897.
"Herrn Förster zur Erwiderung. *GL* V/18.
Christmas editorial, 1897. *GL* V/26.

1898
"Karneval." *GL* VII/4.
"Die Anfänge der Frauenbewegung." *Archiv* XIII.
"Bürgerliche und proletarische Frauenbewegung." *GL* VI/23.
"Warum kann die Frauenbewegung nicht unabhängig bleiben?" *GL* VII/10.
"Mutterflichten im Wahlkampf." *GL* VII/11.
"Das Frauenstimmrecht in England." *GL* VII/13.
"Arbeiterinnenschutz und Frauenfreiheit." *GL* VII/18.
"Die Ziegeleiverordnung." *GL* VII/26.
"Ein Frauendrama." *Zu* XXIV, 1898.

1899
"Ellen Key und die Frauenfrage." *Zu* XXVIII, 1899.

"Der internationale Frauenkongress in London." *GL* IX/16. Also in *Schweizerische Blätter für Wirtschafts- und Socialpolitik*, 1899.
"Die Frauenfrage im Altertum." *Archiv* XIII. Also in *GL* IX/1–2, 4, 6, 9, 12.
"Ein Weihnachtslied." *GL* VIII/26.

1901
"Die Reform der Hauswirtschaft." *Zu* XXXIV, 1901.
"Hausindustrie." *Zu* XXXVII

1902
"Die Lieder der deutschen Frau." *Zu*, 1902.
"Weiblichkeit?" *Zu*, 1902.

1905
"Zeitschriftenschau." *NG* I/3.
"Das ist der Mai." *NG* I/5.
"Schiller und die Frauen." *NG* 1/6.
"Dienstbotennot." *NG* I/7.
"Die gesetzliche Regelung der Heimarbeit." *NG* I/8.
"Hebel oder Hemmschuh?" *NG* I/10.
"Das Problem der Ehe." *NG* I/10.
"Pfingstfahrt." *NG* I/12.
"Die Entthronung der Liebe." *NG* I/20.
"Die Hunnen." *NG* I/21.
"Die Befreiung der Liebe." *NG* I/22.
"Wochenkalender der Gerechtigkeit." *NG* I/22.
"Die Frauen und das Organisationsstatut." *NG* I/25.

1906
"Eine Nacht in der alten Akademie." *NG* II/6.
"Sozialpolitische Luftschlösser." *NG* II/8.
"Der sozial-demokratische Gesetzesentwurf zum Schutz der Heimarbeiter." *NG* II/10.
"Liebesgrössenwahn." *NG* II/11.
"Bürgerliche Sozialreformer und ihre Schleppenträger." *NG* II/13.
"Sich ausleben!" *NG* II/13.
"Auch eine Osterpredigt." *NG* II/15.
"Wider Moral- und Kirchenpfaffen." *NG* II/16.
"Die verletzte Standesehre." *NG* II/18.
"Maifestnummern." *NG* II/18.
"Juristischer Kindermord." *NG* II/20.
"Negerkultur." *NG* II/22.
"Proletarische Mütter." *NG* II/22.
"Preussens Schulen im Lichte amerikanischer Kultur." *NG* II/22.
"Der Trampel." *NG* II/23.
"Vogelfrei." *NG* II/24.

"Nichtraucher." *NG* II/27.
"Kindermund." *NG* II/27.
"Mitläufer." *NG* II/27.
"Meiner 'Meerfahrt' Tagebuch." *NG* II/28.
"Die 'unterdrückte' Frau." *NG* II/29.
"Londoner Tagebuch." *NG* II/29.
"Leid und Leid." *NG* II/33.
"Ein Traum von William Morris." *NG* II/34.
"Allerhand Nachdenkliches." *NG* II/34.
"Sklavenmarkt." *NG* II/35.
"Ausnahmegesetze" *NG* II/36.
"Mutter und Sohn." *NG* II/36.
"Männerkultus." *NG* II/37.
"Erziehungsfragen." *NG* II/39.
"Die Mannheimer Frauenkonferenz." *NG* III/1–2.
"Wochenkalender der Gerechtigkeit." *NG* III/3.
"Zur Dienstbotenfrage." *NG* III/3.
"Dirnen-Streik." *NG* III/4.
"Der Hauptmann von Köpenick als Erzieher." *NG* III/4.
" 'Bürgerliches' und 'proletarisches' Erziehungsprinzip." *NG* III/3.
"Wie wir Ungläubigen Weihnachten feiern." *NG* III/12.
"Der Wahlkamapf und die Frauen." *NG* III/13.
"Auf Agitation." *NG* III/17.
"Eine Konferenz zur Förderung der Arbeiterinnen-Interessen." *NG* III/22.
"Die bürgerliche Frauenbewegung und die Sozialreform." *NG* III/24.
"Jugend von heute." *NG* III/25.
"Gräber." *NG* III/26.

1908
"Die Ehe auf der Anklagebank." *NG* IV/2.
"Abseits vom Wege." *NG* IV/4.
"Ein Aufruf an Deutschlands Frauen." *NG* IV/7.
"Eine ungehaltene Rede." *NG* IV/13.
"Auer und die Frauen." *NG* V/3.
"Frauenstimmrecht und Sozialdemokratie." *NG* V/7.
"Die Frauenfrage auf dem internationalen Kongress." *NG* V/9.

1912
"Die Frau in der Sozialdemokratie." In *Illustriertes Konversations-Lexikon der Frau*, vol. II, pp. 475ff.
"Das geistige Leben des Weibes." In Robby A. Kossmann (ed.), *Mann und Weib, ihre Beziehungen zueinander und zum Kulturleben der Gegenwart*, vol. I, 2nd ed. Stuttgart: Union-Verlag, ND (probably 1912).
"Einführung." In Adele Schreiber (ed.), *Mutterschaft*. München: Albert Langen, 1912.

Reviews *(in alphabetical order by author reviewed)*

Brief review of five books on the Ethical Movement by Felix Adler, William Mangasarian, William Salten, W. L. Sheldon, and S. Burns Weston. EK III/23.

Anzengruber, Ludwig, *Der Meineidsbauer.* EK I/49.

Berliner Tierschutzverein, *Kalender.* EK II/51.

Brasch, Moritz, *Die Ziele der ethischen Bewegung.* EK I/29.

Fischer, Edmund, "Die Frauenfrage." NG I/13.

An article by F. W. Foerster. NG I/10.

Frank, Keiffer, and Maingie, *L'assurance maternelle. Archiv* XI.

Franzos, Karl Emil (ed.), *Die Geschichte des Erstlingswerks.* EK II/50.

Gold, Alfred, *Ausklang.* NG I/7.

Hauptmann, Gerhart, *Hannele.* EK I/48.

Hauptmann, Gerhart, *Die Weber.* EK I/48.

Kempner, Friederike, *Historische Novellen.* EK I/18.

Landmann, Th., *Die Erziehung kleiner Kinder im vorschulpflichtigen Alter.* EK II/50.

Mauthner, Fritz, *Lügenohr.* EK I/12.

Müller-Jahnke, Clara, *Ich bekenne: Die Geschichte einer Frau.* NG I/13.

Naumann, Friedrich, *Neudeutsche Wirtschaftspolitik.* NG II/24.

Nordau, Max, *Das Recht, zu lieben.* EK I/34.

Ompteda, Georg von, *Nach dem Manöver.* EK III/4.

Polenz, Wilhelm von, *Der Pfarrer von Breitendorf.* EK I/24.

Scholten, Oberstlieutnant, *Was uns not thut.* EK I/12.

Sudermann, Herman, *Heimat.* EK I/3.

Thurow, Hr., and H. Ponier, *Was haben wir erreicht? Ein Rückblick auf die Bewegung für die Achtstunden-Arbeit.* EK III/24.

Tolstoj, Leo, *Die Macht der Finsternis.* EK I/19.

Wettstein-Adelt, Dr. Minna, *3-1/2 Monate Fabrik-Arbeiterin.* EK I/6.

Wichert, Ernst, *Aus eigenem Recht.* EK II/2.

Obituaries *(in alphabetical order)*

Susan B. Anthony. NG II/12.

Ignaz Auer. NG V/3.

Henrik Ibsen. NG II/22.

Translations

Elizabeth Barrett Browning, "Arbeiterkinder." EK I/30.

W. K. Clifford, *Wahrhaftigkeit (The Ethics of Belief).* Berlin: Ferdinand Dümmler, 1893.

Biographies

Vogelstein, Julie, *Lily Braun; ein Lebensbild.* Berlin: Hermann Klemm, ND.

Braun-Vogelstein, Julie, *Was niemals stirbt: Gestalten und Erinnerungen.* Stuttgart: Deutsche Verlags-anstalt, 1966.

Braun-Vogelstein, Julie, *Ein Menschenleben: Heinrich Braun und sein Schicksal.* Tübingen: Rainer Wunderlich, 1932.

Victorica, Maria de (Maria von Kretschman), "Autobiography." Typescript written for the U.S. Department of Justice. Leo Baeck Institute, 1919.

Other Works Consulted

Altbach, Edith Hoshino, Jeanette Clausen, Dagmar Schultz, & Naomi Stephan (eds.), *German Feminism: Readings in Politics and Literature.* Albany: SUNY Press, 1984.

Anthony, Katharine, *Feminism in Germany and Scandinavia.* New York: Henry Holt & Co., 1915.

Arendt, Hannah, Review of J.P. Nettl, *Rosa Luxemburg. Der Monat,* XX, p. 243.

Atkinson, Dorothy, Alexander Dallin, and Gail Lapidus (eds.), *Women in Russia.* Stanford, 1977.

Baader, Ottilie, *Ein Steiniger Weg: Lebenserinnerungen.* Berlin: Buchhandlung Vorwärts, 1921.

Bab, Julius, "Geschlechter." *NG* III/5.

Balfour, Michael, *The Controversy over German Industrialization, 1890–1902.* Chicago: University of Chicago Press, 1970.

Bebel, August, *Die Frau und der Sozialismus.* Berlin: Vorwärts Verlag, 1879.

Bebel, August, Review of Lily Braun, *Die Frauenfrage. NZ* XX/1, No. 9.

Beckmann, Emmy, & Elisabeth Kardel (eds.), *Quellen zur Geschichte der Frauenbewegung.* Frankfurt a/M: Moritz Diesterweg, 1955.

Berlin, Isaiah, *Four Essays on Liberty.* London, New York: Oxford University Press, 1969.

Bernstein, Eduard, *Die Voraussetzungen des Sozialismus und die Aufgaben der Sozialdemokratie.* Stuttgart: J.H.W. Dietz, 1899.

Bluhm, Dr. med. Agnes, *Der Einfluss der gewerblichen Gifte auf den Organismus der Frau.* Schriften des ständigen Ausschusses zur Förderung der Arbeiterinnen-Interessen. Jena: Gustav Fischer, 1936.

Bluhm, Dr. med. Agnes, *Die rassehygienischen Aufgaben des weiblichen Arztes.* Berlin, 1936.

Blunden, Margaret, *The Countess of Warwick.* London: Cassell, 1967.

Bramsted, Ernest K., *Aristocracy and the Middle Classes in Germany: Social Types in German Literature, 1830–1900.* Chicago: University of Chicago Press, 1964.

Braun, Otto, *Aus nachgelassenen Schriften eines Frühvollendeten,* Julie Vogelstein (ed.). Berlin: Bruno Cassirer, 1920.

Cauer, Minna, "Kaiserin Friedrich." *FB* VII/16.

Chickering, Roger, *Imperial Germany and a World without War: The Peace Movement and German Society, 1892–1914.* Princeton, N.J.: Princeton University Press, 1975.

Clements, Barbara Evans, *Bolshevik Feminist: The Life of Aleksandra Kollontai.* Bloomington: Indiana University Press, 1979.

Cline, Barbara Lovett, *The Questioners: Physicists and the Quantum Theory.* New York: Thomas Crowell, 1965.

Colomb, Mathilde von, translator of Wendell Phillipps, "Women's Rights." *EK* I/23, 24.

Correspondenzblatt der General-Kommission der Gewerkschaften Deutschlands.

Dernburg, Friedrich, "Lily Brauns Abschied von der Partei." *Berliner Tageblatt,* 12 May 1911.

Deutsche Kunst und Dekoration, Berlin, March/April 1900.

Eckmann, Otto, *Neue Formen: Dekorative Entwürfe für die Praxis.* Berlin: Spielmeyer Verlag, 1897.

Egidy, M. von, "In gemeinsamer Sache." *EK* I/21.

Ettinger, Elżbieta (ed.), *Comrade and Lover: Rosa Luxemburg's Letters to Leo Jogiches.* Cambridge, Mass.: MIT Press, 1979.

Evans, Richard J., "Feminism and Female Emancipation in Germany, 1870–1945: Sources, Methods, and Problems of Research." *Central European History* XI/4.

Evans, Richard J. (ed.), *Society and Politics in Wilhelmine Germany.* New York: Barnes & Noble, 1978.

Evans, Richard J., *Sozialdemokratie und Frauenemanzipation im Deutschen Kaiserreich.* Berlin-Bonn: J.H.W. Dietz Nachf., 1979.

Faloff, Mark, Review of Rosa Luxemburg's Letters to Leo Jogiches, *Commentary,* April 1980.

Fischer, Edmund, "Die Frauenfrage." *SM* XI/3ff.

Foerster, Wilhelm, *Lebenserinnerungen und Lebenshoffnungen.* Berlin: Georg Reimer, 1911.

French, Marilyn, *The Women's Room.* New York: Summit Books, 1977.

Fürth, Henriette, *Die Mutterschaftsversicherung.* Jena: Gustav Fischer, 1911.

Fürth, Henriette, "Entwicklung des Mutterschutzes in Deutschland." In Adele Schreiber (ed.), *Mutterschaft.*

Gärtler, Gina. "Lily Braun, eine Publizistin des Gefühls." Dissertation, Heidelberg, 1935.

Gilman, Charlotte Perkins, *The Home, Its Work and Influence.* New York: McClure, Phillips & Co., 1966.

Gilman, Charlotte Perkins, *Women and Economics.* New York: Harper, 1966.

Gilman, Charlotte Perkins, "The Waste of Private Housekeeping." *Annals of the American Academy of Political Science,* July 1913.

Gilman, Charlotte Perkins, *Concerning Children.* Boston: Sorrell, Maynard & Co., 1900 (Transl. as *Kinder-Kultur.* Berlin, 1906).

Gilman, Charlotte Perkins. See also Stetson, Charlotte Perkins.

Goldschmidt, Henriette, "Erklärung gegen das Frauenstimmrecht." *FB* I/3.

Groh, Dieter, *Negative Integration und revolutionärer Attentismus: Die deutsche Sozialdemokratie am Vorabend des Ersten Weltkrieges.* Frankfurt a/M, 1973.

Grossmann, Stefan, "Geschichte eines geschäftigen Idealisten." *Das Tagebuch,* 15 October 1932 (Review of Julie Braun-Vogelstein, *Ein Menschenleben*).

Hall, Alex, "Youth in Rebellion." In Richard J. Evans (ed.), *Society and Politics in Wilhelmine Germany.*

Harden, Maximilian, "Bebel und Genossen." *Zu,* September-October 1903.

Harden, Maximilian, "Trianon." *Zu,* 19 September 1903.

Hartsock, Nancy C. M., *Money, Sex and Power: Toward a Feminist Historical Materialism.* New York: Longman, 1983.

Hatvany, Ludwig, "Der Kampf um Erfolg." *März—eine Wochenschrift,* 1913, vol. I.

Herkner, Heinrich, "Eine deutsche Beatrice Webb?" (Review of Lily Braun, *Die Frauenfrage*). *Zu* XXXVIII, 1902.

Hickey, Stephen, "The Shaping of the German Labour Movement: Miners in the Ruhr." In Richard J. Evans (ed.), *Society and Politics in Wilhelmine Germany.*

Hippel, Theodor Gottlieb von, *On Improving the Status of Women,* Timothy F. Sellner (ed.). Detroit: Wayne State University Press, 1979.

Hochdorf, Max, Review of Lily Braun, *Lebenssucher.* SM 1916, No. 1.

Holzheuer, Walter, *Karl Kautskys Werk als Weltanschauung.* München: C. H. Beck, 1972.

Honeycutt, Karen, "Clara Zetkin: A Left-Wing Socialist and Feminist in Wilhelmine Germany." Dissertation, Columbia University, 1975.

Honeycutt, Karen, "Socialism and Feminism in Imperial Germany." *SIGNS:Journal of Women in Culture and Society.* 1979, vol. V, No. 1.

Ihrer, Emma, "Die proletarische Frau und die Berufstätigkeit." *SM* XI/1.

Jacoby, Susan, *The Possible She.* New York: Farrar, Straus, Giroux, 1979.

Jaeckel, Reinhold, "Die Stellung des Sozialismus zur Frauenfrage." Dissertation, Tübingen, 1904.

Kautsky, Karl, "Heinrich Braun: Ein Beitrag zur Geschichte der deutschen Sozialdemokratie." *Die Gesellschaft: Internationale Revue für Sozialismus und Politik.* I/1–3. Berlin, 1933.

Kautsky, Karl, "Der mögliche Abschlusss einer unmöglichen Diskussion." NZ XXXII/2, No. 51.

Kautsky, Karl, "Eine Nachlese zum Vorwärtskonflikt." *NZ* XXIV/1.

Kautsky, Karl, "Eine Partei- und Pressfrage." *NZ* XXI/2, No. 47.

Key, Ellen, *Missbrauchte Frauenkraft.* München: Albert Langen, 1898.

Key, Ellen, *The Renaissance of Motherhood.* New York, 1914.

Key, Ellen, *Das Jahrhundert des Kindes: Studien.* Berlin: S. Fischer, 1902.

Key, Ellen, *Rahel Varnhagen.* New York: G. P. Putnam's Sons, 1913.

Kollwitz, Käthe, *Ich will wirken in dieser Zeit.* Berlin: Mann, 1952.

Kretschman, Maria von. See Siémon, Mascha; Victorica, Maria de.

Kuhn, Paul, *Die Frauen um Goethe.* Graz: Berland, 1932.

Landauer, Gustav, "Meine Haltung im Schneiderstreik." *EK* IV/16.

Landes, Joan, "Women, Labor and Family Life: A Theoretical Perspective." *Science and Society,* XLI/4.

Lange, Helene, *Die Frauenbewegung in ihren modernen Problemen.* Leipzig, 1914; reprint Münster: Tendau-Verlag, 1980.

Laufkoetter, Franz, "Die Taktik des Starken und die Taktik des Schwachen." *NG* II/27.

Laws, Theo, *The Darling Daisy Affair.* New York: Athenaeum, 1966.

Ledebour, George, Review of Lily Braun, *Die Frauenfrage. GL* XII/15–16.

Lichey, Margarete, "Sozialismus und Frauenarbeit: Ein Beitrag zur Enwicklung des deutschen Sozialismus von 1869 bis 1921." Dissertation, Breslau: Universitätsverlag, 1926 (?).

Lidtke, Vernon L., *The Outlawed Party: Social Democracy in Germany 1878–1890.* Princeton, N.J.: Princeton University Press, 1966.

Lion, Hilde, *Zur Soziologie der Frauenbewegung.* Schriftenreihe der Akademie für soziale und pädagogische Frauenarbeit in Berlin. Berlin: F. H. Herbig, 1926.

Lösche, Peter, *Arbeiterbewegung und Wilhelminismus: Sozialdemokratie zwischen Anpassung und Spaltung.* Geschichte in Wissenschaft und Unterricht No. 20, 1969.

Luksemburg, Róża, *Listy do Leona Jogichesa-Tyszki,* vols. I, II. Warszawa. Książka i Wiedza, 1968.

Lunn, Eugene, *Prophet of Community: The Romantic Socialism of Gustav Landauer.* Berkeley: University of California Press, 1973.

Luxemburg, Rosa, *Lettres à Léon Jogichès,* vols. I, II. Paris: Denoël, 1971.

Marcuse, Julian, "Mütterheime." *März—eine Wochenschrift,* VI/4.

Marx, Karl, & Friedrich Engels, *Werke.* Berlin: Dietz Verlag, 1964–1971.

Matthias, Erich, *Kautsky und der Kautskyanismus.* Marxismusstudien, No. 2, 1957.

Mehring, Franz, *Meine Rechtfertigung; ein nachträgliches Wort zum Dresdner Parteitag.* Leipzig, 1903.

Meienreis, Dr. R., "Homosexualität und Strafgesetz." *NG* III/10.

Mittelstädt, Otto, Obituary for Georg von Giżycki. *Zu* XI (1895).

Morgan, David W., *The Socialist Left and the German Revolution.* Ithaca: Cornell University Press, 1975.

Niggeman, Heinz (ed.), *Frauenemanzipation und Sozialdemokratie.* Frankfurt a/M: Fischer, 1981.

Nipperdey, Thomas, *Die Organisation der deutschen Parteien vor 1918.* Düsseldorf, 1961.

Oberkirch, Baroness d', Countess de Montbrison, née Baroness Waldner von Freudstein, *Memoirs*, 3 vols. London: Colburn & Co., 1852.

O'Leary, Jeremiah A. *My Political Trial and Experiences*. New York: Jefferson Publishing Co., 1919.

Oppenheimer, Franz, *Die Siedlungsgenossenschaft*. Leipzig: Duncker & Humblot, 1896.

Otto-Peters, Louise, *Das erste Vierteljahrhundert des Allgemeinen Deutschen Frauenvereins, gegründet am 18. Oktover 1865 in Leipzig*. Leipzig: Moritz Schäfer, 1890.

Pivar, David, *Purity Crusade, Sexual Morality and Social Control, 1868–1900*. London: Greenwood Press, 1973.

Plechanow, Georg, "Henrik Ibsen." Ergänzungsheft zu *NZ*, No. 3, 1908.

Popp, Adelheid, Obituary for Lily Braun, *Arbeiterzeitung*, Wien, 13 August 1916.

Quataert, Jean H., *Reluctant Feminists in German Social Democracy, 1885–1917*. Princeton, N.J.: Princeton University Press, 1979.

Rich, Adrienne, *Of Woman Born: Motherhood as Experience and Institution*. New York: W. W. Norton & Co., 1976.

Richenbacher, Sabine, *Uns fehlt nur eine Kleinigkeit: Deutsche proletarische Frauenbewegung 1890–1914*. Frankfurt a/M: Fischer, 1892.

Robinson, Lillian S., *Sex, Class and Culture*. Bloomington: Indiana University Press, 1978.

Roth, Guenther, *The Social Democrats in Imperial Germany*. Totowa, N.J.: Bedminster Press, 1963.

Rover, Constance, *Love, Morals and the Feminists*. London: Routledge & Kegan Paul, 1970.

Rudolphi, Ernst, *Mutterschutz in Theorie und Praxis*. Berlin, 1912.

Salomon, Alice, *Mutterschutz und Mutterschaftsversicherung*. Berlin, 1969.

Salvadori, Massimo, *Karl Kautsky and the Socialist Revolution, 1880–1930*. London: New Left Books, 1979.

Scheffauer, Herman George, *The New Vision in the German Arts*. New York: B. W. Huebsch, 1924.

Schleich, Carl Ludwig, *Besonnte Vergangenheit: Lebenserinnerungen 1859–1919*. Berlin: Rowohlt, 1926.

Schorske, Carl E., *German Social Democracy, 1905–1917*. Cambridge, Mass.: Harvard University Press, 1955.

Schreiber, Adele (ed.), *Mutterschaft*. München: Albert Langen, 1912.

Schröder, Wilhelm, "Berliner Kinderelend." *NG* III/24.

Schult, Johannes, *Aufbruch einer Jugend*. Bonn, 1956.

Sheehan, James J. (ed.), *Imperial Germany*. New York: New Viewpoints, 1976.

Siémon, Mascha (Maria von Kretschman), "Wohnungskünste." *NG* I/21.

Siémon, Mascha, "Kunstgewerbe fürs Volk." *NG* II/9.

Siémon, Mascha, "Traum." *NG* III/2.

Siémon, Mascha, Book reviews, *NG* II/17, XXX/16, V/10.

Slaughter, Jane, & Robert Kern, *European Women on the Left: Socialism, Feminism, and the Problems Faced by Political Women, 1880 to the Present.* Westport & London: Greenwood Press, 1981.

Snell, John, *The Democratic Movement in Germany 1789–1914.* Chapel Hill: University of North Carolina Press, 1976.

Stampfer, Friedrich, "Richtung und Partei." *NZ* XXIV/1/29.

Stanton, Elizabeth Cady, Susan B. Anthony, and Matilda Joslyn Gage (eds.), *History of Women's Suffrage.* Rochester, N.Y., 1887.

Steenson, Gary P., *Karl Kautsky, 1854–1938: Marxism in the Classical Years.* Pittsburgh: University of Pittsburgh Press, 1978.

Steinder, Hans-Joseph, *Sozialismus und deutsche Sozialdemokratie.* Hannover: Verlag für Literatur und Zeitgeschehen, 1967.

Stetson (Gilman), Charlotte Perkins, *Mann und Frau (Women and Economics),* transl. by Marie Stritt. Berlin, 1901.

Stites, Richard, *The Women's Liberation Movement in Russia: Feminism, Nihilism and Bolshevism, 1860–1930.* Princeton, N.J.: Princeton University Press, 1978.

Strain, Jacqueline, "Feminism and Political Radicalism in the German Social Democratic Movement, 1890–1914." Dissertation, University of California, Berkeley, 1964.

Thönnesen, Werner, *The Emancipation of Women: The Rise and Decline of the Women's Movement in German Social Democracy, 1863–1953.* London, 1973.

Trebilcot, Joyce (ed.), *Mothering: Essays in Feminist Theory.* Totowa, N.J.: Rowman & Allanheld, 1983.

Twellmann, Margrit, *Die deutsche Frauenbewegung, ihre Anfänge und erste Entwicklung 1843–1889.* Marburger Abhandlungen zur politischen Wissenschaft, Band 17, No. II. Meisenheim, 1972.

Warwick, Countess Frances Evelyn, "Die Arbeitslosigkeit, ihre Ursachen und Wirkungen." *NG* III/16.

Weber, Marianne, *Ehefrau und Mutter in der Rechtsentwicklung.* Tübingen: J.C.B. Mohr, 1907.

Weinbaum, Batya, *The Curious Courtship of Women's Liberation and Socialism.* Boston: South End Press, 1978.

Winkler, Barbara Scott, "Victorian Daughters: The Lives and Feminism of Charlotte Perkins Gilman and Olive Schreiner." *Michigan Occasional Papers in Women's Studies,* No. 13. Winter 1980.

Zahn-Harnack, Agnes von, *Die Frauenbewegung; Geschichte, Probleme, Ziele.* Berlin: Deutsche Buch-Gemeinschaft, 1928.

Zepler, Wally, Review of Lily Braun, *Die Frauen und der Krieg. SM* 1915, No. 7.

Zetkin, Clara, Editorial: "An die Leserinnen und Leser." *GL* VIII/1.

Zetkin, Clara, *Die Arbeiterinnen- und Frauenfrage der Gegenwart.* Berlin, 1889.

Zetkin, Clara, "Aus Krähwinkel." GL 22 March 1905.

Zetkin, Clara, Christmas editorials. GL X/26, XI/26, XII/26.

Zetkin, Clara, "Frauenrechtlerische Unklarheit." GL VI/13.

Zetkin, Clara, Obituary for Lily Braun, GL XXVI/25.

Zetkin, Clara, "Reinliche Scheidung." GL II/8, 13, 15.

Zetkin, Clara, Review of Eduard Bernstein, *Die Voraussetzungen des Sozialismus.* GL IX/20.

Zetkin, Clara, Editorial welcoming Lily Braun into the SPD. GL VI/1.

Zetkin, Clara, *Zur Frage des Frauenwahlrechts.* Berlin: Vorwärts, 1907.

Zetkin, Clara, *Zur Geschichte der proletarischen Frauenbewegung in Deutschland.* Berlin: Dietz Verlag, 1958.

INDEX